EVERYTHING IN ITS RIGHT PLACE

Everything in its Right Place

ANALYZING RADIOHEAD

Brad Osborn

OXFORD
UNIVERSITY PRESS

OXFORD
UNIVERSITY PRESS

Oxford University Press is a department of the University of Oxford. It furthers the University's objective of excellence in research, scholarship, and education by publishing worldwide. Oxford is a registered trade mark of Oxford University Press in the UK and certain other countries.

Published in the United States of America by Oxford University Press
198 Madison Avenue, New York, NY 10016, United States of America.

Library of Congress Cataloging-in-Publication Data
Names: Osborn, Brad.
Title: Everything in its right place: analyzing Radiohead/Brad Osborn.
Description: New York: Oxford University Press, [2017] | Includes bibliographical references and index.
Identifiers: LCCN 2016022990 (print) | LCCN 2016023712 (ebook) |
ISBN 9780190629236 (pbk.: alk. paper) | ISBN 9780190629229 (hardcover: alk. paper) |
ISBN 9780190629243 (updf) | ISBN 9780190629250 (epub)
Subjects: LCSH: Radiohead (Musical group)—Criticism and interpretation |
Rock music—England—History and criticism.
Classification: LCC ML421.R25 O83 2017 (print) | LCC ML421.R25 (ebook) |
DDC 782.42166092/2—dc23 LC record available at https://lccn.loc.gov/2016022990

Contents

Preface

SINCE *OK COMPUTER* (1997), five of the six records released by the English rock band Radiohead has peaked at #1 on the UK and/or US charts, and these six records have accounted for nearly 26 million of the band's 30 million albums sold. This success in their mature period (1997–2011) is especially notable since, following the generic "Brit Pop" and "Alternative Rock" heard on their first two albums (1993's *Pablo Honey* and 1995's *The Bends*), the band's sound has never piggybacked on any mainstream trends. Their commercial success in this mature period stems instead from an ability to write music that balances expectation and surprise. Though most of their songs present the listener with myriad surprises and disjunctures, they only do so after first setting up rich expectations listeners have inherited from various musical traditions.

This book analyzes Radiohead's studio albums from *OK Computer* (1997) through *The King of Limbs* (2011) to reveal this balance in four musical parameters: (1) song form, (2) rhythm, (3) timbre, and (4) harmony. Songs often begin as if they were in standard verse/chorus form only to replace the expected final chorus with a radically new section at the song's conclusion. Rhythms that initially suggest a standard rock backbeat become stretched or cropped to the point of deforming standard $^4/_4$ meters. Radiohead's music, qua rock music, relies on guitar, bass, drums, and tenor vocal, but those timbres are often digitally manipulated in a manner that disguises the source instrument. Finally, most Radiohead songs exhibit the same Western tonality as Mozart, The Beatles, and children's songs, but dissonant notes do not always resolve in expected ways.

Expanding on recent work in perception, this book approaches Radiohead's recorded music as a sonic *ecosystem* in which listeners participate, react, and adapt in order to search for meaning. Listeners bring into these ecosystems a set of expectations learned (if only tacitly) from popular music, classical music, or even Radiohead's own compositional idiolect, which is largely the product of the band's primary songwriter and lyricist Thom Yorke. Particularly important to this perceptual process are moments in Radiohead's music where a certain expectation—formal, rhythmic, timbral, or harmonic—is strongly cued through recognizable musical stimuli only to be violated by an unexpected realization. Of course, these expectations and realizations are contingent on one's musical background. An augmented sixth chord suggests one continuation to a classical aficionado but quite a different one to a jazz pianist. Hemiola is a novel and fleeting surface rhythm to a baroque oboe soloist but forms the basic meter of entire pieces in post-millennial rock and Ghanaian drumming. Violations of these subjective expectation–realization chains prompt the listener to search more deeply for meaning. Linking these musical details to the corresponding lyrics is often the first step in meaning creation, but an individual listener's search for meaning can also involve biographical details of the band or intertextual relationships with music, literature, or film.

ORGANIZATIONAL LAYOUT

Following the preface, an opening chapter lays out some methodological premises based on ecological perception and semiotics, and argues why Radiohead's music, more than any other commercially viable rock band in the past two decades, deserves such careful study. The book then proceeds through four intensely analytical chapters, each reflecting one of the four parameters named above. Following each of these chapters is a short "analytical coda." Whereas the chapters themselves focus on situating many short examples within Radiohead's catalog, the coda synthesizes the approaches provided in the chapter to illuminate a more comprehensive and interpretive view of one song as a whole. The final chapter animates the theoretical groundwork laid throughout the book in a sustained analysis of one of the band's most popular songs, "Pyramid Song," showing how the same strategies can be used to analyze music videos.

Chapter 1 surveys some of the foundational work in musical semiotics and perception that makes my analytical method possible. Studies of musical perception (e.g., London 2004, Clarke 2005, Huron 2006, Margulis 2013) show that cognitive arousal is maximized by music that meets us somewhere between the expected and the unexpected. Put differently, the brain goes into overdrive when music presents a stimulus that at once draws upon our prior experiences and yet provides some novel twist. In relating this observation to semiotic theory, I suggest Radiohead's balancing of surprise and expectation in form, rhythm, timbre, and harmony—the very balancing act that maximizes a hyperactive cognitive space—can be described in terms of *salience*. Like Beethoven's late music, Radiohead's albums between 1997 and 2011 maximize salience by building upon a host of expectations inherited from classical and popular music while at the same time subverting those expectations several times over the course of a given song. After building a case for how Radiohead's music is so consistently salient in this mature period, the chapter ends with a comparison with the more predictable—and therefore less perceptually marked—two albums that precede this period.

Rock music carries with it a set of formal expectations inherited from the late 1950s (strophic forms), which were transformed by The Beatles and other artists in the late 1960s (verse/chorus). These have remained almost completely unchanged in conventional rock music over the past four decades. Chapter 2 begins by demonstrating these conventional song forms in a handful of Radiohead songs. However, many of their songs begin as a strophic form (AA) or verse/chorus form (ABAB) but replace the expected final chorus with a brand new section of climactic material. The resulting song structure, which I call terminally climactic form, does not appear with any frequency in rock music until after 1990. Radiohead's use of this song form is thus not unique—it situates them within an emergent post-millennial formal trend—but the frequency with which they use it is unparalleled. This is notable because the terminally climactic form, in presenting listeners with a very strong sense of expectation (final chorus) only to subvert that expectation with a surprise realization (terminal climax), which *nonetheless behaves like a chorus* though it uses completely different thematic material, is a clear example of salience—a sweet spot between expectation and surprise.

Chapter 2 ends with a sustained analysis of "2+2=5" (2003–1). What starts off as a repeated strophe (suggesting verse/chorus or strophic form) is merely one of four unrelated sections progressing in an ABCD through-composed formal design. This particularly teleological song form narrates a dystopian future of "progress" (A to B to C to D) in accordance with its Orwellian title. Its withholding of the heavily distorted rock guitar timbre until section C also reflects the band's self-awareness. Fans who missed the guitar-centered band of 1993–1997 are rewarded for their patience not just after two albums (2000 and 2001), but also the opening 1′54″ of what might seem at first blush an equally navel-gazing record. Yorke's petulant cry "you have not been paying attention" can also be read as a dissatisfaction with the mixed critical reviews of their earlier albums *Kid A* (2000) and *Amnesiac* (2001).

Chapter 3 begins with a backbeat, the most prevalent rhythmic expectation in rock music. Though its genesis dates back to 1920s Memphis, it was imported almost wholesale into early rock music in the late 1950s and has remained a steady facet ever since. This chapter addresses all of the moments in Radiohead's catalog that deviate from backbeat-related expectations. Radiohead's most salient rhythms are those that begin with, or contain some elements of, a backbeat, but add or subtract beats from a standard measure of 4/4 time to produce elements of surprise. The repetition of such structures allows a listener to learn to entrain to these rhythms through the process of embodied cognition. Dozens of examples of particular rhythmic manifestations of this principle, including odd-cardinality meter, maximally even rhythms, changing meter, and polytempo, demonstrate that, far from reinventing the wheel in every song, Radiohead consistently alters our backbeat expectations in only a handful of different ways throughout their recorded output.

Two competing metrical layers throughout Radiohead's song "Idioteque" (2000–8) can be read concomitantly alongside the lyrics, which describe a similar battle, struggle, or war scene. Throughout this sustained analysis that ends Chapter 3, I show that a listener's search for meaning within complex grouping dissonance and changing meter can be fruitfully applied to the lyrical narrative in a holistic interpretive framework.

Though formal structure, rhythm, and especially harmony are well-worn territories for music theorists, timbre is a newer area of study that scholars are just now beginning to come to terms with. Chapter 4 demonstrates that ecological perception is well suited for the task of describing how we perceive novel timbral sources. Denis Smalley's concept of *source-bonding* (originally designed for the analysis of acousmatic music) is introduced as a method for describing how we perceive two surprising timbres in Radiohead's music: (1) source-deformation and (2) synthesis. In the first case, two timbral signifiers so essential to rock music—the lead vocal and the electric guitar—are deformed through digital and analog effects. Source-bonding becomes a question of a listener's ability to perceive the invariant properties of the original that remain after digital effects. By exposing the invariant properties of effects pedals and patches used throughout Radiohead's catalog, this chapter also shows that listeners can learn to perceive the invariant properties of the effects themselves over time. Radiohead also uses electronic instruments that transcend the boundaries of normal rock expectations. Synthesized timbres such as those created in and by Pro Tools, MAX/MSP, and the ondes Martenot present formidable boundaries to source-bonding until listeners have gained significant exposure to these timbres and the means by which they are produced.

At the end of Chapter 4 I analyze the bizarre timbres heard throughout "Like Spinning Plates" (2001–10), which was conceived more or less accidentally when a failed demo for "I Will" was played backwards. Inspired by the backwards track, Yorke then went about the convoluted process of recording a new vocal track, reversing it electronically, memorizing it phonetically backwards, recording that backwards version, then reversing the reversed to create a simulacrum of sung English. The only other sound added to the reversed "I Will" demo to create "Like Spinning Plates" is a corrugaphone cut to exactly the length needed to produce overtones harmonically compatible with the backwards "I Will" demo. A listener's ability to recognize these three timbres, despite significant source-deformation, influences the intertextual connections available to that listener in the search for meaning.

The majority of rock music, from The Beatles through post-millennial rock, reflects the same voice-leading structures as those heard in common-practice classical music. Chapter 5 begins by illustrating (through voice-leading graphs) this functional tonal system in Radiohead's music, then moves beyond to define and demonstrate two related systems by which their music deviates from functional tonality: (1) contrapuntal systems and (2) functional modal systems. With this framework in place, I then define four harmonic organizational strategies—absent tonic, double-tonic complex, sectional centricity, and underdetermined—that regularly appear in their music. Brief analyses of two unique voice-leading structures—"Knives Out" (2001–6) and "Paranoid Android" (1997–2)—lead to a sustained analysis of perhaps the most perplexing harmonic design of any Radiohead track.

"Faust Arp" (2007–6) begins squarely in B minor, but the verse quickly introduces modal mixture by juxtaposing B minor and B major triads in an egalitarian fashion. An unexpected turnaround at the end of the verse (C–A♭–D♭) pivots by tritone toward a mode-mixed G-centered chorus. The ending terminal climax brings about yet a third pitch center, but one whose allegiance seems split between B♭ and F. This extraordinary harmonic structure is not only notable for Radiohead, but actually contains two harmonic progressions found nowhere else in the common-practice or rock canons. My approach highlights three different strategies for hearing this structure, which I animate through three hypothetical listeners who differ by degrees in their willingness to hear long-range tonal and/or motivic coherence, as well as their intertextual knowledge of sources as disparate as 19th-century *Lieder* and early 17th-century lament bass.

To create an accurate depiction of what it means to analyze Radiohead, Chapters 2 through 5 each begin with the music itself, organize recurring trends into categories, and present a way of understanding and interpreting those categories. Though painstaking and encyclopedic at times, this bottom-up framework puts us in a position to look at any Radiohead song in context. How do the unique elements of a single song relate to similar phenomena heard throughout their catalog? In Chapter 6, I synthesize and distill the major theories and analytical methods in the book's first five chapters into the analysis of one the band's most popular songs: "Pyramid Song" (2001–2). My aims for doing so are twofold. First, I hope that providing an analysis from all angles will serve as a model for how a listener might analyze any Radiohead song. Second, with the burden of fleshing out all the possibilities within a single analytical domain lifted, I can focus more analytical attention on interpretation and meaning. As in the rest of the book, this chapter illuminates possible meanings by linking analytical details to lyrics and intertextual sources, including not only Dante's *The Divine Comedy* but two films released a few years before *Amnesiac*. The broader scope of this final chapter also allows ample space to address visual cues in the corresponding music video.

RELEVANCE TO OTHER SCHOLARSHIP

Though at times I shed new light on the genesis of certain songs (especially "Pyramid Song" in Chapter 6), readers searching for a general biography of Radiohead will find this book lacking in details surrounding the band members themselves. Relative to extant Radiohead scholarship, the strength of this book is its focus on analysis of the recorded music itself. Most contributions are almost wholly focused on biographical details of the band, media studies, or other considerations not properly music-analytical in nature. This includes Martin Clarke's *Radiohead: Hysterical and Useless* (2006), Mac Randall's *Exit Music: The Radiohead Story* (2011), as well as many of the essays contained within the collections *Radiohead and Philosophy: Fitter, Happier, and More Deductive* (2009) and *The Music and Art of Radiohead* (2005).

Unfortunately, those monographs on Radiohead that have engaged in the analysis of musical details have proceeded in ways which are not engaged at the scholarly level with current music-theoretical research. This includes Marianne Tatom Letts's *How to Disappear Completely: Radiohead and the Resistant Concept Album* (2010), Mark Paytress's *Radiohead: The Complete Guide to Their Music* (2005), Tim Footman's *Radiohead: Welcome to the Machine: OK Computer and the Death of the Classic Album* (2007), and James Doheny's *Radiohead: The Stories Behind Every Song* (2012). *Analyzing Radiohead* not only prioritizes *analysis* of Radiohead's music, but further contextualizes those analyses in recent musical perception and semiotics research, thereby *theorizing* larger trends in each of the four parameters. The result is that the music is not analyzed in a piecemeal fashion, but is rather always aimed at a larger picture that represents Radiohead's idiolect.

Several monographs on Radiohead focus on their early output, often extending no later than *Amnesiac* (2001). This includes Jonathan Hale's *Radiohead: From a Great Height* (1999), Dai Griffiths's 33⅓ volume on *OK Computer* (2004), and Marvin Lin's 33⅓ volume on *Kid A* (2010). *Analyzing Radiohead* supplements this gap by devoting equal amounts of attention to each of their newer albums through *The King of Limbs* (2011). Radiohead's newest album, *A Moon Shaped Pool* (2016), was released as this book was going into production.[1] I occasionally reference features of these new songs that recall Radiohead's work from 1997 to 2011, but, alas, a more sustained analysis will have to wait for a second edition!

While distinguishing itself from competing Radiohead titles, *Analyzing Radiohead* is constantly in dialogue with broader scholarly works which foreground the analysis of pop–rock music from a distinctly music-theoretical angle. This includes Everett's two-volume *The Beatles as Musicians* (1999, 2001). Everett's way of recasting the cultural icons as bona fide composers has influenced my outlook on Radiohead, and I'm not the first to note the parallels between these two groups— both probably the single most influential rock band of their generation. The impact of Allan Moore's 2012 book *Song Means* on the current volume is equally palpable. Though aimed at a more variegated body of music and, arguably, more lyric-driven, readers will find Moore's unapologetically close reading of minute musical detail present in my approach as well. Like Moore, I believe that our personal connections to a piece of music, no matter how idiosyncratic, are valid and valuable so long as they are centered in empirical musical details that others can hear. *Analyzing Radiohead* expands the methodological assumptions laid out by these two works in order to devise a new theory aimed at understanding Radiohead's unique idiolect. Aside from these two monographs, most music-theoretical research on popular music has appeared in peer-reviewed journals and edited collections. This book then sits as one of only a handful of monographs devoted to music-theoretical approaches to modern rock music, and the only one to date on Radiohead.

AUDIENCE

My ideal readership for this book is a Radiohead fan who reads music. That said, there are some things a reader who falls into one of these camps, but not the other, should know about my approach:

1. For Radiohead fans who do not read music (either fluently or at all): I generally assume you all to be a pontificate, cerebral bunch. Rather than water down technical descriptions of this music, the technical apparatus of music theory is wielded with whatever tools strike me as most necessary for addressing the music. Music-theoretical terms such as "beat class," "half-cadence," and "maximally even" are not difficult concepts to understand,

but the jargon may be new. In cases such as these I include definitions and description in a footnote at a term's first appearance. These footnotes also contain citations for scholarly articles that readers may access to learn even more about a given music-theoretical concept.

Readers unfamiliar with notated music may also choose to read only specific chapters. Chapters 1, 2, and 4 use almost no musical notation, and will be completely readable to musicians and non-musicians alike. Chapter 3 will be readable to any musician who can count notated rhythm. My notation of pulses, beats, and hypermeter using dots, open circles, and numbers (respectively) above the rhythm will not only make these easier to follow, but will also serve to deepen a reader's metrical understanding of this music. Chapter 5 is the only chapter in the book that hinges upon the ability to read notated music and, more specifically, voice-leading graphs. A simplified system of voice-leading notation is explained in the text itself. My hope is that readers will come to understand this notation as simply an economical way of showing "*this* note leads *there*." Chapter 6 is necessarily a combination of these approaches.

2. For those readers who read music and are not yet acquainted with the music of Radiohead: welcome! Academic musicians of all subdisciplines will be interested in the approaches to analyzing popular music espoused throughout this monograph. The argument I make in Chapter 1—that a theory of salience justifies a detailed study of Radiohead—connects to other composers who have similarly toed the line between convention and experimentation with great commercial and critical success. Chapter 2's focus not on conventional forms, but on idiosyncratic forms specific to a genre or composer, could be adapted to everything from Beethoven's expansive codas to the pastiche forms associated with Girl Talk and other mashup artists. Chapters 3 and 5 each take a musical parameter present in almost any genre and adapt it to the study of a particular artist. Studies of Elliott Carter's rhythmic practice or of Debussy's voice leading would look much the same in scope and approach, though with wildly different results. Scholars aiming at a broad understanding of popular music will perhaps find Chapter 4 the most rewarding. The study of timbre is a newly emerging and burgeoning field. I am confident that not only the analyses, but also the *theories* of timbre I put forth in Chapter 4 will lay useful groundwork for others attempting to describe this somewhat ineffable quality of popular music.

Whatever training or set of skills readers bring to this book, musical or otherwise, they will be rewarded for doing so. Guitar pedal aficionados will find their knowledge of circuitry rewarded in Chapter 4. Even for readers outside of music, this book has much to offer. Mathematicians' interests will pique in discussions of the Euclidean algorithm in Chapter 3. Cognitive psychologists and perhaps even evolutionary biologists will resonate with my discussion of ecological perception—especially as sustained in Chapters 1 and 4. Historians of both music and popular culture should be interested if for no other reason than the immense market success and influence of the band.

. . . okay, let's rock.

Note

1. My preliminary ideas on *A Moon Shaped Pool*'s similiarities and differences with regards to the band's previous output appeared in a record review I wrote for the Oxford University Press blog shortly after the record's release; see Osborn 2016.

Acknowledgments

FIRST AND FOREMOST, I'd like to thank the musicians in Radiohead for positively influencing me as a composer, a performer, and a listener to a degree that I cannot even begin to express here. In the same breath I'd also like to thank the immense fan base that supports this band (and each other). My interest in Radiohead has been fueled by several fan websites, especially Citizen Insane <citizeninsane. eu>, Green Plastic Radiohead <greenplastic.com>, and The King of Gear <thekingofgear.com>. To all the fans who have contributed to this rich music: this book is for you, by one of you.

I'm grateful for several institutions who provided monetary support for this book. First and foremost, I'm indebted to the University of Kansas School of Music for awarding me summer research funds that allowed for concentrated work on the manuscript. The New Faculty Research Fund, awarded by the KU Hall Center for the Humanities, kick-started my research just as I took the position at KU, and funded a research trip to Denmark. I would like to thank the Society for Education, Music, and Psychology Research (SEMPRE) for a generous travel bursary to support a talk I gave at the University of Liverpool that would become Chapter 1. In the later stages of producing this book, the Society for Music Theory—a beacon of emotional and professional support for me since my first year of graduate school—provided funds to offset the cost of indexing the manuscript. And of course, to my editor at OUP, Suzanne Ryan: thank you for believing in this manuscript, and for helping to guide it in the early stages.

I couldn't have written this book without the wide network of friends and colleagues who have provided intellectual and emotional support in the years since I began this research. First, I'd like to thank those who read my initial chapter drafts. These substantial founts of wisdom include Jake Cohen, Jay Summach, Mark Butler, Ciro Scotto, and Drew Nobile. A short, and woefully incomplete list of the colleagues I've taught alongside who have been willing to let me bounce ideas off them (or buy me a beer when I needed to stop) would look something like: Matthew Balensuela and Misti Shaw at DePauw University; Elizabeth Sayrs, Mark Phillips, and Evan Antonellis at Ohio University; Marie Brown, Jonathan Lamb, Germaine Halegoua, and the entire "write your first book proposal" cohort at the KU Hall Center in 2014; Alan Street and the rest of the theory/comp division at the University of Kansas; the vast network of KU scholars sharing ideas across disciplinary boundaries, especially Colin Roust and Sherrie Tucker. Finally, my colleague and mentor Scott Murphy has shown me not only endless patience and guidance since the day I arrived for my interview at KU, but, just as importantly, kindness.

The intellectual work we do in books such as these is only possible after countless hours spent with world-class teachers. To Michael F. Murray, James Parsons, Matthew Shaftel, Jane Clendinning, Michael Buchler, Evan Jones, Jonathan Bernard, John Rahn, and, more than the others combined, my dissertation advisor Áine Heneghan, I owe everything. Too many members of the Society for Music Theory have generously given their time and energy to transforming me into the scholar I am today. Most responsible for this transformation has been the vibrant community of popular music scholars who've mentored me since graduate school. Lori Burns, Walt Everett, Nicole Biamonte, Mark Spicer, John Covach, Joti Rockwell, Guy Capuzzo, Tim Hughes, Jocelyn Neal, Christopher Doll, Mark Spicer, and Anna Stephan-Robinson, in addition to reading countless drafts of conference proposals and article submissions, paved the way so the rest of us can make a career out of studying popular music, rather than *apologizing* for it. This community coalesced into the SMT Popular Music Interest Group (which, to this day, I cannot believe they let me Chair for a couple years). To those in this network who have always been willing to listen to my crazy ideas and/or share their better-articulated ones, I owe substantial gratitude: Nancy Murphy, Dave Easley, Christine Boone, Cora Palfy, Trevor de Clercq, Robin Attas, Chris Stover, Nolan Stolz, David Heetderks, Megan Lavengood, David K. Blake, Nick Braae, and too many more.

Being able to connect with the larger network of popular music scholars outside of North America has shaped my understanding of what it means to *analyze* popular music. I'd like to thank the Society for Music Analysis (UK) for inviting me to two events—the 2010 SMA Summer School in Durham and the 2013 POPMAC Conference in Liverpool. These venues provided the opportunity to meet and swap ideas with scholars who would become influential to me as researchers and even future collaborators, including Dai Griffiths, Allan Moore, Kenneth Smith, Michael Spitzer, and, before his untimely death, Adam Krims. I'd like to thank everyone participating in the 2014 Sonic Signatures Symposium in Denmark—especially Simon Zagorski-Thomas—for helping to cement some ideas surrounding record production which proved integral to Chapter 4. I'd like to thank the Arbeitskreis Studium Populaerer Musik for putting together the 2011 Osnabrück summer program that would eventually spawn the edited collection *Song Interpretation in 21st-Century Pop Music* (Ashgate, 2014). I spent that week analyzing a PJ Harvey song with Cláudia Azevedo, Chris Fuller, Juliana Guerrero, and Michael Kaler, who taught me when to use music-theoretical tools and, just as importantly, when *not* to. Thanks also to Ralf von Appen, André Doehring, and Dietrich Helms for the warm hospitality in Osnabrück, including the best conference dinner of my career.

On my way home from Osnabrück I sat next to an attractive woman on the plane who, after balking at my unkempt look (I had stayed up all night in Amsterdam), decided the polite thing to do would be to ask me what I was working on. Though largely an exaggeration at this point, I said "I'm writing a book on Radiohead." She married me four and a half years later. My ability to work on this book day in and day out (okay, sometimes not *every* day) was due in large part to a stable yet exhilarating relationship with this intrepid wilderness wanderer who asks out pop music scholars on airplanes: Laura Rossi. Both gifted writers in their own right, my mother Sandy Osborn and brother Kevin Osborn are the first people I call anytime I have something published. Thank you both for always making me feel like a rock star. My father, Richard Osborn, whom I've never seen pick up a book in my life, is now, as we speak, writing a memoir about his half-century of fly fishing. To the man who always encouraged me to try new things, thank you for trying this.

Abbreviations and Notational Conventions

REFERENCES TO TRACK numbers and timings in this book relate exclusively to the original studio releases on CD (or, in the case of *In Rainbows*, the original mp3 downloads). When introduced in the text, albums are indexed by year of release, tracks by order in which they appear on their respective album, and specific passages by track timing at which that passage begins. For example, a reference to the chorus in "Optimistic" would be followed by (2000–6, 1:07), indicating that it is the sixth track on *Kid A* (2000), and that the chorus begins at 1:07. For ease of reference throughout the text, Table 0.1 presents the complete track lists for all of Radiohead's studio albums addressed, however briefly, in this book.

All transcriptions in this book were done by ear using a guitar, keyboard, drum set, and, in tricky cases, a spectrograph. This includes lyrics, which are transcribed as I hear them. Bypassing the various versions of lyrics that appear on the Internet is a no-brainer. However, to truly address individual listeners' perception of musical stimuli, we should also de-emphasize the primacy of Radiohead's authorial intention. Even if we wanted to appeal to intention, we must admit that Radiohead's unique practice of scattering lyrical fragments throughout their artwork makes this a tricky affair.

The book follows American Standard Pitch Notation, wherein the C that sounds between bass and treble clef, also known as "middle C," is called C4. Instruments and voices are typically notated in the clef in which they sound—the convention of notating the guitar an octave above its sounding pitch is ignored. Voice-leading graphs in Chapter 5 follow no octave conventions, with pitch classes notated in the octave that renders the harmonic structure clearest. Drum set transcriptions adhere to the legend shown in Figure 0.1.

TABLE 0.1

Complete track listing of Radiohead's studio albums, 1993–2016

Release year	Album title	Track number	Song title (capitalized and punctuated as per CD liner)
1993	*Pablo Honey*	1	YOU
		2	CREEP
		3	HOW DO YOU?
		4	STOP WHISPERING
		5	THINKING ABOUT YOU
		6	ANYONE CAN PLAY GUITAR
		7	RIPCORD
		8	VEGETABLE
		9	PROVE YOURSELF
		10	I CAN'T
		11	LURGEE
		12	BLOW OUT
1995	*The Bends*	1	planet telex
		2	the bends
		3	high and dry
		4	fake plastic trees
		5	bones
		6	(nice dream)
		7	just
		8	my iron lung
		9	Bulletproof . . . i wish i was
		10	black star
		11	sulk
		12	street spirit (fade out)

TABLE 0.1

Continued

Release year	Album title	Track number	Song title (capitalized and punctuated as per CD liner)
1997	*OK Computer*	1	AIRBAG
		2	PARANOID ANDROID
		3	SUBTERRANEAN HOMESICK ALIEN
		4	EXIT MUSIC (FOR A FILM)
		5	LET DOWN
		6	KARMA POLICE [7 fitter happier]
		8	ELECTIONEERING
		9	CLIMBING UP THE WALLS
		10	NO SURPRISES
		11	LUCKY
		12	THE TOURIST
2000	*Kid A*	1	EVERYTHING IN ITS RIGHT PLACE
		2	KID A
		3	THE NATIONAL ANTHEM
		4	HOW TO DISAPPEAR COMPLETELY
		5	TREEFINGERS
		6	OPTIMISTIC
		7	IN LIMBO
		8	IDIOTEQUE
		9	MORNING BELL
		10	MOTION PICTURE SOUNDTRACK

(*continued*)

TABLE 0.1

Continued Release year	Album title	Track number	Song title (capitalized and punctuated as per CD liner)
2001	*Amnesiac*	1	PACKT LIKE SARDINES IN A CRUSHD TIN BOX
		2	PYRAMID SONG
		3	PULK/PULL REVOLVING DOORS
		4	YOU AND WHOSE ARMY?
		5	I MIGHT BE WRONG
		6	KNIVES OUT
		7	MORNING BELL/AMNESIAC
		8	DOLLARS AND CENTS
		9	HUNTING BEARS
		10	LIKE SPINNING PLATES
		11	LIFE IN A GLASSHOUSE
2003	*Hail to the Thief*	1	2+2=5 (The lukewarm.)
		2	Sit down. Stand up. (Snakes & Ladders.)
		3	Sail to the Moon. (Brush the Cobwebs out of the Sky.)
		4	Backdrifts. (Honeymoon is Over.)
		5	Go to Sleep. (Little Man being Erased.)
		6	Where I End and You Begin (The Sky is falling in.)
		7	We suck Young Blood. (Your Time is up.)
		8	The Gloaming. (Softly Open our Mouths in the Cold.)
		9	There there. (The Boney King of Nowhere.)
		10	I will. (No man's Land.)

TABLE 0.1

Continued

Release year	Album title	Track number	Song title (capitalized and punctuated as per CD liner)
		11	A Punchup at a Wedding. (No no no no no no no no.)
		12	Myxomatosis. (Judge, Jury & Executioner.)
		13	Scatterbrain. (As Dead as Leaves.)
		14	A Wolf at the Door. (It Girl. Rag Doll.)
2007	*In Rainbows*	1	15 STEP
		2	BODYSNATCHERS
		3	NUDE
		4	WEIRD FISHES / ARPEGGI
		5	ALL I NEED
		6	FAUST ARP
		7	RECKONER
		8	HOUSE OF CARDS
		9	JIGSAW FALLING INTO PLACE
		10	VIDEOTAPE
2011	*The King of Limbs*	1	BLOOM
		2	MORNING MR MAGPIE
		3	LITTLE BY LITTLE
		4	FERAL
		5	LOTUS FLOWER
		6	CODEX
		7	GIVE UP THE GHOST
		8	SEPARATOR

(continued)

TABLE 0.1

Continued			
Release year	Album title	Track number	Song title (capitalized and punctuated as per CD liner)
2016	*A Moon Shaped Pool*	1	BURN THE WITCH
		2	DAYDREAMING
		3	DECKS DARK
		4	DESERT ISLAND DISK
		5	FUL STOP
		6	GLASS EYES
		7	IDENTIKIT
		8	THE NUMBERS
		9	PRESENT TENSE
		10	TINKER TAILOR SOLDIER SAILOR RICH MAN POOR MAN BEGGAR MAN THIEF
		11	TRUE LOVE WAITS

FIGURE 0.1 Drum set notation legend.

EVERYTHING IN ITS RIGHT PLACE

1   Analyzing Radiohead

FROM *OK COMPUTER* onward, Radiohead consistently confronts the listener with passages that maximize the balance between banal predictability and sheer surprise. Borrowing from semiotics and neuroscience, I will come to call this balance *salience*. Rather than deal with salient moments on a case-by-case basis, creating a typology of these surprises allows us to observe a thread of continuity in their compositional practice. Radiohead does not reinvent the wheel with every track, and neither should we as listeners. In this chapter I will introduce categories of musical features that the band revisits in multiple tracks that maximize the potential for interpretation. These salient gestures represent musical features which are not too predictable, yet not completely removed from expectations. For example, when Radiohead's songs avoid predictable strophic forms, they do not approximate the free jazz structures heard on Coltrane's *Interstellar Space* (1974). Rather these not-too-conventional, not-too-experimental forms tend to congregate in a few different types such as "terminally climactic" and "through-composed" forms, both of which take verse/chorus and strophic forms (respectively) as their point of departure before moving on to, and ending with, completely unrelated material.

Equally as important as cataloging these surprises in Radiohead's music is understanding how we perceive them. One particular branch of music psychology, ecological perception, can illuminate how these moments both fulfill expectations inherited from rock's stylistic conventions while subverting others. In tandem with close analyses of musical detail, ecological perception can help uncover deeper meaning from this music. In this search for meaning, hermeneutic or interpretive elements serve to answer the "so what?" question rightfully posed of pure theory and analysis. What ecological perception aims to offer are answers to two equally important interrogatives: "why?" and "how?" *Why* does Radiohead's music elicit a high degree of perceptual engagement on the part of the listener, and *how* does a model of ecological perception help us to understand the ways various types of listeners interact with the music?

Markedness and Salience in Radiohead

In neuroscience, an object is said to be most *salient* if it rewards both top-down and bottom-up approaches to interpretation.[1] That is, our attention is drawn to things which are not too similar to what we expect, yet not too different from what we know. From a semiotic standpoint, salience exists somewhere between the unmarked and the marked. Unmarked terms are general, while marked terms offer greater precision.[2] For example, in the opposition between dog/retriever, the latter is marked.

Robert Hatten uses a theory of markedness to identify moments in Beethoven's middle-to-late music which are particularly salient. According to this theory, listeners will not find moments in Beethoven's music which are formulaic with regards to classical style (assuming the listener has the appropriate stylistic competencies) to be salient in any way—and will therefore find little need to pursue any interpretive or hermeneutic strategies. These conventions include regular phrase structure and cadential formulae. On the contrary, this same listener will find nearly incomprehensible a passage of music with irregular phrase structure, non-standard instrumentation, and/or chromatic saturation. Beethoven's most salient themes are the ones that exist somewhere between these two poles, which are marked through *limited* tonal instability and *slightly* irregular phrasing:

> By flirting with one or more instabilities, [Beethoven's] themes acquire the additional salience that comes from stylistically marked oppositions. In turn, that increased markedness creates a greater specificity of content, which enhances the expressive force of such themes.[3]

We might then speak of salience in music as an opposition between the stylistic and the novel, or between predictability and surprise. Somewhere between these oppositions exist salient musical events that are novel to a certain degree, yet still comprehensible to the overwhelming majority of audiences steeped in the appropriate style, be it western classical music, rock music, and so forth. I will show throughout this book that Radiohead's music exploits this salience through a limited number of specific song forms, rhythmic/metric types, timbres, and harmonic organizational strategies used with great frequency throughout their catalog.[4] These salient gestures are thoroughly analyzed and cataloged in Chapters 2 through 5.

Each of these phenomena cue learned expectations, and are especially salient because they occupy a middle space between predictability and surprise. For example, rhythms can range from entirely predictable (e.g., the regular alternation of kick and snare in a backbeat) to wildly sporadic (e.g., the individual articulations in an improvised guitar solo), but Euclidean rhythms, which usually place an odd number of accents over evenly spaced pulses, inhabit a particular zone between those two extremes. In presenting a more sporadic ostinato than the backbeat, yet presenting it in the same repetitive manner, Euclidean rhythms present the opportunity to predict future rhythmic events given significant immersion within the current event. Changing meters also balance predictability and surprise by repeating rhythms which contain evenly spaced pulses over differing period lengths. Radiohead's most salient rhythms each balance predictability and surprise, but do so in only a handful of different ways.

Ecological Perception and Meaning: Invariance, Specification, Affordance

Understanding the core concepts of ecological approaches to musical perception and cognition will help us understand why salience is so relevant to Radiohead's music. It will become clear that a theory of ecological perception is extraordinarily fitting for addressing this music which meets several of our learned expectations from various styles, yet continually assaults us with surprise realizations that cause us to rethink those initial assumptions. The most active state of listener engagement, the one at which the highest levels of meaning-creation will occur, happens somewhere between these extremes. Music psychologist Elizabeth Hellmuth-Margulis echoes this heightened-state hypothesis by suggesting that musical surprise "elevates intensity along some affective dimension."[5] Once our emotional processing reaches this elevated state of intensity, we are primed to search for meaning.

To appreciate just why this is, we must first understand our ancient mammalian brains. Though discussions such as these risk essentializing and perhaps fetishizing the "nature" while dismissing the "nurture," it is important to understand that, while our sound culture has evolved greatly over the past 15,000 years or so, our modes of

perceiving those sounds have not. From an evolutionary standpoint, "musical perception is parasitic on other modes of auditory perception."[6] When we perceive sounds in
the environment, we are programmed to immediately process them for meaning, and
we still do. Most important are two questions: Where is the sound coming from, and
what is making it? Sounds which present very limited novelty will not activate our centers of meaning-processing. We tune out the everyday sounds of our environment and
focus instead on the novel. Benign birds and gentle breezes recede into the background
and become nearly imperceptible, allowing our perceptual systems to concentrate all of
their resources on processing the meanings of more salient sounds that may represent
threat or opportunity (e.g., predatory calls, severe weather, flowing water, herd noises).

At the same time, and in fact *because* our brains are so adapted for this complex process, trying to process too many novel stimuli at one time can lead one to a
situation of "information overload" in which we are unable to process the meaning
of sound effectively. Imagine any number of situations in the wild which would
have (or do now) immerse you in a new sonic environment within a relatively short
period of time. No sooner do we start to make predictions about what one marked
stimulus means and what appropriate actions to take than we are confused by another, distracting us from fully processing the meaning of the first—ad infinitum.

Decoding these complex perception/expectation/realization chains in Radiohead's
music, as well as the meanings we as listeners derive from them, is my central aim in
this book. This analytical process owes a debt to three pioneers in the field of ecological perception. J. J. Gibson pioneered a field known as visual ecology in the 1970s; Eric
Clarke adapted this research into a theory of musical perception, culminating in a 2005
book that remains the central reference on the topic; and Allan Moore's 2012 book was
the first to build a comprehensive theory of interpreting recorded popular song using
these ecological principles. Ecological perception relies a great deal on three important
concepts—*invariants, specification*, and *affordance*. Combined, these concepts help to
solve a perennial problem involving musical meaning: how do we account for the fact
that, though each of us has our own unique interpretation of a piece, there seems to be a
commonly accepted range of meanings shared between many listeners? Put differently,
how do we find a middle space between, on one extreme, pure, unbounded subjectivity among individuals, and, on the other extreme, a single, intersubjective "encoded"
meaning waiting to be "discovered" for each piece of music? Both extremes, demon-
strably false, are riddled with serious philosophical shortcomings. Ecological perception provides us with the tools to carve out a middle space more suited toward human
interpretation of musical stimuli. Jason Summach, in a review of Moore's book, situates
ecological perception's role in this middle space most eloquently:

> . . . meaning is neither entirely imposed by those who make recordings, nor
> entirely constructed by listeners. Instead, meaning emerges in an encounter

between the listener, whose lifetime of musical experiences and associations is necessarily unique, and the track, which presents a unique configuration. [Moore's] chapter title [6: "Friction"] references the "friction" that obtains between conventions evoked by the track, which the listener registers as expectation, and those features of the track that foil expectation.[7]

Ecological perception provides the tools to address this hermeneutic quagmire between subjectivity and intersubjectivity. The invariant properties of a sound are those which remain constant. Invariants specify one of two things. First, the invariant properties of a sound may specify a host of *physical* or acoustical characteristics of the sound source itself. A high-pitched, quickly articulated, dry percussive attack followed by a shower of similar noises occurring within a narrow window of time specifies the sound of glass breaking. The sound created is a direct result of the materials involved, thus the sound specifies exactly the sources involved. Listeners can discern even greater detail in a given glass-break by attending to the invariants of different component sounds.[8] The interval between the initial percussive attack and the subsequent showering is an invariant property of the window's height, while the exact timbre of said showering is an invariant property of the material on which the glass lands. These listening skills are only learned given enough time and exposure to a given stimulus.

Second, the invariant properties of a sound specify a host of *cultural* associations shared by certain groups of people. It may be safe to assume that no culture associates the sound of window glass breaking with comfort and safety (the related sounds heard at weddings and ship-christening not withstanding). In a culture where many personal boundaries of security and property are made from glass, the sound of glass breaking specifies a breach of safety or loss of property. Because this cultural association is so fixed, we may conclude that the loss of safety or property is also an invariant property of the sounds described in the previous paragraph, <glass breaking>.[9] For Clarke, this linkage between the physical and the cultural plays a fundamental role in the theory of ecological perception:

> . . . just as sounds specify the invariants of the natural environment, so too do they specify the constancies or invariants of the cultural environment. The sounds of a muffled drum being struck with wooden sticks *specify* the materials (wood, skin) and physical characteristics (hollowness, damped vibration) of the material source—the drum; and they also *specify* the social event (for instance, a military funeral) of which they are a part.[10]

However, we must also be sensitive to cultural *variants* within different contexts, which then become encoded as invariants within that culture. These may be considered exceptions to the rule, and likely relate not only to particular occasions, but also are applicable only to a smaller culture or subculture. For example, the sonic properties of glass breaking across the hull of a boat means something altogether different for anyone familiar with the convention of christening an ocean liner, and listeners run virtually no risk of confusing this sound with one that specifies personal danger or loss of property. More apropos for the following chapters which analyze form, rhythm, and harmony, cultural sources for Clarke also include "the culturally specific *structural* principles and cultural contexts within which music arises," and these sources are just as integral to the perceptual meaning of sounds.[11]

Invariant properties of a sound are those that are more or less universally understood by listeners, either by understanding the physical construction of an object and its materials or by understanding cultural/structural phenomena associated with that sound. Invariance relies a great deal on specification. Everyday usage of the word specify would not be too far off in this manner. Sounds specify something— either materials of construction or cultural associations. *Specification* is to ecological perception as *signification* is to semiotics and conventional theories of music cognition.[12] While empirical research in the field of music cognition asserts that a fundamentally "bottom-up" cumulative system is at work in our brains when we encounter a discrete musical stimulus (*if* small stimulus A *then* larger concept B; *if* larger concept B *then* larger still image-schemata C . . .), ecological perception is a much more immediate affair.[13] Again, Clarke:

> . . . the standard cognitive approach is to regard perception as simply the starting point for a series of cognitive processes . . . the ecological approach presents the situation entirely differently . . . perceiving organisms seek out and respond to perceptual information that specifies objects and events in the environment, and this perceiving is a continuous process that is both initiated by, and results in, action . . . while mainstream psychology presents the temporal aspect of perception as a stream of discrete stimuli, processed separately and "glued together" by memory, an ecological approach sees it as a perceptual flow.[14]

Sounds in our environment specify their source immediately, without complex cognitive processing schemes, because our relationship to sound is one of *mutualism*. Sounds certainly change us as perceivers over time, and because sound is *only* experienced as a mutual relationship between perceiver and environment, it is also we as perceivers who influence the perception of sound over time, and thus, in a very real way, sound itself. We learn more and more about what sounds specify over time because we have memory. Mutualism thus "rejects those semiotic approaches that assert fixed, arbitrary relationships between signs and referents."[15] Ecological perception illuminates a complex process typically taken for granted when listening to recorded music. Try and recall the last time you thought to yourself something along the lines of "I am experiencing periodic vibrations of tiny columns of air produced by two magnets powered by alternating current, and the reason I am even processing these two sounds as one source is because my brain is compensating for the slight difference in the speed at which those two signals hit my eardrums, which is of course a direct result of my physical placement within this space relative to those two magnets." I am certainly not suggesting that we as listeners *should* preoccupy ourselves with these minutiae, but they are themselves prerequisites for the seemingly instant process of perceiving invariants and the sources they specify.

Most discussions of meaning in recorded music are not merely concerned with invariants or specification, but with affordance, which nonetheless is only possible after accounting for invariants and the sources they specify. Affordance stems from J. J. Gibson's work in visual perception,[16] which is concerned with how we interpret what we are seeing. Gibson reckoned a perceptual system something along the lines of the following three-step process: (1) I see in the distance a narrow, vertically oriented structure (an invariant property of most trees); (2) Though I am too far away to see bark, leaves, and limbs to confirm that the object is indeed a tree, I know from experience that tall, narrow, and vertically oriented are all invariant properties that specify <tree>; (3) Thus, my perception of these invariant properties and the objects they specify *affords* the interpretation <there is a tree on the horizon>. Just as importantly, those same invariants and specifications *do not afford* the interpretation <there is a polar bear on the horizon>, because the invariants needed to specify polar bear do not include those that are narrow or dark in color.

A curious timbral source heard throughout Radiohead's song "Like Spinning Plates" (2001–10) provides the occasion to examine how invariants and affordances relate to the listening experience. <Pulsating amplitude> and <free aerophone attack> are the primary invariant physical properties of the source heard at 1:43. These two invariants afford a number of potential sources, including a flute (aerophone) mediated through a Leslie rotating speaker cabinet or tremolo effect (pulsating amplification). But upon closer listening the *rate* of pulsation in the amplitude is not mechanically consistent, suggesting a human actuator. Furthermore, as the source changes frequencies between $E\flat4$ and $A\flat4$ until 2:53, we can hear the rate of amplitude pulsation consistently increasing on the higher $A\flat4$. When the pitch reaches the higher still $C5$ at 2:53, our predictions about the necessary correlation between pulsation speed and frequency are confirmed. The pattern of the pitches $E\flat4$, $A\flat4$, $C5$, as well as their lack of equal temperament (each higher pitch gets a little flatter), unmistakably specifies an instrument bound to the natural overtone series. The properties of the source's amplitude pattern, manner of attack, and frequency pattern all taken together afford <corrugaphone>—a plastic tube that, when spun in the air at a low speed produces a fundamental frequency relative to its length and diameter and, when spun faster, produces higher overtones of that fundamental relative to the rate of speed at which it is spun. While the invariants specify physical attributes of the instrument directly, they nevertheless only afford <corrugaphone> for listeners who have prior experience with this instrument, and so affordances are always contingent.

Reaching higher-level interpretations of a musical passage is undoubtedly the ultimate goal for a theory of musical perception. The perceptible invariants in "Like Spinning Plates" specify the sound's source—the corrugaphone—but what higher-level meanings does this lead to, and how might different listeners interpret it? A corrugaphone does not suggest any meanings based on percussive attacks such as hitting or punching since neither of these physical movements are linked to the kinesis with which that sound is created. Perceiving the corrugaphone does lead to meanings based on <twirling>, <spinning>, and the like. An individual whose prior experiences include exposure to the track name (not necessarily a given in modern listening practices) might connect the meaning of this event directly with the word "spinning" in the song's title. Like a circus plate spinner, the listener could visualize the gyroscopic effect of spinning the corrugaphone in a recording studio and, without too much imagination, begin to sympathize physiologically with the performer through a process known as embodied cognition. Recent research in cognition theory now suggests that "these patterns take on metaphorical meaning as a result of mapping them onto image schemas derived from bodily experience."[17] The [invariant >>> specification >>> source >>> affordance] chain in "Like Spinning Plates" could thus lead to diverse intersubjective meanings, from the joyous experiences of twirling on a childhood merry-go-round all the way to a listener who, cued by the song's final lyric, remembers a potentially traumatic experience of a "bod[y] floating down the muddy river."

In summation, "invariants afford through specification."[18] The invariant properties of a sound that specify its source and materials do not afford a *single* interpretation, as we have seen, but neither do they allow for an unbounded range of interpretations. We can say that the sonic event affords a limited range of *intersubjective* meanings. Margulis highlights the role of musical analysis in navigating this space between the subjective and intersubjective:

... there is a space between universal, automatic responses and contingent, subjective experience within which analysis can do descriptive work.

Expectation theory, while generally considered a branch of music psychology, positions itself within this space, seeking to explore the ways in which empirically verifiable psychological tendencies might result in rich, affect-full musical experiences that admit variability from person to person.[19]

The affective response to "Like Spinning Plates" that I have suggested above is not a prescriptive endeavor, but rather a description of plausible reactions many listeners might have had. Starting with the assumption that moments of surprise in Radiohead's music often prompt similar affect-full responses, analyzing Radiohead becomes the practice of uncovering possible conclusions a listener might come to in processing these moments for meaning.

Radiohead after *The Bends*

Ecological perception demonstrates the "how" of Radiohead's most marked passages, but what about the *why*? Why does Radiohead's music provide a more fertile ground for musical perception than Britney Spears's "Oops, I Did it Again" (2000–1) or Stockhausen's aggressively abstract 1966 electro-acoustic work *Kontakte*? Radiohead's music provides a more fertile ground for this sort of interpretation of perceptual detail than does music that is either so radically unique (Stockhausen) or so transparently native to an established style (Spears) precisely because it exists between these two marked/unmarked extremes. Their music from *OK Computer* (1997) onward consistently maximizes these ecological and perceptual principles by presenting us with recognizable musical stimuli, which we register as expectation, only to subvert those expectations with potent surprises. Musical tropes (or even familiar pieces) which we encounter frequently and which thus present limited novelty may easily slip into the background of our listening practices. Take, for example, music that is inexorably bound to a common style. Muzak, the company who provides businesses with background sounds for any number of mundane commercial environments, thrives on this assumption. Styles such as "smooth jazz" or "light classical" seem particularly innocuous to our perceptual systems, thus providing us with a warm fuzzy feeling while allowing us to concentrate on choosing the perfect breakfast cereal. On the other extreme, music which bombards our senses with sounds for which we have little to no frame of reference also has a tendency to recede into noise as it alienates the average listener, whose interpretive strategies are continuously fraught with frustration. Music of this caliber includes electro-acoustic music composed in the mid-twentieth century that relies heavily on manipulating found, recorded sounds and synthesized timbres.

Radiohead's music after *The Bends* is particularly suited to a theory of ecological perception because it exists between these two extremes. Recent music psychology suggests that cognitive arousal is maximized by music that meets us somewhere between the expected and the unexpected.[20] We tune out commonly occurring sounds in order to focus on those which are more novel, but we need a familiar base from which to start. Situating novel sounds within a familiar environment helps us to make predictions. Because Radiohead's first two albums—*Pablo Honey* (1993) and *The Bends* (1995)—are in fact too predictable for listeners immersed in rock conventions,[21] their music is far more salient from 1997 onward.

Numerous commentators have remarked on the sheer split between the vision espoused by *OK Computer* and the relatively derivative approaches heard on *Pablo Honey* and *The Bends*. Allan Moore and Anwar Ibrahim show that *OK Computer* exhibits distinct timbral and rhythmic innovation, while *Kid A* begins a distinct phase of formal complexity.[22] While their first two albums place Radiohead squarely in conversation with Brit Pop and Grunge—Nirvana's and The Pixies' influence is not far removed—Moore and Ibrahim note they seem to have "all but forgotten" these influences in their development of a unique voice by *OK Computer*.[23]

Essential to understanding Radiohead after *The Bends* is the distinction between two related terms: style and idiolect. Styles can be very broad indeed, ranging from "rock," to the more narrow "Alternative Rock," to the narrower still "mid-1990s Brit Pop." Generally speaking, styles represent a number of distinct artists. An idiolect is the way that we can, for example, distinguish Radiohead's "High and Dry" (1995–3) from Oasis's "Wonderwall" (1995–3) or Blur's "Country House" (1995–2), three songs released in the same year in the same Brit Pop style. We should also be clear to divorce Radiohead from any sort of "progressive rock" aesthetic with which they may have been associated. Because their music contains none of the surface level stylistic traits from progressive rock bands of the 1970s, Radiohead may be lowercase-p-progressive (read: innovative), but they are not "progressive rock" (read: a genre with its roots in the 1970s). Moore and Ibrahim suggest that the strongest of Radiohead's influences may be the early Pixies albums *Come on Pilgrim* (1987) and *Surfer Rosa* (1988).[24]

An idiolect can be even more unique than a band. For example, we can distinguish between the idiolects of Radiohead (the band) and the individual idiolects of at least two of the group's members—Jonny Greenwood and Thom Yorke—by listening closely to the large body of non-Radiohead projects each has been involved with, as well as by examining more closely those few Radiohead songs not originating from Yorke, the band's primary songwriter. Two standout elements in compositions penned by Jonny Greenwood, namely the prominently displayed Neapolitan sixth chord throughout "Wolf at the Door" (2003–14) and the quotations of electro-acoustic composers Paul Lansky and Arthur Kreiger in "Idioteque"

(2000–8), reveal a propensity for referencing his classical background overtly, a critical difference between Yorke and Greenwood.

Idiolect, at least as it relates to style, is a useful way for us to position Radiohead in the sweet spot along the Spears–Stockhausen continuum. An artist bound to a style with which an individual listener is familiar will offer that listener a lower degree of markedness than an artist either (a) not readily congruent with any style with which said listener is familiar, or (b) drawn eclectically from myriad styles. Notice that the focus here must be on individual listeners for two reasons. First, and perhaps most obviously, different listeners will become more familiar with different musical environments based on their prior subjective exposures, and therefore more adept at recognizing style-dependent stimulus patterns. Listeners in the southern United States may find themselves equally at odds with the harmonic content of a North Indian *Dhrupad* improvisation as the performers of the latter would find themselves with a standard twelve-bar blues progression.

Second, we must focus on individual listeners because the focus of this theory is aimed at musical perception, rather than genre. Though he couches it somewhat empirically, I discern a moral tone when Moore writes, "indeed it is harder to define the idiolect of Bowie, say, than that of Oasis, or of Tony Bennett."[25] What I explicitly *do not* want to recapitulate is anything close to the well-worn axe "experimental music is good, conventional music is bad." First, I think the distinction is finer and more subjective than that, and even if the division were viable, both types of music would serve a particular function. Though I find the *process* of experimental music (a process of experimenting with certain conventions while leaving others intact) useful for distinguishing between genres, I find the more traditional binary distinction between progressive/conventional too coarse for accurately describing most music. Rather than illuminate questions of genre or value, my juxtaposition of style and idiolect is aimed at explaining how Radiohead's juxtaposition of novel and conventional musical stimuli relatively affect a listener's process of creating meaning in their music.

Listeners sufficiently steeped in the stylistic conventions of 1990s rock music will simply not find Radiohead's first two albums—*Pablo Honey* (1993) and *The Bends* (1995)—perceptually salient relative to their music from *OK Computer* (1997) onward. Nearly all of the music on the first two albums conforms too closely to stylistic expectations. Highlighting some examples of these conventional timbres, forms, rhythms, and harmonies used in Radiohead's pre-1997 music will help to contextualize the marked gestures heard in those domains from *OK Computer* onward.

Radiohead's first two albums feature only conventional drums/bass/guitar timbres with one or several acoustic vocal tracks overlaid.[26] Any effects added (e.g., reverb, distortion, delay, phaser) merely color the readily identifiable source, and these are stock timbres heard throughout 1990s rock music. The exceptionally screechy guitar at the end of "Blow Out" (1993–12, 3:12ff.) may be the closest these effects come to source deformation, but because the reverb and distortion (not to mention the multiple guitar tracks) are added gradually, this results in a cumulative build-up process that helps us link later timbres to earlier sources. We can hear Radiohead trying on the ethereal keyboard timbres that will come to define their later music near the end of *The Bends*'s final track, "Street Spirit" (1995–12, 2:48ff.), though its role here is merely to support the arpeggiated electric guitar that dominates the track.

What all conventional song forms have in common is the practice of recapitulation—specifically the practice of ending a song by bringing back some previously heard material. Not one track from *Pablo Honey* or *The Bends* ends in new material. These songs are either strophic, built on the repetition of a single formal unit, or are built from a contrasting verse/chorus pair. Several songs contain at least three choruses, something Radiohead seldom does after 1995. The half-time bridge in "Stop Whispering" (1993–4, 3:24–3:39) that leads to a bombastic third chorus, for example, is a well-worn trope in early 1990s alternative rock music (cf. The Gin Blossoms, Stone Temple Pilots, Smashing Pumpkins, etc.).

Metrically, nearly everything on Radiohead's first two albums fits within predictable two-, four-, and eight-bar phrases anchored through standard backbeats in the drum kit. Occasionally, one hears either a three-bar phrase, as in the recurring signature riff to "The Bends" (1995–2, e.g., 0:12–0:20) and in the verse of "Anyone Can Play Guitar" (1993–6, e.g., 0:43–0:52). The three-measure phrase is minimally disruptive inasmuch it does not affect the half-note level at which backbeat entrainment occurs. In fact, it not only preserves the half-note backbeat level, but the larger measure-grouping as well, only disrupting the two-measure phrase expectation. This ratio of three-when-we-expect-two also appears as a truncated half-measure in the opening riff in "Black Star" (1995–10, 0:09–0:13), which still preserves the backbeat. Only one isolated riff on *Pablo Honey* asks listeners to reorient to a level faster than the backbeat. The recurring intro/verse riff of the opening track "You" (1993–1, e.g., 0:25–0:31) sets up the expectation of a ⁶⁄₈ backbeat by repeating it three times, only to shorten it by one eighth note in the fourth measure, resulting in a ⁵⁄₈ surprise measure.

The myriad harmonic expectations that listeners bring to 1990s rock music is a more complicated affair that will be explained further in Chapter 5. For now, we may note the frequent use of the neighbor IV chord on Radiohead's first two albums, which is an exceptionally common trope not only in rock music, but in blues, classical, and other styles. In "Fake Plastic Trees" (1995–4, 0:13–0:26) adjacent verse phrases dovetail using two consecutive iterations of this IV–I neighbor gesture. When preceded by a supertonic harmony and presented as a loop, this neighbor IV chord becomes part of a conventional rock chord progression I–ii–IV, which is heard in the verse, chorus, and bridge of "High and Dry" (1995–3) and throughout both *Pablo Honey* and *The Bends*. Beatles-esque chromatic alterations, such as the major supertonic and minor subdominant, occur on both albums, awkwardly combined (G♯7–Bm–F♯) in the chorus of "Vegetable" (1993–8, e.g., 0:34–0:47). The D–C–G "Sweet Home Alabama" framework shows up in the verses of "Sulk" (1995–11, e.g., 0:22–0:51) and a "truck driver modulation" pumps up the final chorus of the same song from G (2:03) to A (3:05). Many of the voice-leading gestures heard on these two albums derive specifically from the guitar fretboard—something that changes as their later music becomes more keyboard-influenced. One nearly sees Chuck Berry strutting across the stage in the boogie-woogie-inherited F♯–E neighbor tones over the A chord in the chorus of "Bones" (1995–5, e.g., 1:07–1:10).

Radiohead's music from 1997 onward, as I will show in the following four chapters, transcends the conventions heard on *Pablo Honey* and *The Bends* by providing novel timbres, forms, rhythms, and/or harmonies in nearly every song. But in presenting these surprises within a recognizable style (rock music), the music facilitates a fertile ecosystem for mutual interactions between listening subject and musical object. Subjectivity is once again important here, and we must keep in mind those individuals for whom this relationship holds. Personally, I know several older electroacoustic composers for whom the environment offered by a typical *musique concrète* composition would present more recognizable stimulus patterns than a Radiohead song. The theory I am crafting here, as it relates to Radiohead's music, is only applicable as it relates to listeners familiar with—however passively or actively—the conventions of rock music. Occasionally, what I will have to say is more applicable to listeners immersed in a substyle of rock music or in the general conventions of western tonality. Many listeners may be intimately familiar with harmonic and formal patterns of early 1960s rock music, but have relatively little exposure to the rhythmic conventions that are part and parcel of modern style. Conversely, many will be familiar with some instrument timbres native to Radiohead's music (e.g., the ondes Martenot or Thom Yorke's voice), but have almost no prior experiences with the classical formal units sometimes heard in their phrase structures.

For listeners with prior experience in the musical styles in which Radiohead participates—ranging from rock since its inception in the late 1950s, rock music after 1990, Brit Pop since 1995, experimental rock music in the new millennium, Radiohead's studio albums, to Radiohead's electro-acoustic experiments between 2000 and 2001—the music constantly presents recognizable tropes as a familiar backdrop for more novel sounds. In doing so the music consistently maximizes the

space between expectation and realization so essential to meaning creation according to the principles of ecological perception. In the following four chapters I will
illuminate these surprising passages in Radiohead's music and suggest some ways in
which we might derive meaning from them.

Notes

1. Theeuwes (2012, 24) provides a helpful summary of bottom-up and top-down approaches
to visual perception based on a theory of salience.

2. Edwin Battistella (1996, 9–13) discusses some of the leading definitions for markedness that
have been provided since the 1970s.

3. See Hatten (1994, 117).

4. Hatten uses "strategic markedness" (1994, 118) to convey a similar position in Beethoven.
The internationalist aspect inherent in the word strategic makes this problematic for contemporary music, where the composer could either support or rebut any analytical claims, yet would
have ample motivation to deny, or insufficient memory to recall, the exact motivations behind
certain compositional decisions. My emphasis on these limited types of forms, rhythms, timbres, and harmonies is similar to the two "expressive genres" that Hatten locates in Beethoven's
music ("tragic to transcendent" and "pastoral). I agree with Agawu's critique (1996, 152) that
these two options are limiting, and, in expanding the range of options for hearing Radiohead's
music I hope to broaden the scope of Hatten's original project.

5. See Margulis (2013).

6. See London (2004, 6).

7. See Summach (2014, 184–85).

8. Clarke (2005, 34–35) provides evidence for these sorts of remarkable listening skills of
which we are capable.

9. I use angle brackets for describing invariants and affordances in order to differentiate between the perceptual phenomenon <glass breaking> (read: the perception that glass is breaking)
and prosaic descriptions of glass breaking.

10. See Clarke (1999, 350).

11. Clarke (2005, 126; italics mine).

12. Though Moore (2012) has recently argued for a synthesis of the two approaches, this
particular aspect of musical perception stands in opposition to most theories of cognition, especially linguistically based approaches that claim no sonic understanding can occur without
language to label it.

13. Empirical methods such as these are evinced in most of the work by Diana Deutsch, David
Huron, and Aniruddh Patel.

14. See Clarke (2005, 41–43); reproduced in Moore (2012, 248).

15. Summach (2014, 185).

16. See Gibson 1979.

17. Brower (2000, 324).

18. Moore (2012, 12).

19. See Margulis (2013, 1).

20. For representative samples of such work, see Margulis (2013), London (2004), Clarke (2005), and Huron (2006).

21. Their most popular song from this period, "Creep" (1993–2), is in fact so conventional that the band found themselves on the losing end of a plagiarism lawsuit regarding the song's harmonic progression, which was found to be too closely derived from The Hollies' "The Air I Breathe" (1973).

22. See Moore and Ibrahim (2005, 149–150), which includes numerous references to the critical appraisal of Radiohead's albums from *Pablo Honey* (1993) through *Hail to the Thief* (2003).

23. Ibid., 144.

24. Ibid., 152.

25. See Moore (2012, 167).

26. The occasional string pad is the exception that proves the rule, and is also well within the expectations for timbres heard in rock's harmonic filler layer (see Chapter 4).

2   Form

RADIOHEAD EXPERIMENTS WITH the conventions of Top-40 rock music in order to produce familiar, yet strikingly unique forms. Tracks like "Let Down" (1997–5) exhibit a textbook verse/chorus structure, and thus present few if any surprises in formal design. Indeed, it was song forms like this and "Fake Plastic Trees" (1995–4) that propelled Radiohead into a position of immense market success early in their career.[1] If the goal is to have a song remembered by audiences who may just be flipping through stations (on either the TV or radio), the best shot at doing so is to present a memorable chorus several times throughout the song, thus increasing the chances that a listener will both hear it and commit it to memory.

At the opposite extreme, pieces like "Treefingers" (2000–5) confront us with their unfamiliar formal structure. We have no frame of reference for processing these instrumental pieces that present no familiar macro-design. While these aggressively experimental compositions, including "Pulk/Pull Revolving Doors" (2001–3) and "Fitter Happier" (1997–7), provide no familiar formal signposts, most of Radiohead's forms exist somewhere between plain convention and sheer experimentation. By delivering plenty of new stimuli while at the same time presenting familiar formal signposts along the way, Radiohead's songs continually balance predictability and surprise. Two particularly salient formal designs—terminally climactic forms and through-composed forms—represent the majority of forms heard in these songs.

Musical form may be addressed from two different perspectives. The omniscient or "bird's-eye view" approach may be the most common perspective from which music analysts address formal structure. Songwriters and performing musicians often use this perspective to parse and understand a piece of music, sometimes after hearing the song only once. But I often prefer to address form in terms of real-time listening experiences. Specifically, I am interested in experiences involving minimal-to-no prior exposure. While this certainly includes first auditions, subsequent auditions may still hold a great deal of surprise. In experiencing such forms, interlocking chains of perception–expectation–realization run in a constant loop wherein each formal section leads to an expectation which is either thwarted or realized.

Conventional Forms: Verse/Chorus and Strophic

In order to understand how Radiohead's formal structures experiment with conventions found in Top-40 rock music, we first need to understand what those conventions entail. Two related song forms have been commonplace throughout rock history: strophic forms and verse/chorus forms. To be sure, innumerable variations on these two structures exist if we look more closely at the rock catalog. We might say that there are as many formal types as there are pieces of music, but such a statement, while doing a great deal to validate the richness of conventional music, denies our perceptual systems which evaluate discrete musical stimuli in terms of prior experiences. Listeners have come to expect AABA, strophic, and verse/chorus forms in rock music and come to Radiohead's music bearing those same expectations.

Jason Summach provides a systematic taxonomy of formal types in a corpus of conventional rock music comprising every song in the annual Top-20 charts between 1955 and 1989.[2] This study shows that the overwhelming majority of songs written during this period either exhibit a strophic or verse/chorus design, but it also demonstrates that songs can slip into a space between those two. Summach's system uses letters to represent discrete thematic sections. The most familiar archetype is the AABA form, a strophic form that features a contrasting bridge. Sections labeled "A" are all variations on the same underlying melodic/harmonic framework, while the "B" section provides some sort of contrast, be it different harmonies or melodies. Strophic forms can also occur without such a contrasting section, in which case they bear the lettering system AAA . . ., whereby the number of discrete "A" sections correlates to the number of repeated gestures.

Strophic forms can be traced back considerably further in music history than the origins of rock music, and their archetype can be found in any number of human communication strategies. Take for example a familiar joke archetype: "These three [nouns] walk into a bar. The first [does something], the second [does something related to the first], the third [does something related to the first two, yet does something to bring about a punchline]." Three episodes, all related in crucial ways, follow in series, and the final is modified in some way as to bring about closure to the utterance. Familiar strophic forms can be heard throughout rock history, especially in folk ballads and 1950s and 1960s country- and blues-inspired music. Twelve-bar blues chord progressions can be heard underlying early strophic forms such as Elvis Presley's "Hound Dog" (1956) and Bill Haley and the Comets' "Rock Around the Clock" (1955–1),[3] while later soul and synth-driven hits such as Gloria Gaynor's "I Will Survive" (1978–5) and Blondie's "Rapture" (1980–8) adapt the form to new idioms.

Because this practice persists in the 1990s Brit Pop and Grunge styles from which Radiohead emerges, we can still hear a number of strophic forms throughout their early catalog. Early strophic songs that seem to whole-heartedly adopt the formal convention abound on the first two records, and continue sparingly into the early millennium.[4] The scattered few strophic forms from 2000 onward seem less an adoption of convention and more a formal concession to accommodate a specific purpose. In "Kid A" (2000–2) and "The Gloaming" (2003–8), for example, the strophic form helps to showcase the songs' bizarre timbres, and a decade later the same form helps to rein in the otherwise inaccessible polytempo sprawl of "Bloom" (2011–1).

Whereas strophic forms present a repeated thematically recognizable section, which may or may not be interrupted by a contrasting passage, verse/chorus forms are composed of two thematically contrasting sections called a verse and a chorus. Typically, this contrast serves to spotlight the latter as the more memorable of the two. Verses usually present a linear narrative over the course of the song, sometimes in as few as two installments, sometimes as many as four or more. Verses are separated by a memorable chorus, which often reflects upon the narrative advanced by the verses using a repeated melodic hook, and frequently presents the song's title.[5]

The chorus features both recapitulation and repetition. That is to say, the chorus is presented more-or-less exactly several times over the course of the track (recapitulation), and a single chorus will often present the same lyrical/melodic gesture more than once (repetition). This return to the exact material is the biggest clue in recognizing the chorus. The distinction between repetition (*intra*-sectional) and recapitulation (*inter*-sectional) will become important in later discussions of experimental forms.

Verse/chorus forms often present a second level of contrast by introducing a bridge and, as such, present a hierarchical depth one level more complex than strophic forms. Both forms may contain a bridge for contrast, but the verse/chorus form has contrast built into its two-part thematic nature as well (the verse/chorus pair). Both strophic forms with a bridge and verse/chorus forms each present two different sections, whereas verse/chorus form with a bridge presents three. Therefore, verse/chorus forms with a bridge necessitate a third letter "C" to denote the same bridge that, in a strophic form, would be designated by "B."

Verse/chorus forms, with or without a bridge, become part and parcel of rock music in the mid-to-late 1960s, and by the 1980s had nearly replaced strophic forms on the Top-20 charts.[6] Such explicitly contrasting choruses as Jimmy Buffet's "Margaritaville" (1977–6; "wastin' away in Margaritaville") and Danny and the Juniors' "At the Hop" (1957; "let's go to the hop") highlight the song's title as a way to increase the memorability of the section. Unsurprisingly, the majority of Radiohead's songs that have functioned as singles or quasi-singles (that is, those which have received the most airplay) exhibit this verse/chorus design. On *OK Computer* (1997), songs featuring the clearest rock textures and instrumentation, such as "Let Down" (1997–5) and "Electioneering" (1997–8) are cast in this design, the former featuring the title lyric prominently at the beginning of the chorus. Even on the more abstract early millennial records, the recapitulated choruses and rock-driven accompaniment on tracks such as "Optimistic" (2000–6) and "Knives Out" (2001–6; for which the band filmed a music video) seem tailor-made as singles. Between 2001 and 2011 there are only three songs in the entire catalog that feature such explicit choruses: "We Suck Young Blood" (2003–7), "Wolf at the Door" (2003–14), and "Little by Little" (2011–3). *In Rainbows* does not have a textbook chorus anywhere on the record.

In many cases, it can be difficult to decide which conventional form we are hearing.[7] It is important here to point out a common hallmark of strophes: the presentation of a "refrain," which occurs either at the beginning or ending of the strophe. The Beatles' "Hey Jude" (1968a) begins each strophe with its title-refrain, while the refrain of "Let it Be" (1970–6) closes each strophe. The difference between a verse/chorus form and a strophic form with end-refrain lies solely in whether or not we perceive the part containing a repeated lyric as *autonomous*. In other words, does the repeated lyric function as a section in-and-of itself, or does it function as part of another?

As an illustration, consider two conventional forms on Radiohead's *OK Computer* (1997). In "No Surprises" (1997–10) the listener is presented with a closed harmonic progression (I–IV6–ii–V–I) several times, which is accompanied by the same basic melody but bears unique lyrics each time ("I'll take a quiet life;" "This is my final fit"). Each of these presentations is followed by a repeated lyric featuring the song's title ("No alarms and no surprises please") over a cadential extension of the previous progression (a repeated ii–V finally cadencing on I the third time). "The Tourist" (1997–12) has a very similar design, with each set of unique lyrics ("I guess it's seen the sparks;" "You ask me where the hell I'm going") followed by a repeated lyric ("Hey man, slow down"), but there is *no* harmonic contrast between the two gestures—the chord progressions underlying both sections are identical. So, which is a verse/chorus, and which is strophic with end-refrain? In other words, in which do we sense that the repeated lyric is an autonomous section (chorus), and in which do we sense that it is merely part of a larger one (end-refrain)?

These are serious considerations bearing on a theory of conventional forms, which is not our most pressing concern in Radiohead's music.[8] Instead, we should ask, How do listeners respond to formal structures which lie outside the bounds of these conventional forms? In terms of meaning—specifically intertextuality—it may be meaningful for a listener to categorize "No Surprises" and "The Tourist" as either strophic or verse/chorus designs, because the former (by which I mean the formal design and, by proxy, the song) brings up associations with Tin Pan Alley and early rock and roll music, while the latter does not become commonplace until the later part of the 1960s, bringing up associations with the formal innovations of The Beatles and The Beach Boys. Allan Moore notes that "this process of naming is more important than it is often given credit for being, since by naming a discreet [*sic*] unit, we are comparing it to similar units in other songs, and thus developing the norms by which we understand how to orient ourselves temporally in relation to that to which we're listening."[9] Personally, I hear a strophic form in "No Surprises," since the repeated ii–V chords that accompany the title lyric merely extend the functional harmonic progression of the previous lyrics with no change in texture or rhythm, a common characteristic of an end-refrain. "The Tourist" sounds like a host of other 1990s rock songs that harmonize the verse and chorus with identical chord progressions, but which execute a "breakout chorus" by increasing volume and thickening texture.[10] Typically, the chorus is marked by the title text, but here the repeated chorus lyric "hey man, slow down" is instead a commentary on American tourists Jonny Greenwood witnessed in France who were absent-mindedly cataloging as many sites as they could see without stopping to witness any of the beauty contained therein. "No Surprises" and "The Tourist" therefore differ greatly in terms of their allegiances to similar pieces in the rock corpus.

Regardless of which conventional design we are perceiving—either strophic or verse/chorus—the defining characteristic of all conventional forms is that they rely on *recapitulation*, on a return to some previously heard section to bring about closure. Walter Everett points to the "SRDC" as a defining element of conventional forms: statement, restatement, departure, conclusion.[11] This pattern of recapitulatory closure, whereby some previously heard music is presented as a gesture of attainment, provides the listener with a sense of certainty and satisfied expectation. With the return to closing material, which has been repeatedly presented as the culmination of the SRDC pattern, we can be sure that all musical events that are going to happen have indeed happened, and we can now turn our attention away from the sonic event—the song can end without us perceiving that anything is yet to occur.

From an experiential standpoint, the *lack* of recapitulatory closure in Radiohead's later music stands as the greatest challenge to listeners whose perceptual strategies are attuned to conventional forms. Many song endings eschew the certainty associated with recapitulated closing materials. Instead, they rely on one of two salient formal types: terminally climactic forms or through-composed forms.[12] In terminally climactic form, the piece ends with some goal-directed motion toward strikingly new music which is the climax of the entire song; in through-composed form, the piece simply ends because it is done presenting new material. Some terminally climactic and through-composed songs present the listener with evidence that there is a specific process or trajectory that leads us to these endings on new material, while other endings arrive without precedent, as fractured and fragmented non-sequiturs. These effects are not only embedded within the musical structure itself, but also arise through the listening capacities and prior experiences of the subjective listener.

Terminally Climactic Forms

Terminally climactic forms radically restructure the inherent contrast in verse/chorus forms. But we can also understand terminally climactic forms as the next logical step in songwriters' increasing tendency to use contrast to signal climax across rock history. Strophic forms in the 1950s and 1960s have one optional instance of contrast between strophes (AA**B**A); Verse/chorus forms in the 1960s, 1970s, and 1980s have a built-in contrast between verse and chorus (**AB**) which can be further supplemented with a contrasting bridge (ABAB**C**AB); and terminally climactic forms, which do not appear with any frequency until the 1990s, take the idea of a verse/chorus form and imbue it with a monumental structural contrast at the ending—the song's memorable, climactic highpoint (ABAB**C**). The early archetype for such a form may well be The Beatles' "Hey Jude" (1968a), whose memorable, contrasting sing-along ending ("na, na-na, na-na-na-na") is presented over a harmonic shift that introduces a strikingly new double-plagal progression (I–♭VII–IV–I). This climactic moment is then repeated many times, and could conceivably continue indefinitely.

Terminally climactic form does not always rely upon a verse/chorus beginning. "Hey Jude," for example, is a strophic song with beginning refrain (the title

TABLE 2.1

Terminally climactic form in "Karma Police" (1997–6)

Section	Clock time	Description
intro	0:01–0:25	guitar and piano four-phrase accompaniment, each beginning on A minor chord
verse 1a	0:26–0:51	drums and voice enter; ("karma police arrest this man")
verse 1b	0:52–1:17	("karma police arrest this girl")
chorus	1:18–1:42	drums tacet; ("this is what you get")
verse 2	1:43–2:07	("karma police I've given all I can")
chorus	2:08–2:33	recap chorus
terminal climax	2:34–3:36	new harmonic progression starting on B minor; ("for a minute there I lost myself")
outro	3:37–4:22	continues accompaniment from terminal climax

lyrics begin each strophe). For an example of a true verse/chorus structure with terminally climactic ending, consider the early Radiohead single "Karma Police" (1997–6), the form of which is charted in Table 2.1. The song provides just the right amount of markedness within an accepted range of previous experience, a facet which may have played a part in its blend of both critical and commercial success.

Whereas many introductions frame the verse progression in some incomplete way, sometimes merely elaborating a tonic pedal, by the end of the first verse the listener recognizes that the introduction in fact presented the complete eight-bar chord progression used by the verse. Yorke begins the verse by singing the song title and, in so doing, brings to mind an intertextual connection with any number of strophic songs featuring beginning-refrains (e.g., "Hey Jude"). This set of chain reactions is driven by intertextual formal concerns and by a listener's level of inculcation in rock conventions. After perceiving this intro-verse structure, a listener may well expect a chorus. However, that expectation is not realized, but rather thwarted at 0:52 as the progression in question begins again. There are then three reasonable explanations for this thwarted expectation, each of which has plenty of precedents in Radiohead's catalog: (1) verse one spans two presentations of the progression in question (16 total measures); (2) there is no chorus between these verses (with the expectation that there will be between subsequent verses); or (3) that this is in fact a strophic song, and contains no contrasting chorus.

Expectation (2) is the only one that will be realized. The chorus ("This is what you get") provides a stark harmonic, dynamic, and textural contrast, and is thus reasonably congruent with listener expectations of a standard verse/chorus song. On the other hand, this is certainly not the standard "breakout" chorus typical of 1990s rock music. It is quiet and subdued, reducing the full rock texture of the verse to nothing but voice with sparse piano and guitar accompaniment. Immediately after, we are presented with a second verse (or third, depending on how we count verses).[13] This time, there is no repetition of the eight-bar structure before heading directly for chorus two. Here then lies the answer for the listener who had expectation (1) regarding the verse structure. Rather than assume that there are only two verses and the second was diminished by a factor of one half, listener number one now perceives three verses, each of which is eight measures long, and choruses only follow verses two and three.

Listeners who have no prior experience with terminally climactic forms may have a sense that the chorus is not fulfilling its duty as the memorable high point of the song. For a listener who does have some experience with terminally climactic forms (not in terminology, but in unnamed musical experience), this quiet chorus could be a signal that a much louder and memorable ending section is still to come. Either way, the function of the passage points downstream to a yet-to-be-heard payoff which, surely enough, arrives after the second chorus. This terminal climax shares many features with its archetype, the "Hey Jude" climax. Both feature a sing-along that is repeated many times ("For a minute there, I lost myself, I lost myself"), both raise the volume level to the track's peak, and both introduce a markedly new harmony (in this case, E Major). Additionally, Yorke's vocal ascent to G4 marks the melodic high point of the song's texted material.

Terminally climactic forms pique our perceptual interest precisely because they provide a novel, highly memorable ending only after first activating our sense of prior experience by presenting a familiar framework. Verse/chorus songs present the listener with a sort of contract, and "it is only if the contract were not to be delivered that a strong affective charge would ensue."[14] Each and every terminally climactic form transcends the experiential terms of the verse/chorus or strophic contract, thus bringing about the affective charge.

The link between form and harmony in "Karma Police" is inexorable. As an alternative to monotonality, the song can be heard as expressing tonal centers only active in one of its three sections. The verse draws attention to an A minor tonal center, largely through hypermetric emphasis (each two-bar hypermeasure begins on an A minor triad), which has a consistent lowered third degree but which features both Aeolian and Dorian sixth degrees. Yorke's ascent from E3 through F♯ cadencing on G3, when accompanied by IV–V–I, makes G major a clear center for the chorus, but the lower chromatic neighbor F♯ *major* that follows (a harmonized elaboration of the passing bass F♯ in measure six of the verse progression) complicates this hearing by introducing a parallel tritone relation to the subdominant chord. Finally, the terminal climax, though it features a potential tonic/dominant axis in G, lends itself toward a non-functional D Major hearing through Yorke's consistent falling third progression (F♯4–E4–D4) in which G4 is clearly not tonic, but instead an upper neighbor to the third scale degree. Not only do each of these three sections force us as listeners to reorient to a new tonal center, but each confuses matters further with exactly one chromatic harmony (F major in the verse, F♯ major in the chorus, E major in the terminal climax).

Though terminal climaxes usually take the form of a repeated lyrical/melodic phrase over some sort of contrasting accompaniment, they may also arise through explicit *statistical* means. Here we must distinguish between syntactical climax (e.g., most memorable theme, presentation of song title) versus statistical climax (e.g., loudest/softest volume, thickest/thinnest texture, fastest/slowest tempo).[15] Statistical climaxes may be measured by empirical observation, but syntactic climaxes rely on some sort of aesthetic assessment within the conventions of style.

Statistical and syntactical climaxes often occur in tandem. Table 2.2 shows one of the clearest cases of statistical climax in Radiohead's catalog, "There, There" (2003–9),

TABLE 2.2

Terminally climactic form in "There, There" (2003–9)

Section	Clock time	Description
intro	0:01–0:45	B pedal, accumulative groove build-up (percussion, bass, guitars)
verse 1	0:46–1:15	voice enters on B3–D4–F♯4; ("in pitch dark")
chorus 1	1:16–1:45	new harmonic progression beginning on A; ("just 'cause you feel it doesn't mean it's there")
retransition	1:46–1:53	recap intro
verse 2	1:54–2:23	recap verse with background vocals
chorus 2	2:24–2:54	recap chorus with background vocals
bridge/intro	2:55–3:15	new harmonic progression starting on B, vocals slip from F♯4 to F4
terminal climax	3:16–5:23	voice and full drum set enter; ("we are accidents waiting to happen")

which executes its terminal climax by exploding onto the loudest volume level heard throughout the song. It nevertheless also relies on a subtle thematic transformation of melodic/harmonic elements that unfolds as the song develops. Beginning on a tonic pedal, the song's intro functions very differently than does "Karma Police." Rather than present a complete statement of the verse's progression, this song features an accumulative process, whereby layers of the groove are assembled piece by piece before the vocal entrance.[16] So common is this technique that listeners are very likely to perceive this as an intro, and thus expect a texted verse.

Yorke's opening vocal motive arpeggiates a B minor triad, thus realizing expectations based on the opening tonic pedal. Rock's tonal systems often incorporate submediant pedal points, but the melody and B minor/E minor harmonic axis do not easily reward a hearing in D major. The A major triad at 1:16, a new chord, signals change, but to what? Again, our sense of formal boundaries is challenged as we try to make sense of whether this is part of a larger verse progression, an end-refrain, or a contrasting chorus. But the repeated lyric "just 'cause you feel it, doesn't mean it's there," accompanied by a new functional progression tonicizing the relative D major, strongly suggests a contrasting chorus. So strong is the pull from a verse's putative minor tonic (without leading-tone) to a relative major in the chorus that we can easily hear the entire verse/chorus group monotonally, with the verse representing a progression in D major whose tonic chord is absent. Formal comprehension of the verse depends on a listener's fluency in rock's tonal idiosyncrasies, but also on a listener's expectations, which will be conditioned based on an aptitude for recognizing larger melodic and harmonic patterns. Chorus two marks the realization of an expectation generated by verse/chorus form. After perceiving two verse/chorus pairs, the music at 2:55 will be *prospectively* (that is, in real time) experienced as a textbook bridge. Harmonic contrast is added very subtly, as a thirdless B–D–A progression is paired contrapuntally in the voice by F♯4–F4–E4 (2:55), disrupting a global D major hearing for the first time. When this progression is transferred in full chords to the guitar, Yorke begins to sing what sounds like a texted bridge. But, retrospectively, following the climactic volume explosion at 3:57, a listener must revise this thwarted expectation, and will come to realize that this phrase is actually an independent *introduction to the climax*. It serves a function analogous to the introduction of a verse/chorus form, introducing a key harmonic/melodic element before the full instrumentation and main theme are presented.

During the bombastic climax, drummer Phil Selway's open hi-hats and washy cymbals are heard for the first time, and Jonny Greenwood's distorted new lead guitar riff takes over just before Yorke sings the repeated line ("We are accidents waiting to happen"). The key element in a statistical climax is that we perceive it as such by a measurable sonic parameter instead of a theme. Unlike the previous two examples, the focus here seems not to be on Yorke's voice, but instead on the lead guitar part and the "rock-out" happening in the accompaniment. Jonny Greenwood says of the statistical climax of "There, There," "It's got that Pixies thing that I love, which is a huge build-up of tension and release . . . it's not thinking of things being good in an instant way, but good thinking in terms of five minutes."[17]

A similar process, whereby a basic accompaniment pattern systematically builds and evolves into an explosive terminal climax, can be heard in "You and Whose Army?" (2001–4). Here the ending lyric ("We ride dark ghost horses") is presented over the first emergence of a clear rock-out. The song's lyrics can also be interpreted in conjunction with a shift in tonal system. Leading up to the climax, the protagonist has been taunting, almost teasing the Holy Roman Empire ("come on if you think you can take us on"), and it does so even more convincingly by dodging any steady harmonic position. Like a timid bully juking and strafing to avoid real aggression, a remarkably consistent perfect fifths sequence (D#m–G#–C#m–F#–Bm–E) evades any clear tonic detection. Only in the climax does the protagonist make the first clear threat toward that force ("we ride tonight dark ghost horses"), and it does so with a clear C#m harmonic progression whose Dorian-plagal F#7 chord does little to cloud the tonic radar.

Songs like this, as well as "All I Need" (2007–5), imbue their endings with other characteristics germane to a terminal climax, including the introduction of a new harmony, a repeated lyrical/melodic gesture, and thickened textures, but the focus seems to be on the explosive volume climax. Another way to perceive these statistically driven climaxes is to hear Radiohead withholding the "rock" *trope* for the climax. Distorted guitars, full drum set, and upper-register singing are the clearest signifiers of rock music. Opening with music that is soft, unpredictable, and ambiguous, these climactic endings provide listeners with a trope that finally fulfills rock-centered expectations. Though it features no guitar, "All I Need" does this by moving from a sparse texture—piano and glockenspiel accompanied by a robotic, quiet drum groove—to wide open cymbal washing thickened to the point of utter saturation by a C Major13 chord (2:46) whose diatonic gaps are completely filled by a deafening twelve-tone aggregate on Jonny's overdubbed viola (a technique he associates with Penderecki).[18] Listeners familiar with the song's title will likely perceive that they are receiving "all they need" in terms of rock-out textures, as will the comparatively rare listener who craves dodecaphonic completion.

We sometimes get the sense that Radiohead's terminal climaxes are tacked on. This brings to mind The Beatles' "Happiness is a Warm Gun" (1968b), a song in which Lennon added the title-containing sing-along only after the other two sections had been written and recorded as a demo. The terminal climax of "Faust Arp" (2007–6) seems especially like an appendage to an otherwise verse/chorus song. Table 2.3

TABLE 2.3

Terminally climactic form in "Faust Arp" (2007–6)

Section	Clock time	Description
intro	0:01–0:04	Yorke count-off, guitar arpeggio introduces opening Bm chord with [3–2–3] rhythmic pattern
verse 1	0:05–0:28	voice enters ("wakey wakey") over descending bass starting on B; followed by turnaround moving up to C
chorus 1	0:29–0:38	("guess I'm stuffed") over descending bass starting on G
verse 2	0:39–1:02	recap verse with strings ("squeeze the tubes")
chorus 2	1:03–1:23	double chorus w/extra lyrics
interlude	1:24–1:33	instrumental starting on B♭; fingerpicked acoustic guitar lead
terminal climax	1:34–1:50	interlude progression cont.; voice enters ("you've got a head")
outro	1:51–2:10	chorus progression played on low bowed strings

provides a chart of the song's form. Yorke's quiet, mumbled count-off ("one, two, three, four"), accompanied by the sound of Jonny Greenwood's left hand squeaking on the steel strings of the acoustic guitar, immediately invites the listener into an intimate musical setting. This is achieved primarily through the mix itself, but also through instrumentation. Regarding the mix, the acoustic guitar is panned hard right and left, while Yorke's voice is not only dead-center, but appears "close" in the mix. This front-and-center intimacy (not only the result of volume, but also close microphone placement and careful control of reverberation) is not only a hallmark of folk favorites like Simon and Garfunkel's "The Sound of Silence" (1964–6), but also features prominently on Frank Sinatra's recordings and even Bon Iver's work contemporaneous with Radiohead.[19] Regarding the instrumentation, rarely in Radiohead's music do we hear such sparse instrumentation of acoustic guitar and voice with no significant signal processing. These two related sonic invariants bear a wealth of cultural specifications, including <folk>, <privacy>, <crooners>, and <warmth> to name a few.

These intimate cultural associations link this track to the folk genre and thus encourage a level of participation associated with folk genres.[20] It is through this active and intimate participation that we perceive the standard formal design as the song develops. The opening verse, with its narrative, storytelling lyrical design, gives way at 0:29 to a contrasting chorus, which we perceive by its repeated lyric and harmonic contrast. Perceiving this verse/chorus pair leads us to expect a second verse, which should, in turn, be followed by a recapitulation of the chorus. That expectation is fulfilled, and thus we now expect one of two things from standard rock formal designs. Either a bridge should come after chorus two, which will then give way to a third verse/chorus pair (sometimes just a chorus) followed by an optional outro, or, we should go directly to the ending without an intervening bridge.

Expectations work like something of a chain reaction. If one is fulfilled, we become more certain that related expectations will come to fruition. Thus, having predicted the second verse/chorus pair, and having made expectations about the bridge to follow, the instrumental, guitar-driven music at 1:24 will fulfill our expectation of "bridge" so strongly that, when Yorke's highest vocal note enters at 1:34 for two texted phrases over this music, our realization that this is no bridge, that it is in fact the climactic high point of the song, comes as a shock.

In both "Faust Arp" and "Weird Fishes/Arpeggi" (2007–4) the syntactic and statistical terminal climax is nearly rendered *anti*-climactic by its thematic irrelevance to a significantly more memorable repeated chorus. Prior to the tacked-on climax that ends "Weird Fishes/Arpeggi," Yorke narrates through a five-verse structure describing general subservience to a love interest. These five verses delay the arrival of the song's title-refrain until 3:09. The song's narrative journey now complete, a listener wonders why the repeated lyric, "I'll hit the bottom and escape," really deserves a spot in the terminal climax, its sole function seemingly to make explicit the previous metaphors likening emotional rejection to corporeal decomposition (e.g., "I'm an animal trapped in your hot car . . . I get eaten by the worms and weird fishes") heard throughout the song.

Quite the opposite of these climax-as-appendix techniques, sometimes we can hear an explicit and clear process at work that leads us to *expect* the terminal climax, in a sense making the surprise, ironically, inevitable. "Sit Down, Stand Up" (2003–2) is, by far, the single most goal-directed song in Radiohead's catalog. During live performances of this song the energy is palpable as audience members wait out the first three minutes of the song patiently for the cathartic (and physically chaotic) release that happens at the terminal climax—a frenetic dance beat accompanying the trance-like, seemingly infinite mantra "the raindrops" (3:03). Instead of a standard verse/chorus opening, the entire song can be heard as a single teleological process that builds to this moment.[21] Electronic percussion playing steady eighth notes supports a stripped-down instrumentation of piano and glockenspiel as Yorke accumulates and combines recorded vocal layers over the first two minutes (e.g., when "sit down, stand up" is joined contrapuntally with "we can wipe you out anytime"). A syncopated deep electronic bass pulse enters just before the two-minute mark, giving listeners the sense, along with Yorke's stacked vocal layers, that something is imminent.

Shortly afterward, the previously undifferentiated percussion becomes fuller and more syncopated, building rhythmic tension until 2:53. From 2:53 to the explosive climax ten seconds later that syncopation is gradually overtaken by sixteenth-note snare drum rolls—a common technique heard in the re-transitions of electronic dance pieces. When the four-measure snare roll has completed, right when the listener expects the syntactic volume climax, Radiohead inserts a surprise fifth measure into the previous four-measure framework. This works to momentarily withhold the cathartic climax, making its arrival, just one measure later, all the more powerful. Though this accumulative process is more germane to a song's introduction, "Sit Down, Stand Up" stretches it to the length of more than half the track. Seen differently, the piece amplifies the sense of build-up usually heard only in a song's introduction to span a length usually reserved for a verse/chorus pair.

Terminally climactic forms, which nearly match standard verse/chorus designs and promise their customary recapitulatory endings, only to swerve impetuously at the last moment with endings on brand new, climactic material, occur regularly in Radiohead's music after *The Bends*. This process of matching previous expectations to novel stimuli begins the search for meaning. As music psychologist Candace Brower notes:

> . . . we make sense of the world around us by matching perceived patterns to patterns stored in memory . . . if the match is exact, the search for meaning may end there. If the match is only approximate, however, this may initiate a second step in the cognitive cycle, called *checking*, in which we compare patterns and note their similarities and differences. Checking may then give rise to higher levels of meaning . . . [22]

The meanings of songs in terminally climactic form often come to fruition through our relationship to their lyrical contents, as well as the intertextual associations they bring to mind.

Through-Composed Forms

Terminally climactic forms are so effective precisely because they initially present musical elements that are consistent with the listener's previous experience. But another experimental formal device commonly heard in Radiohead's music—the through-composed form—more thoroughly challenges conventional formal expectations. In through-composed forms, no recapitulation can occur. That is to say, once A arrives it may repeat any number of times, but once a contrasting B section is introduced, A can never return. Lacking recapitulation, through-composed forms ultimately invalidate expectations based in verse/chorus or AABA designs, even though they may initially prompt those same expectations.

In an admittedly more abstract sense, however, through-composed forms amplify and modify the strophic *process* in much the same way that terminally climactic forms amplify the contrast found in verse/chorus forms. Just as strophic forms (without bridge) precede by serial presentation of a given thematic design (AAA . . .), through-composed forms precede by serial presentation of *different* thematic designs (ABCDE . . .) Ironically, this formal device, which presents the listener with nothing except contrast, shares the sense of timeless serial presentation with a form that has, by definition, zero contrast. In the parade of modules, no single module projects a unique closing function; any of them, or none of them, might close the song.

One of the most compact instances of this formal design occurs in the bi-partite song "I Will" (2003–10). What begins as strophic form based on a simple C♯ minor progression turns into a compact through-composed form. Understanding such a concise form (the song clocks in at under two minutes) necessitates hearing divisions of formal structure finer than standard verse/chorus terminology allows. Indeed, these familiar formal sections—verse, chorus, and the like—are absent from Table 2.4. This is because accepted terminology among song forms *relies* on recapitulation. We know that we hear a chorus because it comes back. We know that we hear verse two because the accompaniment is derived from verse one but the lyrics are different. If we are being true to perceptual impulses then, lacking recapitulation, we have no idea what to call a section when it arrives, and thus must settle for a serial labeling system.

Understanding the form of "I Will" at the phrase level allows for a reading of this through-composed form as an emergent process that results not only from the harmonic structure, but from the layered entrances of Yorke's various vocal tracks that gradually saturate the song's ever-expanding pitch space. The primary goal of such a comparatively detailed form graph is to emphasize the role of thematic *development*, rather than mere thematic contrast. That is to say, in "I Will," the varied presentations of the central A theme, labeled A1–A6, are more important to the song's drive than the moment of essential contrast at 1:21, where the A theme gives way to a repeated B theme.

Even with this increased level of focus, a number of the song's defining features are lost in such a chart. Two omissions are most notable. First, section timings are based on the hypermetric downbeat of the section's chord progression, but the corresponding lyrics to each of the A phrases anticipates this downbeat by roughly half a measure. Second, despite the description of pitch space traversed by each new vocal entrance, this is a monophonic assessment of a song that seems nearly defined by the growing territory occupied by several polyphonic vocal entries over the course of

TABLE 2.4

Through-composed form in "I Will" (2003–10)

Section	Phrase	Clock time	Description	Vocal ranges (low to high)
A	intro	0:01–0:02	one measure anacrusis; solo electric guitar strums G♯ major	
	A1	0:03–0:15	("I will lay me down") over C♯ minor progression	lead vocal: C♯4–G♯4
	A2	0:16–0:28	("in a bunker underground"); two independent voices created when lower part extends lower than 8vb	2nd voice down to D♯3
	A3	0:29–0:41	("I won't let this happen to my children"); two-voice texture continues	
	A4	0:42–0:54	("meet the real world comin' out of your shell")	
A′	A5	0:55–1:07	("white elephants, sitting ducks"); third voice added	3rd voice: A3–E4
	A6	1:08–1:20	("I will rise up")	
B	B1	1:21–1:30	("little baby's eyes"); 3-voice texture with melody in lowest; guitar progression begins on A; 3-measure phrases	lowest voice: G♯2–C♯3
	B2	1:31–1:40	repeat of B1	
	B3	1:41–1:59	repeat of B1 with 2mm. interpolation and extension; ends on strummed C♯m triad	

the track. It is this latter key feature of the song that guides its motivic development, and thus the shape of the through-composed form.

Doubled perfectly in parallel octaves for the first two phrases, it is impossible to tell which of the two voices—high, starting on G♯4, or low, starting on G♯3—is the melody and which is the harmony. It is only on the lyric "underground" where a sense of labor division emerges. While the high voice ascends to a half-cadence on G♯4, the lower voice text paints the syllable "-ground" by burrowing more than an octave below the high voice, down to D♯3, for the first time in the song. "The Sound of Silence" comes to mind, namely the spirited debates which attempt to settle once and for all which singer has the "melody." Ontologically, the case here is different (all vocal takes in "I Will" are recorded by Yorke), but the question from the listener's perspective remains the same: With which voice should we sing along? The answer could simply be practical (range considerations), but when our monophonically entrenched brain plays back the melody throughout the day, the question remains, Which line will we hear?

Questions regarding the primacy of a certain melody would not endure if they were not, to a certain extent, subjective. My ear is drawn to the warm, intimate chest voice heard in sections A1–A2, that is, until the moment at which the two lines disentangle at the end of the phrase. From here until the end of the A section, the bell-like falsetto upper voice seems to articulate the clearest idea of melodic structure, always aiming for the goal-tone G♯4 over dominant harmony, while the lowest voice wanders in an improvisatory fashion in the depths of Yorke's range. An added middle voice in phrases A5 and A6 doubles the guitar's characteristic 4–3 suspension from C♯ to B♯.

As a through-composed form, once "I Will" departs from this A material and arrives at B, it must never recapitulate A. Section B provides motivic contrast in three ways: (1) through the new melismatic, quasi-improvisatory vocalese beginning at 1:21; (2) through the new chordal progression presented by the guitar at more than double the previous rate of harmonic change; and (3) through a new texted vocal melody, which arises through a yet-unheard tetrachord (G♯2 to C♯3) featuring a yet-unheard pitch, the Dorian-inflected raised sixth scale-degree A♯. This final and contrasting repeated lyrical/melodic phrase, repeating three times at the song's end, has more than a whiff of terminal climax about it. Yet the song cannot be said to be a textbook terminally climactic form because it does not supplant a previously heard chorus with a more memorable terminal climax. It is a through-composed song (AB) that begins like a strophic form (A1, A2, A3 . . .) and ends with a terminal climax (B).

Franz Schubert's shorter through-composed songs were among the first to utilize this kind of motivic development. "Halt!" from *Die schöne Müllerin* (1823), develops repetitions of each C major motive in a process that shapes the song more than the brief foray into G, which serves as the song's B section. Like "I Will," this song's drastically short duration (Dietrich Fischer-Dieskau's 1951 recording lasts a mere 1′32″) still leaves room for an ending that repeats a given lyrical/melodic segment exactly three times at its conclusion. Schubert's through-composed song, which ends in novel material rather than recapitulatory certitude, is thus the perfect setting for Müller's poem, which ends by asking repeatedly, "did you lead me to the right place?"

Although the forms of "I Will" and "Halt!" pursue the development of lyrical/melodic phrases, many of Radiohead's through-composed forms appear in the purely instrumental tracks. One strategy for understanding Radiohead's instrumental pieces is to hear them as constant variations on a single theme, what I have elsewhere called a monothematic form.[23] Rather than set up discrete, contrasting sections—something heard in strophic, verse/chorus, terminally climactic, and many through-composed forms—a monothematic form has *no sections*. It is a constantly evolving single idea, a thematic kaleidoscope. "Feral" (2011–4), for example, starts with a two-drum-set groove that seems to be pulled directly from a funk break, accompanied only by a set of whole-note chords. Over this single theme, a series of events is layered over the course of the track. Yorke's voice appears, but sparingly, not as a sung melody of any sort, but as yet another sampled texture. A low, rolling bass part joins the mix at 1:30, adding to the sense of driving kinesis in the funk drum parts. Accumulation is not a guiding factor in "Feral." Just as there is no intro, there is no outro—the piece simply ends after adding and subtracting layers and samples.

"Fitter Happier" (1997–7) is Radiohead's first experiment with a monothematic form. The background is composed only of ethereal string samples that accompany Yorke improvising at the piano. We hear no percussion or bass instruments, and instead of sung vocal samples, we hear only two *spoken* narratives. One of these, which appears faintly and sparingly in the right channel, is a short repeated spoken sample taken from the 1975 film *Three Days of the Condor* ("This is the Panic Office . . . section 9–17 may have been hit. Activate the following procedure").[24] The focus for most listeners will undoubtedly be the computer-generated voice, loud in the center channel, which speaks a linear narrative throughout the song.[25] Fragmented in its recommendations for a better everyday life ("keep in contact with old friends, enjoy a drink now and again"), the computer voice sometimes strays from this supposedly helpful advice as if a glitch in its program swerves it toward apocalyptic and poetic prophecies ("Like a cat / tied to a stick / that's driven into / frozen winter shit").

Two tracks from the early millennium push the limits of developing a single theme even further. In "Pulk/Pull Revolving Doors" (2001–3) a pounding, chest-rattling electronic beat undergirds the entire track, accompanied only sparsely by melodic electronic sounds. Against this backdrop, Yorke ruminates about various types of doors, but his voice is filtered through an auto-tuner, which is programmed to snap every frequency he speaks to the closest note of a predetermined musical scale. Detectable auto-tune, as a foreground stylistic feature rather than a discreet production tool, was made popular by Cher's hit "Believe" (1998–1). Yorke's distortion of this aesthetic predates its widespread use in post-millennial hip-hop by several years. It appears here as neither a source of polished aesthetics, nor as a tool of stylistic identification. Instead, it seems to cause only confusion, though listeners may interpret the gesture retrospectively if they have experienced the late 2000s meme "auto-tune the news," where various newscasters are made to "sing" by third party fans using the technology. Barring these culturally specific experiences, listeners will likely be confused as to whether they are interacting with a speaking or singing subject. The timbre of the voice is one of speech, while the fundamental frequencies, added artificially, are those of an equal-tempered major scale.

Unlike these monothematic forms in which development is guided by a voice of some sort (however modified), "Treefingers" (2000–5) is purely instrumental. It evolves gently and glacially, much like the icebergs and mountains experienced visually on the *Kid A* cover art. Functionally, "Treefingers" serves as an abstract, monothematic conduit between two tracks on the album ("How to Disappear" and "Optimistic") whose verse/chorus forms pose almost no barriers to formal understanding.

Blended Forms, Idiosyncratic Forms

While most of Radiohead's experimental formal types can be described as terminally climactic or through-composed, a few exist in a unique space much their own. "Paranoid Android" (1997–2) is a famous example which many have likened to the progressive rock formal practice of composing a "suite" of related ideas (cf., Queen's "Bohemian Rhapsody"). "Paranoid Android" is quite nearly through-composed, but recapitulates a middle section as a way to bring about closure.[26]

Parts I, II, and III of the song are not only completely independent of one another thematically, but also feature different organizational strategies. It would be one thing to have three unique verse/chorus suites in a song, but by rethinking formal structure itself between each of these three parts, Radiohead challenges the listener to approach form in a unique manner for each section.

Though Table 2.5 casts Part I as two verses, each with the same end-refrain, we could easily conceive of the same structure as two verse/chorus pairs. The repeated lyric "What's that?" which occurs at 0:51 and 1:41, seems too short to be an autonomous chorus, and the preserved texture and groove of the previous music suggest to me a varied continuation of the verse. However, some listeners may interpret the subtle harmonic and timbral changes as suggestive of a chorus. Additionally, a higher guitar part enters, repeatedly emphasizing the same (D–E) motive in the lead vocal melody; a new hypermetric emphasis is placed on the provisional G minor tonic for the first time; and, if you listen closely enough, the same computerized voice heard in "Fitter Happier" is intoning the words "I may be paranoid, but not android," providing the only instance of the song's title, an attribute many listeners associate with the typical chorus.

TABLE 2.5

Three-part "suite" form in "Paranoid Android" (1997–2)

Section	Clock time	Description
intro to part I	0:01–0:17	quiet drum and guitar groove
verse 1	0:18–1:07	end-refrain ("what's that?") at 0:51
verse 2	1:08–1:56	recap verse and end-refrain
intro to part II	1:57–2:19	signature riff, ¼, quiet [A–C–A, G♯–C–D]
episode a1	2:20–2:41	vocal entrance ("ambition makes you look pretty ugly") over signature riff, followed by ⅞ riff
episode a2	2:42–3:03	variation on episode a1 ("remember my name")
outro a1	3:04–3:32	part II intro riff in ¼ followed by ⅞ riff with new guitar lead
intro to part III	3:33–4:03	sets up passacaglia [C–B–B♭–A . . .]
chorale	4:04–5:35	three times through passacaglia with increasing layers (4:04, 4:35, 5:05)
outro a2	5:36–6:23	recapitulate part II outro twice (w/modifications)

Immediately after this conventional structure, the song swerves to what sounds like instrumental bridge material. Two main grooves are present here. First, a benign groove in common time at 1:57, featuring a guitar part that sounds like a modified A minor pentatonic blues riff with a foreign lower semitone (A♭ or G♯?) added. The voice soon enters over this ("ambition makes you look pretty ugly") just before the previous groove modulates to ⅞ time featuring a groovier, undulating bass part. This compound unit repeats, only now the guitar seems to get angrier along with the irritable voice statement ("you don't remember"), now articulating the A minor pentatonic riff with heavy distortion before also usurping the previously bass-driven ⅞ riff with a swirling, maelstrom-esque lead guitar part that will later serve to close the song. Thus, the form of part II is less like a pair of verses, and more like two vocal "episodes" staggered by instrumental interruptions.

Undoubtedly the most striking formal characteristic of "Paranoid Android" is the extended chorale-passacaglia that spans more than two minutes of the track (3:33–5:35). More than a hint of classicism shrouds this passage. The baroque practice of passacaglia is one where a repeated bass line (called a "groundbass") forms the basis for a set of variations to be overlaid in the upper parts. Halfway through the chord progression, the C minor "lament bass" (a descending bass line, in this case by semitone) shifts gears impetuously toward a distant D minor tonic. And, because of its repeated nature, just as soon as we cadence in D minor the passacaglia begins again on the previous C minor bass progression. Over four presentations of this dizzying loop a choir of voices provides a curtain of chorale-style oohs and ahhs as Yorke progressively adds variations to a plaintive melody presented in full at the onset ("rain down"). The piece then ends with an instrumental outro borrowed from the end of part II.

Although "Paranoid Android" presents a formal structure for which there is almost no external comparison (the comparison critics draw to Queen seems driven only by the stylistic heterogeneity), other idiosyncratic forms such as "Exit Music" (1997–4) and "Hunting Bears" (2001–9) do have formal precedents, though not in rock music. Their alternations of a main theme with two different contrasting themes, closing with a recapitulation of the original main theme (ABACA) suggest a *rondo*, a form common in classic-era instrumental music. The main A theme in "Exit Music" is beset on either side by two different ideas: a B theme starting at 1:26 ("breathe, keep breathing") featuring a mellotron choir; and, following a second presentation of A, a C theme at 2:50 ("you can laugh a spineless laugh") that gradually builds volume and texture until it presents the song's only cacophonous outburst, featuring overdriven bass, washy cymbals, and Yorke screaming a full octave higher than all previous A sections. The opening quiet guitar part then recapitulates for an outro with Yorke now praying "we hope that you choke" in the sweetest manner one could possibly express those sentiments.

Recognizing well-formed archetypes for a few common song forms, both in conventional rock music (strophic and verse/chorus) and experimental rock music (terminally climactic and through-composed), serves the listener well in terms of fitting the listening experience to listener expectation. But sometimes the drive to do so leads us to Procrustean motives, whereby we imaginatively reshape what we hear to fit a previous archetype. However, there *is* no perfect archetype of a strophic form, nor a terminally climactic form, nor any other song form. Instead, a number of songs display a shared set of characteristics—what Wittgenstein called "family resemblances." Epistemologically, humans' "organizing system and something waiting to be organized are hopelessly intertwined," and so we perceive these unique song forms as individual utterances of some common form.[27]

Trevor de Clercq shows that a number of verse-like, chorus-like, or bridge-like sections heard in rock music cannot be categorized as one or the other, but instead only as "blends" of both.[28] Expanding de Clercq's theory from the level of individual sections to the song as a whole, we can find many "blended forms" in Radiohead's catalog which derive inspiration not from one standard formal type, but which display prominent characteristics of at least two different archetypes. Such is the case in "Bodysnatchers" (2007–2) and "Go to Sleep" (2003–5). Interestingly, both are best experienced not only as blends of two distinct formal types, but in fact as a blend of one conventional formal type (verse/chorus or strophic) and one experimental formal type (through-composed or terminally climactic).

"Bodysnatchers" begins with two verses, each of which contains an end-refrain ("I've no idea what you are talking about") at 0:41 and 1:38. The music then swerves toward a seemingly straightforward contrasting bridge, which decreases the volume from the previous loud verses. The listener will here perceive a conventional formal type, and has thus been conditioned to expect a recapitulation of some previous section (probably either the verse, refrain, or both) following the conclusion of this bridge at 3:09. So ripe is the expectation for an AABA form, dare I say some listeners will actually start to sing a third verse. But the music does not return to a loud third verse. It instead remains quiet as Yorke murmurs indecipherable syllables until 3:31 when the music becomes loud again, but not for another verse. Instead, the loud music presented here is more like an extended outro or "playout" as Yorke continues to sing nonsense syllables in a new melody, before finally warning us repeatedly, "I see it comin'!" (possibly the ending?). The AAB[C/A] form, which ends in more-or-less new material is thus best described as a strophic/terminally climactic blend. The expected straightforward recapitulation of strophic forms has been removed, while the would-be unprecedented terminal climax is foreshadowed in many significant ways by the altered A section accompaniment that returns.

A meter-changing groove that alternates between ¼ and ¹²⁄₈ in the beginning of "Go to Sleep" sounds like it could be the first verse of a conventional form, complete with end-refrain at 1:22 ("I'm gonna go to sleep / and let this all wash over me"). But the music that follows at 1:29 is utterly new. Featuring a steady ¼ groove, it lacks the rhythmic complexity of the previous "verse." As such, when an extended end-refrain returns at 2:19, seemingly orphaned from its expected second verse, what are we to expect afterward? A return to the previous verse (ABCBA, yielding a rondo structure)? Or, perhaps something new (ABCBD, like a through-composed form with an end-refrain hiccup in the middle)? Though both have precedents in Radiohead's catalog, the answer is somewhere in-between. What actually recapitulates at 2:48 to end the song is the *accompaniment* of the surprise music that followed the first end-refrain (C), a technique reminiscent of the recapitulation of an interior contrasting section to bring about closure in "Paranoid Android." "Go to Sleep" is thus best described as a through-composed form that retains remnants of its strophic genesis.

Radiohead's most salient song forms evoke but regularly transcend the normative formal structures we expect from rock. If Radiohead uses no recapitulation at all, they almost surely forego any chance at comprehensibility. And, if they constantly rearticulate standard verse/chorus designs, they undoubtedly would not receive the study and scrutiny that they do.

Radiohead's Use of Formal Types, 1997–2011

Table 2.6 shows Radiohead's five basic formal types. On the Y axis we see the six albums within our statistical sample (organized top to bottom chronologically), and on the X axis, the percentage of each of those albums that may be reasonably represented by each of the five formal types. For example, approximately half of the songs on *OK Computer* (1997) are best described as verse/chorus forms, and there are no terminally climactic forms to be heard on *The King of Limbs* (2011).[29]

Table 2.6 also demonstrates a significant *inverse* correlation between experimental formal structures (e.g., terminally climactic, through-composed) and albums in which we hear more experimental timbres and rhythms. As a way to interpret this correlation, we may understand this as a case of Radiohead (consciously or not) avoiding a sort of "information overload." When Radiohead presents unconventional or experimental timbres or rhythms, they do so within song forms that are recognizable; or, conversely, when composing experimental song forms, there is less room for confusing rhythms or timbres. Note for example the spike in terminally climactic forms that occurs on *In Rainbows* (2007), which features some of the most straightforward instances of traditional rock timbres and rhythm section grooves. And, conversely, the profound departure from traditional rock timbres on *Kid A* (2000) is accompanied by a statistically significant spike in the number of strophic and verse/chorus forms on the album. An unprecedented 90% of songs

TABLE 2.6

Frequency of formal type by percentage of album

	Strophic	Verse/ chorus	Terminally climactic	Through- composed	Other/ blended
1997	25%	50%	8.3%	8%	8%
2000	45%	45%	0%	10%	0%
2001	27%	41%	4%	23%	18%
2003	36%	25%	21%	21%	7%
2007	55%	0%	33%	4%	8%
2011	56%	25%	0%	12%	6%

on *Kid A* are composed in these conventional forms. In accounting for this inverse correlation from an ecological standpoint, attention to timbre and rhythm must balance with the perceptual debt needed to process formal structure. When we are not burdened with understanding a complex or unconventional formal structure, we have more cognitive facilities to devote to understanding novel timbres and rhythms.

Another complementary way to understand this data involves thinking about Radiohead's stylistic evolution over the course of these 14 years. As the band traces a gradual path away from traditional rock and roll conventions from 1997 through 2011, note the steady decrease in the number of verse/chorus forms. However, the other hallmark of rock formal structures, the strophic form, appears to rise proportionally alongside this decline in verse/chorus forms. Strophic formal designs account for over half the songs on *The King of Limbs*, in which entire tracks are structured around a single groove. It might be tempting to interpret these as balancing one another, thus keeping the same level of conventional structure in place over time. But strophic forms operate very differently from a perceptual standpoint. Verse/chorus and AABA forms are easily recognizable because of their inherent contrast. Once we hear a recapitulation of A following a presentation of B, the form is clear. Monothematic through-composed forms, on the other hand, have the ability to constantly keep us listening for processes and developments. As we are presented with elements that sound similar to elements we have already heard, yet are significantly different, we tune into the differences. Our perceptions tune into the novel, leaving familiar elements to recede into the background. "Bloom" (2011–1), though best described from a "bird's-eye view" perspective as a strophic structure, is experienced as a process of development involving the confusing and gradually evolving polytempo present in the percussion section. A processual understanding takes over when I hear "Codex" (2011–6), but the process is one of a textural build over the course of several strophes, sections which are only apparent to me as I analyze retrospectively.

An ecological approach to understanding and perceiving form necessarily happens in time. First-listening experiences, during which we improvise a map of musical events, offer valuable insight into that approach. Subsequent hearings are also interesting, as we continually balance real-time and retrospective experiences in an attempt to make sense of the whole from the parts. After years of interacting with Radiohead songs, I find that the real-time experience of formal perception rubs against or enhances what I now *know* the song will eventually do, and I still listen for new ways to understand those larger structures in relationship to the perceptually immediate parts. The experience is truly an ecological one, just as intimate and interactive as dancing in a familiar space, noting how your ever-changing position with regard to other elements and organisms affects your understanding of the space as a whole.

Analytical Coda: "2+2=5"

Nowhere else in Radiohead's catalog does a listener encounter such a formal tour-de-force as "2+2=5" (2003–1). Unlike "I Will" (2003–10), which balances experimental form with relatively conventional harmony; or "15 Step" (2007–1), which offsets its experimental rhythm with a comparatively conventional song form, "2+2=5" offers no such concessions. Its through-composed ABCD form, broken out in Table 2.7, is as challenging to grasp as is its odd-cardinality meter, polytempo, and chromatic harmony. But like "Karma Police," the song does offer several signposts along the way if we are willing to consider timbre and harmonic design as potential avenues into its unusual form.

TABLE 2.7

Through-composed form in "2+2=5" (2003–1)

Section	Clock time	Description
intro 1	0:01–0:13	low D with channel switching, spoken text ("that's a nice way to start, Johnny")
intro 2	0:14–0:24	guitar riff [Fm–Csus4/E] establishes F minor key and 7-beat groove
A1	0:25–0:52	vocals enter ("are you such a dreamer"); F–E neighbor tone elongated to F–E–Eb–D . . .
A2	0:53–1:21	("I lay down the tracks"); section A's two-part structure now apparent
B	1:22–1:53	("it's the Devil's way now"); voice/hi-hat and guitar polyrhythm
C	1:54–2:25	abrupt change to rock-steady ¼; full band, overdriven guitars; voice yelling ("you have not been paying attention")
D1	2:26–2:38	instrumental interlude; parallel 6th dyads (F/Ab and G/Bb); establishes D groove
D2	2:39–3:19	voice enters over D groove, parallel 6th dyads now Bb/Db and F/Ab, each phrase ends on G7

Two such harmonic and timbral signposts are most revealing. First, a bewildering change of harmony in the A section—a clue that something new is coming in the form—explodes into an intertextual odyssey that encompasses not only George Orwell's novel *1984* but, perhaps less predictably, George Frederic Handel's setting of Psalm 69 in his 1741 Oratorio *Messiah*. Second, a sudden mid-song timbral shift proves to be telling not only in terms of formal design, but also as a window into Radiohead's rather tenuous relationship with timbre around the turn of the millennium.

Sections A and B (0:01–1:53)

Following the spoken introduction, the first 25 seconds of the track are occupied by a two-chord riff, alternating a root-position F minor triad with a first-inversion C major triad, the inner-voice pedal F suspended despite the leading-tone E in the bass. For the purposes of an experientially oriented theory of form, the perception this riff affords, <introduction>, is most important. Identifying it as such leads to a complete perception–expectation–realization chain confirmed when Yorke enters with "are you such a dreamer," signaling the onset of a verse.

A standard introduction accumulates various instrumental layers until a completed accompaniment—both rhythmic and harmonic—emerges fully formed for the vocal entrance. Given this inherited set of expectations, the harmonic change at 0:42, which begins at the seventh measure of Figure 2.1, will be perceived as a surprise. This surprise sets off a chain reaction having much to do with intertextuality and harmony. From a formal standpoint, what has occurred is something of a bait and switch. What we previously understood as the complete two-chord verse riff has turned out not to be so, prompting the question, Is this a new section, or were we only given part of the complete riff in the introduction?

The answer to this formal question involves text-painting—the practice of adding meaning to lyrics through pitch—as well as rock's harmonic conventions. Modern rock music rarely utilizes leading tone scale degrees such as the E♮ here necessary to form a C major triad in the key of F minor. Because this leading tone is inherited from western art music, its presence here affords the *learned style* topic. It is within the orbit of this classical sphere that we ultimately must understand the surprise, at once formal and harmonic, that occurs at 0:42. Foreign to rock's harmonic vocabulary, the progression [F7/E♭–D7–Gm] that sets off this formal surprise belongs not to Harrison or Hendrix, but to Handel. Figure 2.2 shows the same harmonic progression, also in F minor, in the tumultuous recitative "Thy Rebuke Hath Broken His Heart" from *Messiah*. Yorke's lyrics over this progression are not George Handel's selection from Psalm 69:20, but are in fact George Orwell's from

FIGURE 2.1 A section progression in "2+2=5" (2003–1, 0:25).

FIGURE 2.2 Handel, *Messiah*, Pt. 2, no. 29 "Thy rebuke hath broken His heart".

1984 ("Two and two / always makes five"). As if the reference to *1984* were not clear enough, Yorke's melody text-paints the Orwellian lyrics. "Two and Two," sung on the dyad C4 to F4, a perfect fourth, highlights the true sum of the integers, unbridled by a government regime bent on distorting the truth by any means necessary to advance the party line. Yorke continues, starting again on C4 but reaching a step higher into falsetto register for G4 ("always makes") to form a perfect fifth—the totalitarian total of two and two which, for Orwell, epitomized the sort of double-speak he envisaged as the logical conclusion to communism.

But how exactly are we supposed to process meaning within a tangled web of associations as seemingly disparate as the dystopian masterpiece *1984* and the ever-hopeful *Messiah*? In "Conceptual Integration and Formal Expression," cognitive theorists Turner and Fauconnier propose a model for integrating and assimilating ideas between disparate sources such as these. Figure 2.3 places Orwell's and Handel's texts into one of Turner and Fauconnier's "conceptual integration networks" (CIN).[30] CINs consist of four "mental spaces." Most notable are the "input spaces"—the east and west nodes—which describe meanings associated with each individual source. The generic space guides the manner in which the two input spaces interact with one another, resulting in the core output of the network, the blended space.

Essential to my CIN are three concepts shown in the "generic space" (truth, control, and individual will), which control the resultant mapping between the two inputs: Orwell and the psalmist articulate these generic concepts in opposed ways, but the blended space reveals intersections of agreement across the two inputs: (1) truth is not in the control of the individual; (2) we individuals are ever at the will of some

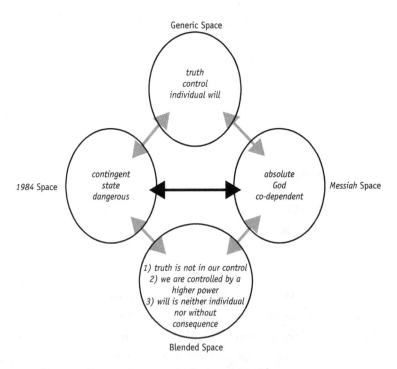

FIGURE 2.3 Conceptual integration network of *1984* and *Messiah*.

higher power; and (3) an individual's free will is always compromised, either onto-logically (it was really God), or because it will be met with punishment (from the state). The meanings in this blended space resonate strikingly well with those ex-pressed through the song's lyrics, as well as what we know of Yorke's own political beliefs as revealed through several interviews. Replace Orwell's fears of communism with Yorke's distrust of multinational capitalism and a nearly perfect correlation emerges. Yorke's environmental concerns, especially climate change (N.B., section A2's lyrics: "sandbag and hide / January has April's showers") result from the same kind of human affront toward Mother Nature that God endures in Psalm 69:20.

This tangled Handelian/Orwellian moment of intertextual significance takes us from the surprising F7/E♭ harmony all the way to the über-classical half-cadence at 0:49.[31] When the phrase restarts at 0:53—Section A2—we now understand the true phrase length of this verse unit. Perceiving Yorke's repetition of the opening double-neighbor motive [C4–D♭4–B4] primes us to expect a repetition of this full verse unit, which is realized exactly, taking us to the end of the A section at 1:21.

After these two passages the song moves to a quiet B section at 1:22 where the driving seven-pulse odd-cardinality rhythm has been replaced by a *polytempo* at 1:22. That is to say, the guitar and hi-hat are playing in two different tempi which are not related by rational ratios (e.g., the standard 3:1, 2:1, or, less commonly, 3:2 and 4:3 rhythms common to rock music). Suffice it to say for now that by the B section skep-tical listeners may be wondering where all of this soupy, ethereal noise is headed. Any verse/chorus- or strophic-based expectations cued by the two-part verse (A1 and A2) are now thwarted.

Appreciating the full import of the timbral shift that characterizes the next sec-tion entails recognizing "2+2=5" as the opening track on *Hail to the Thief* (2003), an album which, upon its release following *Kid A* (2000) and *Amnesiac* (2001), was to be pivotal for guitar-loving Radiohead fans. To say that this moment at nearly two min-utes into the album is crucial is an understatement. Even though they gained a new generation of fans following the release of two electro-acoustic albums at the begin-ning of the millennium, Radiohead lost many fans of their early rock and roll albums *Pablo Honey* (1993), *The Bends* (1995), and, to a lesser extent, *OK Computer* (1997). During the B section, it is this latter camp of listeners who is wondering whether or not Radiohead has just made a third cerebral/electro-acoustic album, which could perhaps be the third and final nail in the coffin for this particular fan base.

Sections C and D (1:54–3:19)

A volume explosion at the onset of the C section marks the arrival of the track's sta-tistical climax. Figure 2.4 shows that the statistical climax, a result of the song's peak

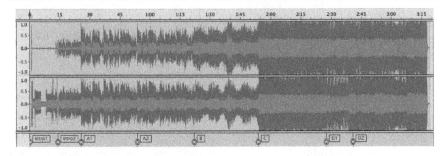

FIGURE 2.4 Waveform analysis of "2+2=5" (2003–1).

amplitude, coincides perfectly with the arrival of section C. Here at 1:54 the band launches into a bombastic rock-out, entirely without warning.[32] Yorke shouts "because" at the end of the B section, and a split second later it sounds like *The Bends* all over again (maybe more like Pearl Jam, ca. 1996). Fully overdriven multiple guitars and backbeat up-tempo drums accompany Yorke shouting "You have not been paying attention" in his signature yell-scream. The meaningfulness of this moment is substantial within the scope of Radiohead's career up to this point. Within the first two minutes of the album, we hear a profound *synthesis of styles* in the music. The band begins in a contemplative, cerebral mood (ca. 2000–2001), then brings back the rock (ca. 1993–1997) just in time to keep *The Bends* fans on board, while still managing to give the *Amnesiacs* something to remember.

Yorke's nagging, almost petulant cries throughout the C section may also describe the frustration the band experienced after *Kid A* and *Amnesiac* were dismissed by fans and critics alike for not "rocking" enough. Recalling the virtual schism Radiohead's electronic-driven albums created in the rock community, Allan Moore notes,

> One might posit that the determined anti-rock evolution of Radiohead suggested for a while a renewed interest in the difficult, in music which needs working at (as did most of *Kid A* and only a little less of *Amnesiac*), even in music whose ultimate rewards will outlast initial incomprehension (and if this sounds like a return to the avant garde aesthetics of 1910 or 1950, maybe that's food for thought), were it not for the comparative safety of *Hail to the Thief*.[33]

Though lasting only a split second, traversing the break between B and C sets into motion meanings that span four albums in Radiohead's catalog.

This rock-out trope continues for the remainder of the song, though the exact thematic elements constantly shift and evolve in a through-composed manner. While the D section maintains the general full-rock texture of the C section, there are no shared thematic elements. Beginning with a two-dyad alternation in parallel sixths (F over A♭ and G over B♭) in D1, the G/B♭ dyad is replaced by B♭/D♭ in section D2. Having shed its Orwellian/Handelian learned and cerebral intertext in favor of 1990s-era rock aesthetics, the D section subtly resurrects at least the Orwellian song title through its progression of parallel sixths. The pitch distance between D1's dyad pair (F/A♭ to G/B♭) is two semitones (or, if you'd prefer, two frets on the guitar), and the pitch distance between D2's dyad pair (B♭/D♭ to F/A♭) is five semitones. Two instances of Orwellian text painting bookend the track in (inter)textual significance.

Conclusion

Through-composed forms such as "2+2=5" allow artists to reinvent their timbral, rhythmic, harmonic, and even formal identity from section to section. Unlike terminally climactic form, the song is in no way goal-oriented toward one meaningful moment. Instead, each passing serial succession of themes (A–B–C–D) is as meaningful and perceptually potent as the previous. This rebirth between sections is what then makes "2+2=5" a different through-composed form than "Feral" (2011–4) or "Fitter Happier" (1997–7), both of which are monothematic formal developments over the course of the track. "2+2=5" is instead a *polythematic* through-composed form, which nevertheless unifies thematically diverse sections by shared timbral and rhythmic parameters. The A and B sections, though thematically diverse, are grouped together by a lower volume and tumultuous rhythm, while C and D, different among themselves and from sections A and B, are grouped together by their rocking opulence. "2+2=5" relishes in sudden changes of dynamics and themes with no regard for organic unity, and thus provides listeners the opportunity to process meaning on a section-by-section basis. The musical/literary/political meaning in the A section is categorically different than the self-reflexive creation of inter-album meaning exacted at the onset of the C section, and so are the means through which those meanings are created.

Notes

1. Moore and Ibrahim (2005, 150) underscore the point that, contrary to the formal experimentation begun on *OK Computer* (1997), which becomes fully maximized by *Kid A* (2000), the formal designs heard on *Pablo Honey* (1993) and *The Bends* (1995) are not a unique part of Radiohead's idiolect, but rather an inherited style trait.

2. See Summach 2012.

3. Ibid., 23–24.

4. *OK Computer*'s opening track "Airbag" (1997–1) exhibits a clear strophic structure, as does "Morning Bell" (both 2000–9 and 2001–7 versions).

5. Jocelyn Neal (2007, 45) has written extensively on the narrative functions of verse/chorus and related conventional forms.

6. See Summach (2012, 107).

7. Especially when bridges are present (AABA in strophic, ABABCB in verse/chorus) the two forms can be heard as variations on the same basic formal principle. As John Covach (2005, 74–75) has pointed out, a standard verse/chorus design with bridge can be understood as a "compound AABA" form, with each verse/chorus pair standing in for "A." Understood this way, both conventional forms thrive on the (re)presentation of some central body of music, either the strophe or the verse/chorus pair.

8. Jay Summach's study (see 2011 and 2012) does this exceptionally well, as does Trevor de Clercq's (2012) dissertation.

9. See Moore (2012, 82)

10. See Doll 2011.

11. See Everett (1999, 16).

12. I have explored extensively these two formal types in post-millennial experimental rock in two articles; see Osborn 2011 and Osborn 2013.

13. My preferred method of numbering verses, following conventions I have previously outlined, aligns a verse's number with that of its subsequent chorus, sometimes resulting in verses 1a and 1b in Table 2.1. For more on this convention, see Osborn (2010a, 261).

14. Following this statement, it is ironic that Moore (2012, 82) analyzes no songs in which this is the case.

15. See Meyer (1980, 194).

16. For more on accumulative beginnings, see Spicer (2004, 33).

17. See Robinson (2003, 35); quoted in Moore and Ibrahim (2005, 147).

18. Bailie (1997, 42) and Hale (1999, 102) have each proposed connections between Greenwood and Penderecki relating to techniques of chromatic saturation. It is unclear which piece(s) Greenwood is thinking of here. The technique of chromatic saturation through cluster chords is more readily associated with Penderecki's contemporary Gyorgy Ligeti, or even earlier in the music of Henry Cowell.

19. Amanda Lewis (2011) offers a technical analysis of the microphonic techniques used in Bon Iver's song "Skinny Love" (2007).

20. This linkage is along the lines of what Feld (1984, 12) called "interpretive moves."

21. A remarkably similar form can be heard in "Ful Stop" (2016–5, 3:19), where a gradual build-up leads to a terminal climax that repeats the mantra "truth will mess you up."

22. See Brower (2000, 323–4).

23. See Osborn (2011, 7).

24. Phil Rose (2016, 50) points out the discrepancy between this film and the one cited in the *OK Computer* liner notes as "Flight of the Condor," which is not the title of the movie, but rather a cut from Dave Gruson's soundtrack for the film.

25. The timbre of this voice reminds me of the 1983 film *WarGames*, in which a hacked defense-department computer asks the question, "Shall we play a game?" and the hacker replies

(not realizing what he has hacked into) "Let's play global thermonuclear war"—an intertextual reference which, though driven primarily by timbre, is topically apropos to *Three Days of the Condor* (thanks go out to Jason Summach for bringing this relevant film to my attention in a personal communication). Younger listeners will likely associate this timbre more readily with Stephen Hawking's adaptive speech apparatus, or with any number of later Internet-based text-to-speech bots in the early 2000s such as "Grape Ape."

26. Nathaniel Adam (2011, 35) has argued convincingly for a three-part reading of the song's form, though he refers to the outro at 5:36 as a "Part IV." Alternatively, Nicole Biamonte (2014, 7.9) demonstrates that the same three-part schema can be read as a more conventional form beginning with two verses, and whose bridge, constituting all of Adam's "Part II," returns as an outro to close the song.

27. This snapshot of Donald Davidson's epistemology is quoted in Lehrer (2008, 71).

28. See de Clercq (2012, 213–286).

29. In an earlier study Moore and Abrahim (2005, 151) suggest a gradual reduction in the formal complexity of Radiohead's songs between 1997–2003. However, their methodology, in which complexity is measured by the number of distinct sections, is not grounded in recent research on form in popular music. Such a method would, for example, rank a standard verse/chorus form as more 'complex' than a monothematic through-composed form.

30. See Turner and Fauconnier (1995). Lawrence Zbikowski (1999) has adapted CINs for the analysis of Schubert, and provides a more comprehensive literature review of the subject.

31. This does not account for the F^{add6} chord that directly precedes the half-cadence, which serves only as consonant support for Yorke's 4–3 suspension (F4–E4). This non-functional set of suspensions, which functions analogously to a cadential six–four, would be reduced out in even the closest of foreground readings.

32. In this way, the volume explosion is very different than in the following track, "Sit Down, Stand Up" (2003–2), whose incipient terminal climax is foreshadowed long before its arrival.

33. See Moore (2012, 160).

3   Rhythm and Meter

PERHAPS THE MOST characteristic interactions associated with the experience of rock music since its inception in the 1950s involve vigorous rhythmic movements. Whether shaking our hips or nodding our head, rock music has traditionally provided the steady pulse conducive to aligning our bodily movements with the musical pulse with little to no conscious thought. Certainly it was this characteristic that led the elder generation to distrust rock music based on their observation that it seemed to whip the youth into a Dionysian frenzy on the dance floor. A generation later, distorted guitars and double-kick drums only grafted this movement upward as headbanging became an emblematic gesture of heavy metal and rock. Still others among us enjoy the same beat at the same pace while leisurely sitting in our chairs at home or in the car. Whether patting our feet, tapping our fingers, or full-on air drumming, experiencing rock music unquestionably involves a kinesthetic interpretation that usually takes place only because of the regular and predictable steady beat happening throughout the music.

When rock music does *not* provide us with this predictable beat, what do we do? As listeners moving with the music, our first instinct will be to search for a beat or pulse with which we can interact. Privileging kinesthetic involvement with rhythm does not, however, entail the absence of cognitive action. Rather the two are blended in a process known as "embodied cognition." Cognitive scientists couch this mind–body link in terms of human evolution: "[s]ensory processes (perception) and motor processes (action), having evolved together, are seen therefore as fundamentally inseparable, mutually informative, and structured so as to ground our conceptual systems."[1] Of the four distinct speeds of bodily motion that connect directly to our cognition of rhythmic structure, two are most evident when listening to Radiohead: beats and subdivisions.[2] These two primary speeds of rhythmic cognition have direct correlates in human physical motion. Various beat-speeds in Radiohead's music (this is true for almost all music) align with the speed of our heartbeats, chewing, walking, head nodding, and sexual intercourse. Subdivisions, a much faster rate of kinesis, align more properly with speech, hand gestures, and digital movements such as finger tapping.

Music psychologist Maria Witek's survey of participant kinesis in popular music reveals how salience might influence our understanding of rhythm. In her study,[3] the rhythms which most encouraged dancing among listeners were "not the ones that have very little complexity and not the ones that had very, very high complexity, but the patterns that had a sort of balance between predictability and complexity."[4] Tracks like "2+2=5" (2003–1, ⅞ time) and "15 step" (2007–1, ¾ time) exhibit a level of complexity at the beat-level which is balanced by predictability at the subdivision level (or, as in the maximally even palindrome "Pyramid Song" (2001–2), vice versa). By refusing to conform to our expectations of a steady beat in rock music, yet usually providing us some type of beat (however asymmetrical or unsteady), we will observe yet another parameter in which Radiohead's music achieves balance between expectation and surprise. From my years of interacting with the rhythmic structures in Radiohead's music—as a listener, as an analyst, and at the drum set—I hear five distinct ways in which their music escapes the orbit of conventional rock rhythmic structures thereby reaching a higher level of salience: odd-cardinality meter, changing meter, maximally even and/or Euclidean rhythms, grouping dissonance, and polytempo.

For each of these five rhythmic/metric types, it will be interesting to understand exactly how they obscure our sense of steady beat, and how, at the same time, they nevertheless retain a faster pulse stream shared by all instruments (in all examples except those which exhibit polytempo). Figuring out the ways in which these faster subdivisions group into larger beats allows our bodies to "move with the changing sounds of the groove, responding to a basic unit that [is] constantly repeated, but never the same."[5] To facilitate reader interaction with these rhythmic structures, I utilize a novel dot-based diagram that should make *feeling* these beats clearer. After all, the heart of the matter in rhythmic interpretation lies in how we interact kinesthetically with the music, whether through dancing, headbanging, tapping our toes, or drumming on the steering wheel.

Expectations regarding Regular Meter and Backbeat in Rock Music

Meter can be defined most broadly as the ways in which we group smaller units into larger ones.[6] In most pop and rock music, the ways in which *beats* (the primary kinesthetic level containing two to three *pulses* which subdivide the beat) are grouped into larger *measures* and *hypermeasures* usually remains steady throughout most of the song. This often results in units at multiple levels that adhere to groups of binary numbers, particularly two, four, and eight. Defining more rigorously some of the above terms, as well as establishing a notation system to be used in the musical examples throughout, will give us a consistent base for the analyses to follow:

Beat: Also known as "tactus."[7] The primary kinesthetic level present in the music, usually between 60 and 180 beats per minute (hereafter, BPM).[8] Listeners will typically pat their foot or bob their head at this metric level. Beats may be numbered within a measure, such that "beat one" is the first beat in any measure, while "beat four" is the last beat in a measure of 4/4 time. Beats are notated with open circles, with each open circle encompassing all pulses beneath it.

Pulse: Related to "subdivision." A level faster than that of the beat, which subdivides the beat, commonly in half (binary meter), sometimes in three (compound meter), and rarely into four (only within very slow tempi ~60 BPM). Though too fast to be felt as properly metric, some faster grids (>4 per beat) often form the lowest common denominator of all slower syncopated rhythms, and thus still act as the underlying pulse. Pulses are notated with filled circles below the beats they comprise.

Measure: Also known as "bar." The span of music which would, if notated, exist between two bar lines in a certain meter signature. Only relevant to non-notated music if a meter signature can be inferred through backbeat, backbeat deformation, or some other paradigmatic rhythmic/metric structure. Perceived measures are notated with bar lines in the transcription.

Hypermeasure: Related to "hypermeter" and "phrase." A pattern, either recurring or irregular, by which measures are grouped together based on recurring motives or accents. Hypermeters are notated using sequential numbers (e.g., "2" represents the second measure of a perceived hypermetric grouping) above the notated pulses and beats that measure contains.

Two beats, each of which is divided into two pulses, are often grouped together by a paradigmatic structure such as the backbeat. In such paradigmatic rhythmic structures, we can speak relatively uncontroversially about rhythm in terms of musical notation. In the backbeat, for example, we take for granted that the snare drum plays primarily on beats two and four of a measure which lasts four beats—even without transcribing or reading from a score.[9] Radiohead's music, like most rock music, does this with some regularity. We might even say that, from the standpoint of musical culture over the past century or so, Radiohead's music carries with it the "important relationship between the backbeat and the body, informed by the African-American culture of the ring shout."[10] Backbeats sometimes form the metric background for entire songs in Radiohead's catalog, including "Karma Police" (1997–6), "The National Anthem" (2000–3), "There, There" (2003–9), and "Bodysnatchers" (2007–2).

Figures 3.1 and 3.2 demonstrate the two most common types of backbeats: eighth-based and sixteenth-based. In nearly all backbeats, quarter notes, notated with open circles, form the primary beat level. This is the beat to which most listeners experience primary entrainment, seen primarily as head bobbing or foot patterns on the dance floor. In Figure 3.1, the fast tempo (quarter=167) restricts the underlying pulse to the eighth note. This layer might be drummed with the fingers, for example, but is too fast to be the primary beat. Figure 3.2's slower tempo (quarter=91) enables not only the eighth-note level, but also activates a faster sixteenth-based syncopated layer beneath (sixteenth=364), which forms the underlying pulse. This layer could be interpreted by fingers or hands on a table, but does not affect the primary beat we interpret with the feet or head: the slower quarter note. Relating Figure 3.2 back to my definition of pulse, note that at 364 BPM, the sixteenth note is too fast to be the properly metrical pulse. Nevertheless, it is the lowest common denominator which encompasses all notes in the kick drum and signature bass guitar riff. A listener comfortably drumming on the steering wheel with one hand will likely

FIGURE 3.1 Eighth-based backbeat in "Jigsaw Falling Into Place" (2007–9, 0:16).

FIGURE 3.2 Sixteenth-based backbeat in "The National Anthem" (2000–3, 0:12).

tap an eighth-based pulse (two per quarter-note beat) while nevertheless situating themselves cognitively within a steady stream of sixteenth notes anchoring the rampant syncopations. Embodiment shapes all understandings of meter and rhythm, even those too fast to (comfortably) be expressed by our extremities, "automatically ground[ing] cognitive processes that might normally be considered disembodied."[11]

Odd-Cardinality Meter

One way in which Radiohead's rhythms frequently subvert this expectation of regular meter is through measures which contain an odd number of beats or pulses, as opposed to binary numbers such as two and four. The most common odd-cardinality meters in Radiohead's music involve five or seven pulses grouped into asymmetrical beats (also known as "non-isochronous" beats) of two to three pulses each.[12] In ⅞ time, for example, we experience three beats, one of which lasts three eighth-note pulses, the other two lasting two eighth-note pulses. These three beats can occur in any order. The 2+2+3 ordering of this ⅞ meter is heard clearly in the opening guitar riff of "2+2=5" (2003–1). Alternating between two chords, each of which lasts two measures, the opening version of this riff sets up a four-measure hypermeter (though this changes after the voice enters when new chords are given only one measure each).

This example should make clear that there is no necessary correlation between odd-cardinality meter and hypermeter. Odd-cardinality measures such as the above often group (if only temporarily) into binary hypermeters, and binary meters are sometimes grouped in non-binary numbers, resulting in odd-cardinality, non-binary, and/or irregular hypermeter. For instance, though each measure is in a steady ¼ time, the first verse/chorus pair of "Paranoid Android" (1997, 0:17–1:06) consists of four hypermeasures lasting, in order, six, four, four, and three measures each.

Groupings of five in Radiohead's music often exhibit an interpretive richness that requires more flexibility in the otherwise two-layer concatenation between beat and pulse. Tempo allotments we would normally regard as belonging to the tactus often allow for five units—which we might then call beats—but which we might then group metrically as two "hyperbeats" plus three beats (or vice versa), despite the fact

FIGURE 3.3 ⅞ 2+2+3 odd-cardinality meter in "2+2=5" (2003–1, 0:14).

that we have already named a unit at some other tempo the beat. The beginning of "15 Step" (2007–1), transcribed in Figure 3.4a, illustrates this most clearly. There are five beats per measure, each of which is subdivided by two pulses in the percussion, and the accent structure suggests hearing this is as a 3+2 hyper-beat grouping (notated with smaller integers) within each repeating measure. Because of these three distinct levels within each measure,[13] it makes sense to speak of this as ⁵⁄₄ time, rather than ⁵⁄₈, since each measure of ⁵⁄₄ allows for the quarter-note beat to be subdivided into eighth-notes and the resulting asymmetrical metric structure to be notated as a dotted half-note followed by a half-note.

There are really three different ways of feeling this odd-cardinality meter. Perhaps the most energetic listening strategy (Figure 3.4a) feels only the 188 BPM quarter note beat, which, though not strongly articulated in the guitar, kick drum, or snare drum (on the contrary, these layers are mostly responsible for the faster syncopated pulses), is plainly present in the steady hi-hat. The most relaxed strategy, shown in Figure 3.4b, is one clued in almost exclusively to the guitar, feeling its larger 3+2 division as the non-isochronous beat itself (the first longer beat lasting 62.66 BPM, the faster second at 94 BPM), with even quarters in the hi-hat serving as the pulse. Since Listener B's hierarchy has been "flattened" to only two dimensions, devoid of Listener A's hyperbeats, it might make more sense notated in ⁵⁄₈, the groups of three and two eighth notes composing two unequal beats of dotted and standard quarter notes.

The most complex strategy is that shown in Figure 3.4c, in which we begin by feeling the guitar's four durations as the non-isochronous beat structure, the two fastest being just as quick as Listener A's beats, the other two slower at 125.33 BPM.

FIGURE 3.4 "15 Step" (2007–1, 0:41).

FIGURE 3.4 (Continued)

Dividing Listener B's two beats into four then opens up an extra hyperbeat metrical layer, shown as smaller integers in the first bar of Figure 3.4c. Once a listener becomes accustomed to this faster beat, the first beat of 3.4b feels so comparatively slow relative to the 188 BPM pulse (188/3=62.66 BPM) as to render it nearly non-metrical.

Whether entraining to five equally spaced faster beats or two non-isochronous slower beats, conceiving of the rhythm in ⅝ facilitates a way of thinking about rhythm that I call *backbeat deformation*. If we begin with the axiom that backbeats involve snare accents on beats two and four, contain beats that last one quarter note, and can be notated within a measure of ⁴⁄₄ time, then we can understand this rhythm, at least in part, through its relationship to the backbeat. Like most of Radiohead's most salient music, this rhythm conforms to some expectations while subverting others. There is a snare attack on the last beat of the measure, but that beat is no longer the fourth but instead the fifth due to an internal expansion of a standard four-beat measure by one quarter note. Being attuned to the invariants in predictable environments, such as the backbeat, leads to a heightened sensitivity in cases such as these when we encounter deviations from those invariants.

Odd-cardinality meters vary in terms of how actively the engaged listener must search to find recurring patterns. In backbeats, our level of expectancy matches very closely the music we hear, so this is a non-issue. At slower tempi, an odd number of beats per measure creates a minimal challenge for a listener only interested in tapping the beat. If all we are doing is tapping our foot to the primary pulse, there is no difference between ⁴⁄₄ and ⅝. In cases such as these, it is only the next level "up" that is affected—listeners not paying attention to anything slower than the beat will fail to notice that, while their alternating steps divide a ⁴⁄₄ measure into even half-notes, that same pattern divides a ⅝ measure unevenly into a dotted half note and an undotted half-note (in either order). Given that they feature beats at approximately the same tempo, this listener will not notice the difference between, for example, the opening beats of "15 step" (2007–1) and the opening beats of "Bodysnatchers" (2003–2).

Faster tempi, where the beat itself is subdivided by alternating two- and three-pulse units, present a more formidable challenge for any listener wishing to keep the beat. Returning for a moment to "2+2=5," let me posit three options for a listener's kinesthetic engagement. The most active listener notices the 2+2+3 pattern shown in Figure 3.3, and pats a foot three times per measure, with the final pat lasting 50% longer than the previous two, since it contains three pulses instead of two. A listener who does not notice this (or perhaps does not wish to entrain at such an "uneven" level), might then choose to attempt to pat all seven pulses per measure. Because patting our foot at 296 BPM is rather uncomfortable for even one measure (proof that this is not the level of the beat, but rather the pulse), this listener either gives up kinesthetic involvement or moves to tapping one or multiple fingers instead of feet. A third option, somewhat disengaged with the musical structure, would involve tapping to every other of these pulses. As Figure 3.5 demonstrates, this has the rather unfortunate effect of putting the barline exactly *between* two beats, or, rather, of elongating the measure to 14 pulses and seven beats of equal length, all of which ignores the guitar's recurring 2+2+3 pattern.

But, this option—patting to a steady pulse despite the 2+2+3 structure—does have some merit. In patting to every two pulses (in effect, the quarter note), the seven eighth-note structure cycles through twice for every seven quarter notes. Thus, the hypermetric downbeat for such a listener would coincide with the metric downbeat every other time through the 2+2+3 structure. However, these seven evenly spaced pulses may not constitute meter, at least the hierarchic definition we are used to. Even though these seven pulses form an underlying "grid" to group the faster 2+2+3 rhythm, they are themselves not grouped into twos and threes, and form no larger structure other than the sum of their single beats. They form nothing more than a one-dimensional string. For background pulse layers such as these, potentially felt underneath odd-cardinality meters, I prefer the term *non-metrical beat layer*. Since this beat would represent the primary level of metrical engagement, the 2+2+3 structure is then felt as properly *rhythmic* over it, and we are no longer using meter to organize rhythm or beats.

FIGURE 3.5 "2+2=5" (2003–1, 0:13) with non-metrical beat layer overlaid.

Maximally Even and/or Euclidean Rhythms

Odd-cardinality meters in Radiohead's music are often staging places for Euclidean and/or maximally even rhythms (usually, in the case of odd-cardinality meters, "and"). The main piano riff from "Codex" (2011–6), transcribed in Figure 3.6, clearly illustrates the principle of Euclidean rhythms. In each bar, stylistically competent listeners will sense an underlying stream of 16 pulses per bar, which we may then interpret as sixteenth notes. That is to say, the lowest common denominator that encompasses all rhythmic onsets in the voice, piano, and quiet kick drum involves sixteen evenly spaced time points per notated measure. Observing the underlying piano rhythm in this section, notice that there are five onsets per measure, meaning that there are five onsets played for every sixteen possible time points. But, these are not just *any* five onsets within that space of sixteen. In fact, the particular spacing of those five onsets represents a maximally even spacing of five onsets within a grid of sixteen evenly spaced time points. That is to say, although we cannot divide sixteen by five evenly, the rhythm we hear in the piano is the *closest-to-even* distribution possible of sixteen units into five sets (<33334>, regardless of order). There exists only one such possible distribution given k onsets over n evenly spaced time points, and this distribution is known as a Euclidean rhythm.[14]

Euclidean rhythms exhibit a tenuous relationship with traditional theories of meter. Perhaps the most conservative definition of meter relegates meter to time signatures, which divide the total number of pulses into beats. This means that all beats are composed of two to three pulses. Furthermore, before 1900, all beats in the meter were uniform. Euclidean rhythms such as that in Figure 3.6 would thus seem like only a surface embellishment, a decidedly non-metric rhythm against such definitions of meter. Once odd-cardinality meters began to appear in notation, a perfect correlation between Euclidean divisions and meter signature arises. Figure 3.3 demonstrates this correlation. There is no difference between the 2+2+3 customary metric subdivision of ⅞ and the Euclidean rhythm present in the guitar's accent pattern, wherein seven equal pulses are distributed among three beats in the closest-to-even manner possible (two beats get two pulses, one gets three).

FIGURE 3.6 "Codex" repeated Euclidean/maximally even rhythm, piano (2011–6, 0:03).

FIGURE 3.7 "The National Anthem" (2000–3, 0:02) 2+2+3+2+2+2+3 maximally even Euclidean bass.

FIGURE 3.8 "Morning Bell" (2000–9, 0:08) riff with 3+3+2+2 non-maximally even Euclidean rhythm.

Somewhere between these two extremes, we might describe the role of Euclidean rhythms as "metric-ish." This is what is meant by the asterisk symbols used to group all pulses in Figures 3.6–3.9. They are not beats in the traditional manner indicated by the open circles in all other examples, but neither are they wholly unworthy of metrical status. We can use meter signatures to influence the way these rhythmic/metric chimeras are felt. In cases where a regular meter is suggested—especially through backbeat as in Figure 3.7—a regular meter signature such as ¼ cues us to entrain to even quarter notes. Figure 3.8, on the other hand, utilizes the composite meter signature 3+3+2+2 in order to highlight the Euclidean distribution that outshines any possible regular meter.

But what does maximal evenness have to do with Euclidean rhythms/quasimeters? Maximally even rhythms are a subset of Euclidean rhythms. The Euclidean rhythm in "Codex" is also maximally even because the longer beats are spread out as far as possible from one another—in this case necessarily so because there is only one longer beat. But, what about when there is more than one beat which spans more pulses than the rest? In Euclidean distributions where there are two larger beats, these rhythms can be either maximally even or not.

An example of a maximally even Euclidean rhythm can be heard in the opening bass riff to "The National Anthem" (2000–3). As in "Codex," we should sense 16 evenly spaced pulses underlying this unaccompanied riff, but the rhythm is much more complex: [2+2+2+1+2+2+2+2+1]. We can hear this rhythm in a more metrically sound way by grouping the singletons with an adjacent double, producing the tidier rhythm [2+2+3+2+2+2+3] shown in Figure 3.7. In this grouping we may now recognize the Euclidean distribution of sixteen pulses into seven units: five units of two and two units of three. We call this a maximally even Euclidean rhythm because the longer groupings (those comprising three pulses) are spaced as far apart as possible. Given a sixteen-pulse cycle of five twos and two threes, there is only one way to partition those two threes as far apart as possible, and this is known as a maximally even rhythm, keeping in mind that all maximally even rhythms are also Euclidean.

But not all Euclidean rhythms are maximally even. Whereas the "National Anthem" rhythm spaced its larger units as far apart within the cycle as possible, the recurring keyboard riff in the *Kid A* version of "Morning Bell" (2000–9), transcribed in Figure 3.8, places the largest beats adjacent to one another at the beginning of the bar. Entraining to the accompanying hi-hat rhythm, we feel ten subdivisions present in each bar, and the keyboard accents occur in a 3+3+2+2 grouping.[15] While it is true that the Euclidean distribution of ten pulses into four beats involves two twos and two threes, a maximally even version of that distribution would separate each three with a two in order to spread them out evenly over the bar. This rhythm, however, does not, in a sense front-loading all of the larger beats at once. As such, it is a non-maximally even Euclidean rhythm.

The key interpretive moment for the non-maximally even Euclidean rhythm in "Morning Bell," for me, comes at 1:37, when Yorke repeatedly sings the lyrics "cut the kids in half." Central to my interpretation of the rhythmic/lyrical meaning is a passage from 1 Kings in which King Solomon declares, "cut the living child in two, and give half to one woman and half to the other." Imagine a rather large family which contains ten children. The parents are going away on vacation, and four volunteers are each clamoring to babysit as many of the ten children as possible. Since the parents cannot rightly sever the bodies of two of these ten children in order to distribute 2.5 children to every babysitter, they must settle for the Euclidean distribution of whole children. Thus, two babysitters receive two children each, and two lucky babysitters each receive three—the exact rhythmic figure we hear throughout "Morning Bell."

For many Radiohead fans, lyrics are surely the first place to turn for interpretation. The same might be said of any texted music. However, another avenue for interpretation might turn toward things we know of the individual band members. The underlying rhythmic counterpoint of "The National Anthem," starting at 1:57, transcribed in Figure 3.9, is largely the product of a maximally even bass riff (recorded by Yorke) and Jonny Greenwood's ondes Martenot melody. Greenwood is undoubtedly the member of the band with the most formal composition experience. He composed the scores to Paul Thomas Anderson's films *There Will Be Blood*, *The Master*, and *Inherent Vice*; shared a premiere with Penderecki in 2011; and most relevant to our purposes here, is also something of a moonlighting Messiaen enthusiast.[16]

FIGURE 3.9 "The National Anthem" (2000–3, 1:57) bass and ondes Martenot.

When I hear the ondes Martenot part enter, my mind first registers something like <this is Greenwood's favorite instrument>, then I go to <Greenwood loves the ondes Martenot because of Olivier Messiaen's use of it in the *Turangalîla* Symphony>, and then my mind becomes stuck on Messiaen for a while. Once I find myself pondering Messiaen, I hear the pitches in the ondes Martenot part as one of his modes of limited transposition—in this case, a subset [679t] of the octatonic scale.[17] The highly symmetrical octatonic collection is also a maximally even Euclidean distribution of eight pitch classes in twelve-tone equal temperament. That is to say, given the twelve keys on a piano, the most even way to distribute an eight-note scale is by alternating half and whole steps: [in semitones: 1+2+1+2+1+2+1+2].[18] And this correlation is not a simple coincidence. In fact, Greenwood's use of the octatonic scale is a clever solution to the problem presented by Yorke's mode-mixed bass riff. In the first two measures we hear Greenwood using the dyad A/F♯ to reinforce the D major half of the riff, then transposing that dyad up a semitone in the second two measures to complement the D minor portion.

Admittedly, this mode of meaning acquisition, based both on intertextuality and extra-musical interpretation, and grounded in a firm understanding of the mathematics of both pitch and rhythm, may seem idiosyncratic. Creating a mental map of the foregoing interpretation may yield something like the following four steps: recognize the bass rhythm as the Euclidean distribution of 7 in 16; recognize the ondes Martenot pitches as an octatonic subset; simultaneously recognize the link between steps one and two, as well as the link between step two and Messiaen's modes of limited transposition; recognize the autobiographical connections between Messiaen and Greenwood.

Two justifications may be provided for this process. First, the process is far from immediate, and is a result of listening to and thinking about the music for an extended period of time. In other words, it is not so much how we hear the first time, but how we can *learn* to hear over time. Second, the process of learning to hear this way is the product of kinesthetic engagement with the piece. Performing this bass part necessitates *feeling* the maximally even rhythm in my picking hand. As a singer I feel the muscular movements needed to transpose that minor third in the ondes Martenot up a semitone in the second measure. Far from a mathematical abstraction, the meaning is intimate, interactive, and the direct result of embodied musical experience.

As Table 3.1 shows, Radiohead's music provides many occasions to interpret the meanings behind maximally even and Euclidean rhythms. To me, the underlying metaphor in maximally even rhythms is a spatial one (the beats are as far apart as possible), and this can be leveraged for any number of hermeneutic purposes. However, with Euclidean distributions, there is also something of an egalitarian ethic present (the pulses are evenly distributed across beats), which could also play an important role in our interpretive strategies.

Changing Meter

In most popular music, the underlying pulse stream to which a listener entrains remains steady throughout the song, as does the underlying beat, providing a steady

TABLE 3.1

Selected Euclidean and maximally even rhythms in Radiohead's music

Song	Time, instrument	Grouping	Maximally even?
"The National Anthem" (2000–3)	1:57, bass	2+2+3+2+2+2+3	yes
"Pyramid Song" (2001–2)	2:07, piano	3+3+4+3+3	yes
"Morning Bell" (2000–9)	0:08, keys	3+3+2+2	no
"Dollars & Cents" (2001–8)	0:01, bass	2+2+3+2+2+3+2	yes
"2+2=5" (2003–1)	0:13, guitar	2+2+3	yes
"Sail to the Moon" (2003–3)	1:56, drums	3+2+2+3	no
"15 Step" (2007–1)	0:40, guitar	3+3+2+2	no
"All I Need" (2007–5)	2:45, piano	1+2+1+2+2	yes
"Reckoner" (2007–7)	0:09, guitar	3+3+3+4+3	yes
"Codex" (2011–6)	1:04, piano	4+3+3+3+3	yes
"True Love Waits" (2016–11)	0:10–0:17, keyboard	2+3+2+2+2+3+2	yes
"True Love Waits" (2016–11)	0:18–0:30, keyboard	2+3+2+2+2+2+3	no

framework by which to group larger metrical structures such as bars and hyper-measures. Changing meter involves moving from one system of grouping beats to another (we could call this a change in time signature if referring to notation). Changing meter sometimes involves a change in the steady beat, and sometimes does not. When the underlying tactus does not change, all that changes is the way in which the larger structures are grouped. While this does suggest some change in kinesthetic involvement (for example, in a meter change from ¼ to ¾ with the underlying quarter-beat remaining steady, a listener still has to negotiate the change from two equally weighted strong and weak beats per bar to one strong and two weak), a more intricate change involves two meters which ask listeners to renegoti-ate the underlying beat.

"Packt like Sardines in a Crushd Tin Box" (2001–1) provides a steady beat in the electronic percussion that strongly suggests primary kinesthetic involvement at the quarter-note level through its paradigmatic backbeat structure. The quarter-note beat, annotated with open circles in Figure 3.10a (and clarified with beat numbers "1" or "2"), remains steady throughout the passage, and so we can hear this as a *beat-preserving* meter change. Beginning at 0:15, we perceive beats one and two by strong attacks in the kick and snare, respectively. This pattern of kick–snare occurs twelve consecutive times until 0:26. With such a high degree of repetition, the lis-tener will either interpret this as six measures of ¼ time (if two backbeats constitute a bar), or twelve measures of ²⁄₄ time.[19] In either case, the attentive listener has already quickly developed two expectations: an inculcated bodily involvement

FIGURE 3.10A BP-meter change in "Packt..." (2001–1, 0:15) with single-beat interpolation.

with the quarter-note beat, and a high level of anticipation for a half-note grouping of those beats qua backbeat. Only one of these changes at 0:26.

From 0:15–0:26, each snare attack has been preceded by two kick-drum attacks. At 0:26, the snare-drum attack is preceded by four kick-drum attacks. Since in a backbeat we would interpret this as even numbers of eighth notes leading up to the snare, all that has been disrupted by this four-kick pattern is the half-note grouping. The primary beat—the quarter note—remains unaffected. This means that a listener patting her foot to the quarter note beat can continue to do so throughout the passage, despite the meter change. Beat-preserving (hereafter, BP) meter changes such as these do not ask us to reinterpret the primary beat, but only to consider (if we are so willing) what sorts of larger metrical structures are affected. My transcription in Figure 3.10a interprets these metrical changes as interpolations of a single beat. Listener A wishes to hear all possible kick–snare backbeat structures as occurring on beats one and two, respectively, and so adjusts to these interpolations accordingly.

What is so interesting about "Packt" is that, very quickly after this metrical disruption at 0:26, the music rights itself and the original measure is restored. In fact, if conducting in 2⁄4 time, we can choose to simply "float" over Listener A's one-beat interpolations and land back in exactly the right place, as is shown in the alternative transcription in Figure 3.10b. We can imagine three different listeners' reactions to this passage. Listener A senses the backbeat grouping (perhaps interpreting beat one with one appendage and beat two with another), and thus feels the meter change at 0:26 very strongly as it thwarts her kinesthetic interpretive strategy.[20] She learns over the course of repeated listenings to interpolate ¼ measures in the right places

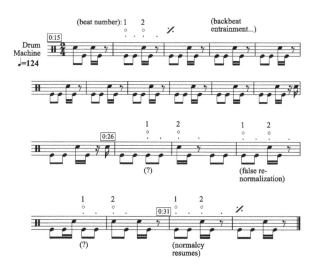

FIGURE 3.10B BP-meter change in "Packt . . ." (2001–1, 0:15) with backbeat preservation.

to maximize entrainment with as many backbeats as possible. Listener B senses the same backbeat as Listener A, but is perhaps more resilient. When the disruption at 0:26 happens she clutches to the preserved quarter-note pulse like a ring buoy and floats along until her original backbeat is restored at 0:31. Along the way she gets faked out in the fifteenth measure in Figure 3.10b by what I've labeled a "false re-normalization"—a premature moment where it appears that the backbeat has been permanently restored.[21]

Listener C, whose interpretation is not notated, has little to no engagement with the backbeat, preferring to bob her head in an egalitarian fashion to every quarter-note beat. Unlike Listeners A and B she feels no disruption in this passage because she's entraining only to the preserved beat in the beat-preserving meter change—in other words, a non-metrical beat layer. These three potential listening strategies in "Packt" reveal that, while it has been customary in the scholarly literature to reify meter by indexing it with meter signatures (a properly notational element, which is certainly related to the felt phenomena), there is also an experiential element to meter which is highly contingent upon our individual listening strategies. In other words, meter is just as much an emergent attentional state as it is a notational vestige.[22] Beat-preserving meter changes happen throughout Radiohead's catalog. For the sake of space, Table 3.2 takes the notational shortcut, identifying them only by the meter signatures I perceive most readily.

Beat-changing (hereafter, BC) meter changes throw a wrench in all three interpretive strategies Listeners A–C exhibited in "Packt." While all three relied on the quarter-note beat remaining consistent throughout, some of Radiohead's changing meters do not allow for this. Instead, they ask listeners to entrain to some unit smaller than the beat which will act as a pivot between two different meters. This faster pulse level, which I call the pivot pulse, acts as a sort of lowest common denominator to which the attentive listener may entrain in order to maintain bodily engagement with some rhythmic facet in passages such as these.

By starting with an obvious backbeat, "Go to Sleep" (2003–5) foregrounds a BC-meter change rather explicitly on the musical surface. The kick–snare pattern notated in the first measure of Figure 3.11 strongly suggests a quarter-note beat and ¼ meter. However, after only one measure this pattern is discontinued and we hear a paradigmatic compound meter—either ⁶⁄₈ or ¹²⁄₈ depending on whether you hear it as one full measure or two.[23] In either case, the kick drum still begins each beat, but the snare no longer behaves as a beat itself, but rather acts as an anacrusis to the next beat. Since compound beats comprise three pulses, we must actually change the length of the beat to which we entrain.

Navigating changes of meter such as these, which involve beats of different speeds, involves hearing, feeling, or visualizing a faster pulse which is actually preserved

TABLE 3.2

Beat-preserving meter changes in Radiohead

Song	Time/section, instrument(s)	Meter change
"Paranoid Android" (1997–2)	5:47, ensemble	4/4(×2) to 7/4
"Idioteque" (2000–8)	0:11, percussion	6/4 to 4/4
"I Might Be Wrong" (2001–5)	2:37, voice and guitar	4/4 to 2/4*
"Sail to the Moon" (2003–3)	0:01, ensemble	7/4 to 2/4 to 7/4; 6/4 to 2/4 to 6/4; 5/4 to 2/4 to 5/4**
"Go to Sleep" (2003–5)	verses, drums	4/4 (150 BPM) to 6/4 (150 BPM)
"Faust Arp" (2007–6)	verses, ensemble	4/4 (186 BPM) to 3/4 (186 BPM)
"Videotape" (2007–11)	0:45, ensemble	4/4 (x3) to 4/4 (x2)***
"The Numbers" (2016–8)	3:18, ensemble	4/4 to 2/4

* A listener entraining to the hi-hat rhythm—recurring eighth-notes directly off the beat with an "e-and" after beat two only—can actually keep conducting 4/4 throughout this. Since the voice hyper-rhythm changes from 4/4 to 2/4 twice during this section, the two groupings will line up immediately afterward.

** Each hypermeasure is a palindrome *x–y–x*, with the meter of *y* remaining constant at 2/4 for each hypermeasure, while the number of beats per measure in *x* decreases from 7/4 to 6/4 to 5/4 from one hypermeasure to the next.

*** This is more properly a hypermetric change since the 4/4 grouping in each measure remains constant. This could also be interpreted as a hypermetric grouping dissonance between the piano and voice, which occurs more rampantly throughout the track.

FIGURE 3.11 BC-meter change in "Go to Sleep" (2003–5, 0:43).

throughout the meter change. The pivot pulse acts as a pivot between two meters of different cardinality and/or subdivision in much the same way as a pivot chord helps smooth modulations between keys by playing a harmonic role in each.[24]

The pivot pulse that connects each recurring ¼ and ¹²⁄₈ bar in "Go to Sleep" is the eighth note. While the beat cannot be preserved between the two meters, the level of disruption felt in this meter change is minimal since the pivot pulse is only twice as fast as the beat in the first measure. Radiohead's meter changes never involve a pivot pulse that quarters the beat, a facet heard in some math-metal and progressive rock (e.g., the 16th-note pivot pulse involved in Tool's song "Intolerance" (1993–1, 0:21)). Because pivot pulses between meter A and meter B are commutative, the pivot from the ¹²⁄₈ bar back to the ¼ bar is indeed the same pulse speed as before (eighth=300 BPM). This makes the quarter-note beat in the ¼ measure 150 BPM (300/2) and the dotted-eighth beat in the ¹²⁄₈ measure 100 BPM (300/3).

Though it involves the same pivot pulse, the situation in "Faust Arp" (2007–6) is ultimately more complex due to the lack of a percussion layer. Without this percussion layer present, the underlying beat structure is underdefined. The 3+2+3 rhythm in the guitar is the closest thing to a steady metrical framework in the first two verse/chorus pairs.[25] As such, it acts like a maximally even meter, the second shorter beat sandwiched together between the two longer beats in each measure. While it may be tempting to notate this in ²⁄₄ meter given the eight sixteenth notes in each bar, there is no underlying rhythm section layer to support such a hearing—any ²⁄₄ or ⁴⁄₈ time signature imposed upon this music is, at best, a notational convenience.[26]

So, to which beat will an attentive listener most likely entrain in this passage, and how does that decision affect what happens in the subsequent meter changes? Again, we can imagine three different listening strategies, all of which will use the eight sixteenth notes in every bar as the underlying pulse by which to group larger beats kinesthetically.

Unsurprisingly, the simplest strategy is also the least musically sensitive. Listener A merely pats every other sixteenth note in an even eighth-note beat throughout this meter change, as shown in Figure 3.12a. This strategy interprets the last two attacks of the maximally even 3+2+3 groove in the guitar as a syncopation against a quick, regular, and imagined ⁴⁄₈ beat (186 BPM). She then maintains this beat throughout the ⁹⁄₈ bar, which then really becomes three bars of ³⁄₈ with very little metrical structure because the only thing faster than this beat is the recurring first syllable in Yorke's "a-gain" on the second of every three beats. "On again, off again" aptly describes Listener A's strategy in sticking to her guns throughout this meter change, as the two primary accents in each group of three (measures 5–7) would be the downbeat (beats 1, 4, 7) and the "offbeats" between the second and third beats of each measure (2.5, 5.5, 8.5).

FIGURE 3.12A BP-meter change in "Faust Arp" (2007–6, 0:02) with consistent 186 BPM beat.

Listener B finds Listener A's quick eighth-note pulse too fast to be comfortable, opting instead for the half-speed interpretation of two quarters per bar shown in the beginning of Figure 3.12b. This works well enough in the first four bars, with the guitar's 3+2+3 again acting as a sixteenth-based syncopation, but utterly falls apart in the ⁹⁄₈ bar. Because Listener B pats every other one of Listener A's beats, and nine is not divisible evenly by two, Listener B ends Yorke's "on again, off again, on again" in-between beats, which she realizes when the original meter returns ("watch me fall like"), now flipped exactly halfway off the beat. After learning from this "mistake," Listener B perhaps attempts Listener A's faster beat to navigate the ⁹⁄₈ bar (shown in the second system of Figure 3.12b) rather than let it flip the beat around. The half-beat in Listener B's first bar is preserved as the pivot pulse for the ⁹⁄₈ measure. Tempo changes in the transcription (quarter=93, to eighth=186, and back) clarify this pivot pulse.

A third strategy involves interpreting this 3+2+3 guitar figure as a maximally even *metrical* entity, as a sort of composite meter built of two three-pulse beats separated by a two-pulse beat. Of the three possible orderings of two threes and one two relative to an eight-pulse cycle, this is by far the rarest.[27] By already entraining to two different beat speeds in the first bar, Listener C is primed to hear a beat in the meter change unavailable to Listeners A or B. Because no single duration comprises the beat, Figure 3.12c foregoes any regular meter signature in favor of two *different*

FIGURE 3.12B BC-meter change in "Faust Arp" (2007–6, 0:02) with 186 BPM pivot pulse.

FIGURE 3.12C Euclidean rhythm in "Faust Arp" (2007–6, 0:02) interpreted as two different beats.

tempo markings: one for the two-pulse beat, one for the three-pulse beat. The three-pulse beat heard twice in the first bar can be preserved throughout the entirety of the meter change. Doing so transforms Listener B's ⅝ bar into three small measures of a faster ⁶⁄₁₆ (124 BPM).[28] Yorke's "on again, off again, on again," which now swings gracefully as the <long–short–long> pattern germane to fast compound meters, is clearly the payoff for this active entrainment to the pivot pulse.

Listener C's strategy, which features eight three-pulse beats and only one two-pulse beat, sheds harsh light on Listener A's regularity: Why superimpose a beat layer that is not only imagined, but which captures only one out of every nine rhythmic groupings? Though it may seem like I am advocating for a certain way of hearing the verse of "Faust Arp," I ultimately believe that each entrainment strategy, regardless of the chosen beat and pulse, offers something of value. Even in choosing a beat layer which is imagined, Listener A gets to feel jazzy, accented syncopations that Listener C interprets as stable downbeats.

Grouping Dissonance

Each of the preceding phenomena, for the most part, relies on having one referential meter at a time against which all else is measured.[29] More commonly than changing meter, however, Radiohead employs two different meters or groupings at the same time, resulting in a grouping dissonance.[30] Prevailing psychological research suggests that western listeners are only able to entrain to one grouping structure at a time, which means that the other metric grouping will be perceived as dissonant against the one to which we choose to entrain.[31]

The most common grouping dissonances in western music are two against three (notated as 2:3 or 3:2) and 3:4/4:3. The first of these, known as *hemiola* (a Greek term which refers not only to the rhythmic proportion 3:2, but also to the pitch interval 3:2—a perfect fifth), is relatively common. Especially common in compound meters, where each beat comprises three pulses, a grouping of two is often heard, creating a 2:3 grouping dissonance. In naming grouping dissonances, I will follow strictly a system which places the most resilient and steady meter as the final number, so that "2:3" may always mean a dissonant two-pulse grouping heard against the backdrop of an established three-pulse meter.

The hemiola is so common in compound meters that it hardly constitutes a salient rhythmic gesture. Particularly notable 2:3 hemiolas in Radiohead's oeuvre include the midrange guitar in "Subterranean Homesick Alien" (1997–3, 1:25), and the signature grooves heard throughout both "How to Disappear Completely" (2000–4) and "Daydreaming" (2016–2). In these last two examples, the hemiola forms such a repeated and constant figure that it is tempting not to classify it necessarily as 2:3 or 3:2, but either—a figure/ground relationship that can be flipped in the listener's mind at different points throughout the song.

Less common grouping dissonances, including 3:2, 3:4, and others, are sufficiently outside the normative expectations inherited from backbeat-based rock music to be perceived as marked. A relatively straightforward 3:4 occurs in the opening guitar part from "Weird Fishes" (2007–4, 0:07–0:59). Though simple in its design, the metric dissonance is notable for its persistence. Pop–rock songs use this 3:4 figure from time to time over the span of a two- or four-measure phrase, after which the dissonant grouping tends to right itself and realign with the dominant meter. This grouping dissonance, however, does not realign itself at any of the expected hyper-metric downbeats along the way. Instead, it continues articulating every third of the drum set's four eighth-note groupings—four hi-hats which mark off a recur-ring strong–weak backbeat—for the entirety of the introduction and first half of the verse.

Already from this example, we might extract something mathematical and kin-esthetic about recurring dissonant grouping streams. They realign at specified in-tervals, and the moments in which they align feel like a hypermetric arrival point. Such a persistent grouping dissonance as "Weird Fishes" also creates a hypermetric dissonance—a sort of chain reaction where smaller grouping dissonances at the level of the beat compound to make larger *embedded grouping dissonances* at the level of the phrase.[32] To understand embedded grouping dissonance, we must understand the mathematical relationship between cycles of four and cycles of three. Since there is no common denominator between three and four, the lowest common multiple (hereafter, LCM) is the point at which the two groupings line up. The LCM of three and four is of course twelve, which means that the backbeat and the guitar line up every twelve eighth notes. However, given the exact kick–snare pattern which, de-spite a perceptible half-note backbeat only articulates a downbeat in the kick drum every two measures of 4/4, this 12-eighth period of alignment clashes with the 16-eighth note period that composes each two-measure unit. As such, the guitar will only line up with the downbeat of a two-measure unit every six measures because the LCM of three (guitar grouping) and 16 (two-measure grouping) is 48, or six measures of eight eighth notes each. Patient listeners may not be satisfied with just any kick-articulated downbeat in the drum part, but instead hold out for the two successive kicks that begin only every fourth measure, rendering the repeating unit twice that length; it takes twelve measures for a high note in the guitar to coincide with the beginning of the four-bar drum pattern (LCM of three eighths and 32 eighths is 96 eighths).

The rest of the musical cues in the introduction and verse point to a regular hypermetric rhythm of four (the complete recurring drum pattern) and 16 measures (the four distinct guitar chords, labeled A–D in Figure 3.13, which last approximately four measures each). Though it is clear from the example that the guitar does not alter its *rhythm* to align with any regular hypermetric downbeats, we can observe the chords changing roughly every four measures and, given that the LCM of any multiple of two—a backbeat, a measure, a two- or four-measure pattern—and three cannot be 16 beats, this means that the changes of harmony are driven by something else.

Examining the number of three-note groupings played on each chord reveals an inconsistency. Some chords are played ten times, others eleven. If the chord starts

FIGURE 3.13 3:4 embedded grouping dissonance in "Weird Fishes . . ." (2007–4, 0:07).

before a four-measure drum grouping, it is played eleven times, because 11×3=33 and the "head start" that is gained by beginning prior to the hypermeasure allows it to finish before the next 32-group begins. If a chord begins after a four-measure hyper-bar is already underway, however, it is only played ten times (10×3=30), allowing it to finish before the next begins. This concern for the preservation of a four-measure hypermeter imbues the passage with a sense of irony, given the overt lack of concern for any smaller groupings, including the measure and beat. Furthermore, this irony seems linked to the lyrics ("I'd be crazy not to follow / Follow where you lead"), which we might imagine as text-painting the guitar's failure to follow the surface-level grouping in the drums despite reluctantly keeping pace ever-so-roughly with the larger hypermeter.

From time to time, Radiohead creates grouping dissonances which involve more complex ratios than 3:4. Most of these *x:y* dissonances involve at least one prime number, which means that the LCM—the place at which the two meters should re-align—will be as long as [*x*y*]. More often than not, however, some musical detail overrides this mechanistic procession of metric groupings. "Weird Fishes" is thus something of an anomaly. The ⁵⁄₄ opening guitar riff in "Let Down" (1997–5) inter-faces with the otherwise straightforward ⁴⁄₄ introduction and verse in a manner far more musically idiosyncratic than purely algebraic.

Though there are multiple electric guitar layers present in this song, this riff tran-scribed in Figure 3.14 is the most recognizable since it forms a regular, repeating ostinato.[33] A listener who begins counting at the beginning of the track in ⁵⁄₄ will be rather surprised when the rest of the rhythm section enters on what feels like beat four. Perhaps then we should retrace our steps, measuring the full band's downbeat as the downbeat of the ostinato instead. This would mean that the excerpt begins with three beats of anacrusis and has the unfortunate consequence of casting the tonic pitch A4—the highest pitch and arguably the melodic goal of each pair of five-beat bars—as the weakest beat in the measure. With an underdetermined "down-beat" to the five-beat ostinato, a listener might as well do the pragmatic thing and consider the first heard beat the downbeat. This seems to fit within expectations we have for ⁵⁄₄, since the A4 goal pitch is now heard as the second intra-measure strong beat of a 2+3 subdivision.

A few notational quirks in this example deserve further explanation. Since it seems unlikely that a listener will continue to hear ⁵⁄₄ as the dominant meter once the drum set's backbeat enters, the meter signature for both parts changes to ⁴⁄₄. Yet the guitar's exact five-beat grouping persists, as the slurs over the guitar riff highlight. Integers at the onset of each slur represent the numbered beat in ⁴⁄₄ on which each five-beat grouping begins. Since the five-beat grouping is one beat longer than the ⁴⁄₄ meter, the beat on which the guitar begins will appear to transpose forward one

FIGURE 3.14 5:4 grouping dissonance in "Let Down" (1997–5, 0:01–0:35).

beat each time it repeats. This could be expressed as a grouping dissonance between two interval cycles, the five-cycle superimposed onto the four-cycle. Kinesthetically, this means a listener conducting in 4/4 time will sense a secondary accent on a different beat each measure. This persists until Yorke's syllable "stop" ("star-ting and then STOP-ping"), which seems a fitting place to cease the misalignment if only for a measure.

A more straightforward, though less persistent case of 5:4 can be heard throughout the handclaps in "Lotus Flower" (2011–5). From the beginning of the track, the bass and drum set establish a 4/4 groove. Heard only faintly at first, pairs of handclapped eighth notes grate against this grid of quarter-note beats. As the claps get louder, they also settle into a more regular pattern of two eighth-note attacks followed by three eighth-note rests. Though we could hear these in ⅝—two at-tacked pulses for every five—given the quarter-note beat in the bass and percussion, we are more likely to hear this grouping dissonance as a five quarter-note grouping with each pair of five doubled as a group of ten eighth notes.

Dissonant metric groupings can be described most succinctly as beat-class modu-lations.[34] Subdividing the 4/4 meter into its constituent pulses at a level that encom-passes all of the handclaps means subdividing it into eighth notes. If the integers 0–7 represent these numbered eighth notes in a measure of 4/4, then 0 is the initial downbeat and 7 is the final eighth note. Set <2,3> then represents the two handclaps that occur on beat two (read: third and fourth eighth-notes of the measure), but since we are hearing the pattern in 5/4, the full four-clap pattern—two attacks followed by three non-attacks, doubled—would be represented as <2,3,7,0> as shown in Table 3.3.

Because the period of that repeating handclap gesture is 5/4 (ten eighth notes) instead of 4/4 (eight eighth notes), the beat-class notation of the handclaps, relative to the mod-8 4/4 framework, will transpose "forward" two units (notated as "T2") relative to the 4/4 period. This yields the sequence shown in Figure 3.15, in which the beat-class notation can be seen alongside the notated grouping dissonance.

This cycle is completed within the first five measures (about nine seconds) of the recording, after which it continues for some time. Since the T2 cycle started on beat two of the 4/4 measure, it obviously recycles on beat two as well. Relating beat-class theory to traditional notation, notice that, like the "Let Down" example, since the period of the handclaps is five beats and the meter four beats, the beat on which the handclaps begins is transposed forward one beat (read: two eighth notes) in each measure. Perhaps surprisingly, I do not feel the fourth iteration of the handclap sequence, where it crucially aligns with the 4/4 downbeat <0,1> as the completion of any process. Rather, I hear the fifth iteration as the point of arrival, where the

TABLE 3.3

T2 transposition of grouping dissonance in "Lotus Flower"
(2011–5, 0:01)

Grouping	0	1	2	3	4	5	6	7
Grouping A (bass and drums) 4/4	0	1	2	3	4	5	6	7
Grouping B (handclaps) 5/4		[	2	3				7
Grouping A (bass and drums) 4/4	0	1	2	3	4	5	6	7
Grouping B (handclaps) 5/4	0	]		[	4	5		
Grouping A (bass and drums) 4/4	0	1	2	3	4	5	6	7
Grouping B (handclaps) 5/4		1	2	]		[	6	7

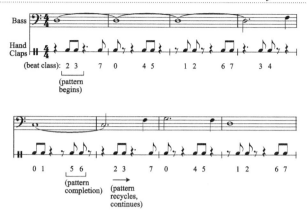

FIGURE 3.15   T2 beat-class modulation in "Lotus Flower" (2011–5, 0:01–0:14).

original <2,3,7,0> beat-class sequence recycles, marking the "full circle" return after a T2 journey through mod-8 space. And because five is co-prime relative to the eight-unit modulus, this means that a cycle of five will generate every member in the set of eight before repeating any (e.g., the ordered set <04512673>). Conducting through this example in ¼ with one hand while tapping the handclap rhythm in the other is a particularly effective way to interact kinesthetically with this cyclical journey.

In Radiohead songs involving grouping dissonance, embodied musical experience and mathematical intuition can combine to create higher-level meanings. Humans exhibit a deeply binary structure. We are bipedal creatures with bilateral symmetry. In order to keep our balance while dancing, we must dance in twos (even when waltzing one step takes longer than the other). Unless actively analyzing the mathematical proportions in this music, listeners feel these frictions cognitively engaging them. When considering the physical/spatial ecosystems in which these perceptions occur, whether alone in a bedroom or in a crowded, sweaty discothèque, the bodily actions and reactions incited by these rhythmic structures interact in real time with that ecosystem, and, in the case of the dance club, instantly influence and are influenced by the dancing bodies of other listeners in that environment.

Polytempo

While metric dissonances present synchronous journeys through pulses and beats, only presenting interpretive challenges at the level of measure and hypermeasure, instances of polytempo in Radiohead's music flip that relationship upside down. In most of these cases, the larger repeating period of two competing pulse streams is the same, yet the pulse streams that compose that larger period are different in both speed and cardinality.

One way of visualizing polytempo as it differs from metric dissonance involves a running track. Imagine that you are sitting in the stands and the metrically dissonant layers in "Weird Fishes" (let's call them Runner three and Runner four for their respective groupings) both started at the same place directly in front of you. Runner three is farthest from you on the innermost ring of the track, Runner four is closest to you on the outermost ring of the track. Though they run at exactly the same pace, Runner three appears back in front of you much earlier than Runner four until Runner three eventually laps Runner four and the two line up together again. This would be Runner four's third lap and Runner three's fourth lap, which personifies the metric dissonance in "Weird Fishes." Polytempo presents the opposite situation. If both runners begin together, run exactly once around the track, and return in front of you at exactly the same time, the runner in the longer outside lane had to run faster. The time both runners took to complete the entire track was the same, but the outer runner moved at a faster pace to do so.

Such is the case in *The King of Limbs*'s opening track, "Bloom" (2011–1, 0:08). The electronic percussion backbeat transcribed in the top staff of Figure 3.16 quickly draws the listener into a fast ¼ (quarter=149) engagement. Just seven seconds later, a second rhythmic layer begins to emerge. Performed on what sounds like two differently tuned snare drums,[35] this layer begins by adding what seems to be just a triplet-based layer. On its own, this creates a grouping dissonance at the quickest level—each half note now subdivided by both sixteenth notes and quarter-note triplets (3:8). If this were the extent of it, we would not have a case of polytempo. As notated by the arrows in the first measure, however, this triplet-based notation does not quite capture the sound of the two rhythmic streams beginning at 0:15. The span of time that it takes the drum machine and snares to complete their measure is the same, but there seems to be no shared pulse stream that captures the internal tempi of each part. The top line, in a sense, has to "run faster" to reach the end of the measure.

The forward-pointing arrow in my transcription indicates that the would-be second note of a quarter-note triplet is displaced later in the measure by a rhythmic interval impractical to notate by any conventional standards. It is necessary to

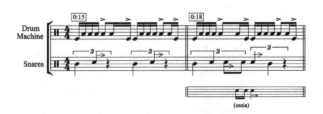

FIGURE 3.16 Polytempo organization in "Bloom" (2001–1, 0:15).

understand just how small of a time window we are talking about here. If it were the second note of a quarter-note triplet, it would occur 0.333 of the way through the first half-note. On the other hand, if it were participating in the same sixteenth-note tempo as the electronic percussion, it would be the fourth sixteenth note, occurring 0.375 of the way through the first half note. Instead, what the arrow connotes is that this note usually occurs (keeping in mind it is performed by a human and is subject to microtiming variation) actually between those two easily notatable values. At this quick tempo, that means we are talking about a profound phenomenological difference occurring in the tiny space between 0.2657 of a second and 0.3019 of a second.

This repeated group only lasts a few seconds before the second, related groove begins at 0:18. This "mature" form of the groove then forms the repeated backdrop for the rest of the song. The approximate quarter-note triplet rest in the immature form is now filled by two quicker notes. There seems to be more performer variation in this second groove, and sometimes the part itself is double-tracked, meaning that at various points it sounds like (1) the two approximate triplet-eighths notated in the main staff, (2) the two approximate sixteenths notated in the *ossia* staff, or (3) both approximations simultaneously. Note that even the half-note subdivision within the measure—sovereign in the immature form—is now obscured, seemingly pushed later in the bar. This groove, heard throughout "Bloom," is most easily experienced as a polytempo because, while each measure begins and ends with the beginning of two separate pulse streams—one in the electronic percussion, one in the acoustic—there are no shared subdivisions present in the bar, and thus we are given the choice of hearing one of two competing, irreconcilable pulse streams of different tempi throughout each measure.

The polytempo in "Bloom" catches our attention so immediately partly because the track begins with such an engaging rhythm—the backbeat. Such is also the case in "2+2=5" (2003–1, 1:22), which begins with the odd-cardinality meter instead of a backbeat. Later in that song, the hi-hat transcribed in Figure 3.17 provides the underlying eighth-note pulse (296 BPM) by which we were able to measure that ⅞ meter in the lead guitar. After this section ends at 1:21, two new electric guitar layers enter over this preserved hi-hat pulse.

If we take the easily discernible hi-hat pulse as the new eighth-note, then we see that each vocal phrase in this new B section is composed of five measures of ¼, or 20 total beats. Comparing the recorded artifact with a live performance of the song at the 2009 Reading Festival is instructive in this case. Physiologically, it is clear to see that the whole band entrains to Phil Selway's preserved eighth-note pulse in the hi-hat in groups of twenty, but instead of the polytempo organization of the two guitars heard on the album version, Jonny Greenwood plays a more recognizable

FIGURE 3.17 "2+2=5" (2003–1, 1:22) polytempo B Section.

1+2+1+2 rhythmic syncopation on the same pitches. In this live performance a steady stream of eighth notes persists in both layers and thus there is no polytempo. We might then wonder how the album version's guitar part was recorded, perhaps through a delay or sampling pedal? Listening more closely for timbre, the guitar line that shadows Yorke's vocal melody (A♭–G–F . . .) does bear an articulation closer to tape manipulation than a pick or fingers.

Once a listener visualizes this hypothetical in-studio technique, it is easy to see how it might come together. Against the steady flow of the hi-hat, the guitarist plays each of these notes once at the beginning of each measure (eight hi-hat articulations), and the delay pedal is set to a certain tempo value. If the tempo on the delay pedal were also set to 296 BPM (or if the guitarist were using a tap-tempo pedal and was tapping the tempo of the hi-hat), then we would not have polytempo and everything would move at the same speed. However, if the speed on the delay pedal were set to a tempo slower than 296 (it sounds about right when I play it around 220 BPM), then each of the guitarist's attacks at the beginning of the measure would be repeated fewer than eight times, creating a polytempo relationship against the hi-hat.

But the question still remains, How was this part actually recorded? I will counter this question with another question: Does it matter? A listener familiar with guitar pedals and/or signal processing will recognize the sound of the guitar as a sampled or delayed signal rather than a performed one. From there, everything else falls into place. Is the signal moving at the same speed as the hi-hat? No. Is there, however, some coordination with the repeating period of the hi-hat and the repeating period of this guitar motive? Yes. This could then be expressed as a polytempo, although guitarists will also interpret it experientially as a familiar phenomenon that occurs when altering the speed of a delay pedal against a given source. I find this thought experiment to be far more musically engaged than resorting to intention or simply looking up the answer to a fact-based question.

Having presented five categories of rhythm and meter in Radiohead's music that lie just outside of our expectations surrounding the backbeat, we are now set to observe how these play out in the analysis of an entire song. But the foregoing has been more than just a theoretical setup to this analysis. There is much to be gained from holistic analysis of an entire song, but there is also value in paying attention to how our bodies react to specific moments in a song, however fleeting. Sometimes, the expressive rhythms that I have described form the backdrop for entire songs, and so our perspective on them may change as the song evolves. But, even when that is not the case, even when songs only present us with short, interesting passages, we should not shy away from paying inordinate amounts of attention to those passages. After all, they grabbed our attention, and our bodies, for a reason.

Analytical Coda: "Idioteque"

"Idioteque" (2000–8) derives its name from a rather obvious portmanteau involving the French *discothèque*, and thus engenders embodied sensations of dance. This pre-auditory expectation is realized in the track's opening seconds by a bass-heavy drum machine pounding out a highly danceable club beat. Especially as it relates to dance, counting beats (either analytically or as embodied cognition) is an integral part of the listening process for this and similar tracks. Empirical analysis of the rhythmic features of "Idioteque" alone—including changing meter and embedded grouping dissonance—yields a captivating study, but a more intimate understanding of the piece can be reached by blending rhythmic analysis with a concomitant hermeneutic reading of the lyrics. When applied to this song, such an interpretation reveals a rich plot structure in which two opposing metrical forces representing the assumed characters "Six" (portrayed by the percussion) and "Twenty" (portrayed by the voice and sampler) battle throughout the song for metrical control. Familiar formal structures in Table 3.4 have been divided into finer rehearsal letters A–K. Aside from subdividing verse, chorus, and the like, these rehearsal letters also mark important moments in the song's dramatic arc.

Exposition

The story of "Idioteque" opens with the percussion, a protagonist of sorts, stating its central ostinato. Percussion's ostinato, transcribed in Figure 3.18, is decidedly concrete, stable, and brief, consisting of only six beats (the ³⁄₂ meter signature only clarifies that the meter is not compound, which ⁶⁄₄ usually connotes). It is decisive, and

TABLE 3.4

Macro- and micro-form of "Idioteque" (2000–8)

Section	Letter	Clock time	Description	Dramatic form
intro	A	0:01	percussion 6-beat ostinato	exposition
	B	0:12	sampler 20-beat ostinato	
	C	0:38	percussion solo with tambourine	
verse 1	D	0:59	voice entrance, modified percussion	rising action
chorus 1	E	1:34	"Here I'm allowed / Everything all of the time"; percussion modifications continue	
verse 2	F	1:52	100-beat structure; 20*5 in sampler	climax
chorus 2	G	2:35	recap chorus with 5*4 vs. 4*5 grouping dissonance in voice	falling action
transition	H	3:10	modified "heads and tails" percussion	
outro	I	3:14	percussion solo, same 100-beat structure	resolution
	J	4:05	sampler and voice re-enter	
	K	4:49–5:09	sampler, voice, and percussion tacet; non-metrical "shrieking" sounds	

FIGURE 3.18 Percussion's ostinato in "Idioteque" (2000–8, 0:01).

proclaims an identity for the percussion that appears as steady and unshakable as the perfectly metronomic rhythm its digitally programmed performance provides.[36]

But all is not stable here, as the story's antagonistic sampler has simultaneously revealed itself, albeit in a passive way.[37] The ambiguous synthetic sounds lurking in the background from 0:01–0:11 are not part of percussion's metric identity—in fact, they pose a threat to its stability. By means of a crescendo entrance into rehearsal letter B, the sampler reveals its plan to metrically destabilize the percussion, which serves as the main conflict in the song's narrative. At B, the sampler now has a clear metric identity, a ¼ meter clearly organized in groups of five measures to form an overall identity of 20 beats, shown in the middle two staves of Figure 3.19.[38] The percussion, sensing the approach of the sampler back at the crescendo into B, has also gotten stronger in terms of amplitude, but has failed to retain its metric identity of 6 beats with the onslaught of the sampler's well-formed 20. All the percussion can do to protect itself from the bombardment of these 20 beats in this ½ to ¼ meter change is put up a shield of mechanically alternating hi-hat and snare for the remaining 14 beats, which represents a mere fragment of its once stable identity. At this point, the percussion appears to be no match for the more advanced sampler, not being able to meet the challenge of a higher grouping structure.

With a surprisingly quick retreat, provoked only by the entrance of the percussion's ally (the tambourine), the sampler leaves the conflict abruptly at rehearsal letter C. Left completely unchecked, the percussion recovers from the attack by immediately executing a reverse meter change back to ½, stating its ostinato without metric opposition for the longest duration yet, with the tambourine providing a steady cover fire of sixteenth notes atop a strong six-beat platform. It would appear at this point that the conflict has been resolved, leaving the percussion standing victoriously unharmed in metric identity, but as the tambourine retreats in the penultimate measure of rehearsal letter C, the listener wonders what may have scared it off.

FIGURE 3.19 Voice entrance in "Idioteque" (2000–8, 0:59).

Rising Action

At rehearsal letter D, the sampler also gains a metrical ally, Yorke's voice, and with this new force begins to make its first real offensive against the now outnumbered percussion. The voice sounds as a leader or figurehead of sorts for the sampler/voice team, which we can now understand as "Twenty," its dominant metrical identity.[39] Figure 3.19 transcribes the voice's proclamation of the oncoming battle between Twenty and Six (percussion).[40]

Twenty's metrical grouping is unchanged, but has been given greater definition by the hypermetric accents in the voice part. With two strong hypermetric downbeats falling at the onsets of measures one and three, the voice continues to split the five-measure structure into a 2+3 grouping for the rest of the piece. A graphic analysis of the beat, subdivision, and hypermeter involved in the newfound subdivision of Twenty's five-measure structure is shown in Figure 3.20.[41]

With the continued absence of the tambourine, the percussion is left in a familiar position; it is completely unable to formulate any sort of counter-attack. Once again, as in rehearsal letter B, all it can muster is to fill the void of 14 beats with an alternating hi-hat and snare. Here it seems that the percussion is simply not able to meet the challenge of Twenty's higher grouping structure. It may only be a matter of time before percussion gives up its Six identity completely, assimilating to something better fitting what Twenty is demanding to relieve the grouping dissonance and tension forced upon it.

Rehearsal letter E, the chorus, is a joyous dance of sorts. It represents Twenty celebrating a victory in realizing that the conflict is nearing conclusion, that the percussion's weak attempts at fighting off the 20/2+3 structure are futile. In the same metric structure as the preceding verse, the voice, now outlining a triumphant, almost major melody,[42] announces that Twenty is clearly the supreme ruler of this metrical and temporal space while percussion remains struggling.

As shown in Table 3.5, this lyrical declamation in Figure 3.21 can be read as an obvious text-painting of the metrical conflict if we choose to interpret the lyrics as a double entendre with "all of the time" being a member of the set "everything," meaning Twenty is allowed all of the [musical] time.

At this point, the listener may be almost positive that Twenty's continued assaults and recent taunting will have worn down the percussion. As the second verse of the

FIGURE 3.20 (Hyper)metric analysis of 20-beat structure in "Idioteque" (2000–8, 0:59).

TABLE 3.5

Double entendre in chorus lyrics

Possible interpretations	Things Twenty is allowed	... at frequency
A	everything	all of the time
B	everything, including all of the [musical] time	(not stated)

FIGURE 3.21 Repeated chorus lyrical-melodic gesture in "Idioteque" (2000–8, 1:34).

song begins, we might expect to hear a new approach from the percussion aimed at living more peacefully in this new metric order.

Climax

The climax of this narrative, as well as the most violent grouping dissonance in the piece, occurs at rehearsal letter F. Here the percussion, apparently infuriated by the boastful arrogance of Twenty's lyrical provocations in the chorus, attempts a significant counter-attack for the first time in the piece. The percussion is finally successful in retaining its Six identity while simultaneously under the metric regime of 20/2+3. This results in a 6:20 grouping dissonance. To make this work, the percussion must surmount a counter-attack on the battleground already established, which in the second

FIGURE 3.22 Truncated percussion in "Idioteque" (2000–8, 0:10).

verse consists of the 20/2+3 structure being articulated five times for a total of 100 beats. This presents an inherent problem for preserving the identity of Six, since the closest the percussion can get to 100 beats without breaking its meter is 102 beats (17×6=102). Since getting Twenty to break its incessant metric pattern seems impossible, the percussion must somehow drop two beats without significantly altering its identity.

The listener may have noticed that the percussion has already performed this meter change once in the ultimate bar of rehearsal letter A, transcribed in Figure 3.22. It goes by almost unnoticed because, in shedding its last two beats, the percussion leaves behind a paradigmatic backbeat appearing after stating its true identity for several measures before.

With this precedent set, it seems a likely hypothesis that the percussion may reuse this truncation as a way out of the metric predicament. Accordingly, the outline of the percussion's metrical plan of attack for rehearsal letter F would involve stringing together 16 statements of its Six identity (96 beats), followed by the 4-beat tag transcribed in Figure 3.22 for a total of 100 beats.

After the premature victory celebration in the chorus, Twenty is caught severely off-guard by this counter attack. While Twenty does manage to retain its metrical identity through the climax, it senses that said identity is now unstable, not as dominating as before. With this sobering realization, the voice of Twenty is noticeably shaken, and has shed its arrogant demeanor in favor of a more alarmist "run for the hills" tone. The lyrics in this second verse clearly depict a leader who is fully aware of the metrical situation at hand. Especially metaphorical to this narrative are the text-painted announcements "let me hear both sides," which can be read as relating to the simultaneity of the 6:20 grouping dissonance, as well as "we're not scaremongering, this is really happening," which shows a leader telling his forces that this is not to be taken lightly, that their metric stability is in serious danger.

As percussion's strategy in this crucial battle for metrical control of the piece unfolds, the 96+4 meter change hypothesis proves to be an incorrect one. Furthermore, analyzing the metrical framework of the percussion in this climax reveals how its failure to follow the given hypothesis ends up costing it this integral showdown.

Hypothetically it would have been completely feasible for the percussion to string together ten groups of six to form 60 beats, at which the two characters' grouping structures would have lined up, yielding a larger 3+2 division (60+40).

TABLE 3.6

Altered placement of percussion's 6-beat ostinato within 20(×5) (2000–8, 1:52)

Twenty	20				20				20				20			20		
Six	6	6	6	4	6	6	6	6	6	6	6	6	6	6	2	6	4	
Hypermeter	2								3									

After that, the percussion would need 6 groups of 6 followed by the ¼ measure articulated in the opening ((6×6)+4 vs. 20×2) to round out the climax. This means percussion must alter nothing until the ultimate measure of the section; it must do nothing to mask its identity, to disguise its purpose. However, as shown in Table 3.6, the percussion acts upon the ¼ meter change prematurely in the fourth measure, and this hypermetrical faux pas proves to be its downfall in this climactic battle.

When the percussion drops these two beats in the fourth measure of Table 3.6, the percussion and sampler now share a hypermetric downbeat at 40 ((6×3)+4+(6×3) vs. 20×2) and 100 beats, instead of the predicted 60 and 100 beats. Remembering the rising action, this is exactly the 2+3 grouping that Twenty started employing with the entrance of the voice at D. What has happened here, from a metrical, hermeneutic, and even Freudian standpoint, is repression. All that the percussion has worked so hard to fight and repress, that being the metrical structure of Twenty's 2+3, has come out hypermetrically in larger form. Without the necessary hindsight to evaluate its decisions, the percussion has inadvertently outlined two strong hypermetric downbeats that coincide both with the downbeats of Twenty itself, and the 2+3 metrical ideology of Twenty. Had the percussion waited until beat 96 to insert the ¼ bar, the hypermetric downbeats 60 and 100 (which reduce to 3+2) would have inverted Twenty's 2+3 identity, and perhaps inverted the battle for metrical control.

Before moving into the falling action, where the percussion is powerfully disheartened by this realization, it exhibits a decline in morale at the end of the climax as it begins to waver from its Six identity in the last three measures. The 2-beat antepenultimate bar in Figure 3.23 features the tail-end of percussion's Six identity, while the ultimate measure presents its remaining 4-beat head.[43] The antepenultimate and ultimate measures together thus form a disfigured 2+4 beat retrograde collage of the 6-beat ostinato. Percussion also drops in amplitude at the end of the ultimate measure, creating a depressing, crushed decrescendo into the return of Twenty's boastful chorus.

FIGURE 3.23 Disfigured collage of 6-beat percussion ostinato in "Idioteque" (2000–8, 2:30).

FIGURE 3.24 Twenty's recombinant identity: 4×5 and 5×4 simultaneously, chorus 2 of "Idioteque" (2000–8, 2:35).

Falling Action

From a formal standpoint rehearsal letter G is merely a repetition of the boastful chorus and would ostensibly be labeled the same, but from a hermeneutic standpoint, this celebration by Twenty comes in a drastically different context. The difference between the first appearance of the chorus and this one is of paramount importance to the plot's development. While the first appearance was clearly a premature celebration, Twenty is fully confident that there is no chance of metrical power going back to the percussion at this point.

As a demonstration of this victory, Twenty celebrates the outer core of its identity, 20, in a yet unheard way. Having previously only subdivided its 20-beat unit as five units of 4 beats, it now combines that dominant identity with the inverse of itself, four units of 5 beats, resulting in a 5:4 grouping dissonance. Figure 3.24 shows this boastful, virtuosic celebration of Twenty's identity, which marks the resolution of the metrical conflict in the track. Following the second chorus, the percussion seems to mount a counter-attack at 3:13, stating its Six identity several times, but misplaces a measure of 4/4 at 3:21, articulating exactly the same hypermetric gaffe as in Table 3.6. With Six clearly in repetitive death spasms,[44] Twenty articulates the same full 20*5 structure from 4:04–4:48, the re-entrance of the four sampled chords now heard as a victory song.

Marianne Tatom Letts has argued that much of the musical sparring in *Kid A* (2000) can be "parsed into the binary oppositions of nature versus technology."[45] Given that the dominant metrical identity in this piece, Twenty, is composed of both technological (sampler) and organic (Yorke's voice) elements, this binary division may be too simplistic a reading. Indeed, the grouping dissonance that celebrates the second chorus is so powerful because it *blends* the technological with the organic. We hear Yorke's "natural" voice, but cut-and-pasted in four groups of 5 using a sampler, recombined with a more "organic" version of his chorus sung in five groups of 4. Metrical analysis—specifically analysis of grouping dissonance and changing meter—can be interpreted hermeneutically to reveal a more nuanced interaction between the technological and the organic in this piece.

Notes

1. See Varela, et. al (1991, 173); quoted in Iyer (2002, 389).

2. Vijay Iyer's (2002, 393) other two speeds of embodied cognition include one too slow to be considered properly metric (phrase-level) and another too fast to be considered a primary unit of rhythm or subdivision (grace notes).

3. See Witek et. al (2014, 8).

4. Interview for NPR's *Morning Edition*; see Michaeleen Doucleff, "Anatomy of a Dance Hit: Why We Love to Boogie with Pharrell." Transcript at: http://www.npr.org/blogs/health/2014/05/30/317019212/anatomy-of-a-dance-hit-why-we-love-to-boogie-with-pharrell (accessed May 30, 2014).

5. See Attas (2011, 1). I should be careful to note that both Attas's approach (inspired by Hasty, rather than London) and her chosen genre of music (dance/soul-inspired music that rarely escapes $\frac{4}{4}$ meter, instead relying on microtiming for its groove feel) differ substantially from my project. Nevertheless, her method for mapping heard rhythmic and metric phenomena onto bodily experience is a useful one.

6. Of course, many scholars have advocated for more specialized definitions of meter, some of which are tailored toward specific musical styles, such as Ghanaian, as opposed to common-practice European, conceptions of meter. See London (2004, 3–6).

7. London (2004) prefers the term tactus throughout his work.

8. London (2004, 29) surveys much of the literature surrounding experimental data for this point and comes up with a wider number, aimed at assessing what is "possible" to count as the beat. After some consideration, he settles on 30 BPM as the slowest beat possible, and 240–300 BPM as the fastest.

9. Though the backbeat is most strongly associated with $\frac{4}{4}$ meter, we can also speak of compound meter backbeats in $\frac{12}{8}$ and $\frac{6}{8}$. Dividing the top number of each of those meters by three reveals the number of beats in each measure, and the snare attack occurs on even-numbered beats, with $\frac{12}{8}$ acting like a doubly long $\frac{6}{8}$.

10. See Iyer (2002, 407).

11. Iyer (2002, 389) draws on Varela et. al (1991) in this assertion.

12. London (2004) prefers the term non-isochronous for this phenomenon throughout his work. I greatly prefer it to the commonly used "odd" (which implies that a great deal of world music is somehow strange) and "asymmetrical" (which I've always found troublesome since the line of symmetry in a series of 5 actually falls on one of the elements as opposed to the line of symmetry in a series of 4, which falls between two of the elements).

13. Based on the harmonic progression there is also a larger four-measure hypermeter in this example, of which I have only notated the first two measures.

14. Toussaint (2005, 4) introduces this term for a rhythm which is the product of the Euclidean algorithm—an ancient, and purely mathematical conception—which he also relates to other applications, including the calculation of leap years in calendar design, drawing digital straight lines, and other non-musical applications. Euclidean rhythms are related to London's idea of "non-isochronous meters" (2004, 100ff.), as well as Jay Rahn's "diatonic rhythms" (1987, 25ff.)

15. Victoria Malawey (2014, 12) analyzes each measure in this rhythm as a slower composite 3+2 structure and notes how this 3+2 structure is also present in the hypermetric rhythm between the verse and chorus. The two-chord pair transcribed in Figure 3.8 is presented three times, followed by two presentations of the chorus's alternation of G and D chords.

16. Olivier Messiaen (1908–92) was a French composer and theorist most notable for incorporating birdsong into his compositions. Jonny Greenwood sheds light on his connection to Messiaen in a 2001 interview: "I heard the *Turangalîla* Symphony when I was fifteen and I became round-the-bend obsessed with it" (see Ross 2001).

17. In this integer-based pitch notation, C=0, C♯/D♭=1, D=2, and so forth. Furthermore, ten is notated as "t" and eleven as "e" to avoid confusing single- and double-digit pitch classes.

18. Jay Rahn's work on isomorphisms between pitch and rhythm (1987) forms the foundation for most connections between pitch and rhythm. Rahn is especially interested in rhythms he calls "diatonic," which makes them maximally even—a property they share with the diatonic scale.

19. I have chosen to notate the example in 2/4 rather than 4/4 because each half-note in the central groove is exactly the same, which to me suggests no higher grouping structure.

20. In analyzing this "accumulative" beginning, Spicer (2004, 33) notes that "it 'stutters,' for lack of a better description."

21. This reminds me of the phenomenon known as "false recapitulation" in Classic-era sonata forms, where the opening theme seems to come back prematurely, often in the wrong key.

22. Gjerdingen (1989) prefers the expression "mode of attending."

23. It is possible, though I might argue not musically sensitive, to hear the second measure of this example not in 12/8, but rather as two measures of 3/4. In this case, there would not be a pivot pulse at the beat level, only the double-beat level. I ultimately disagree with this hearing because it ignores the paradigmatic long–short pattern in the kick and snare that is so essential to compound meter. Furthermore, a 3/4 (or 6/4, preserving the 12/8 bar length) interpretation necessitates hearing a 2:3 hemiola without any grounding in those three beats to begin with, which I would strongly argue is then not a hemiola at all because there is no three already present "against" which we could understand the two.

24. Pivot chords facilitate key changes by playing a role in each of the two keys, often functioning as predominant. For example, in a modulation from C major to G major, the A minor triad can simultaneously sound like vi in the former and ii in the latter.

25. The notation of this guitar part in Figures 12a–12c is a rhythmic reduction that highlights this Euclidean structure by omitting the quiet, muted articulations in the lower strings. For a more intricate transcription, consult my analysis of the Euclidean structure itself in Osborn 2014.

26. I don't consider Yorke's mumbled "1,2,3,4" count-off that begins the track sufficient metric grounding for a regular-meter interpretation. For one, his tempo, the same as Listener B's, only

works in the first and third measures. Second, count-offs for changing-meter pieces often sacrifice complexity for the practicality of beginning together.

27. 3+3+2 is the most common, heard in the main riff of Coldplay's "Clocks" (2002–5), and 2+3+3, less common, is heard in the first measure of Thursday's "Understanding in a Car Crash" (2001–2).

28. Since Listener B's beat moves at 186, Listener C's $^6/_{16}$ beat can be derived by: 186/3=62; 62*2=124 BPM (the math here is the same as if a single listener were experiencing a metric modulation).

29. Or, at least, that the two different meters are exact multiples of one another (e.g., Listener A's quarter-note beat in "Faust Arp" is exactly twice as fast as Listener B's half-note beat). Given certain mathematical constraints, it may be possible to hear certain Euclidean rhythms themselves as metrical, or, at least, to switch in a figure/ground fashion between a regular meter with the rhythm as syncopation and vice versa.

30. Harald Krebs (1999) differentiates between grouping and displacement dissonances. The latter is less applicable to Radiohead's music, in which analogous structures have been historically discussed in terms of rock's characteristic syncopation.

31. Taylor (2009) relates this to a familiar "figure/ground" illusion where the viewer can either choose to see two faces or a vase, but not both simultaneously. Poudrier and Repp (2013) present experimental evidence that this metric simultaneity may be somewhat possible, though only under very strict conditions.

32. Mark Butler's conditions for this situation include not just the co-existence of metric and hypermetric dissonance, but in fact the "causal relationship" (2006, 158) wherein the former results in the latter.

33. Indeed, the other layers are so thickly overdubbed that it is difficult to tell which notes constitute a "part" or if that is even a viable concept for this level of studio-centered composition. My ear is personally drawn to the repeated C♯5, but I cannot decide which of the other notes outside of the main ostinato "belongs" with it to constitute a riff.

34. Beat-class sets and beat-class modulations have been developed as analytical tools by Roeder 2003 and Cohn 1992.

35. Live, Jonny Greenwood can be seen playing variations of this part on a snare drum and tom.

36. Although this piece originates from a demo recorded by Jonny Greenwood, Moore and Ibrahim (2005, 145) note that Thom Yorke had acquired the entire back catalog of the Warp label during the recording of *Kid A* (2000) and that "the more abrasive end of the output of Aphex Twin (that label's most celebrated artist) has a clear influence on the beat-driven 'Idioteque' [2000–8]."

37. The characters "Percussion" and "Sampler" are assumed characters. It is also important to note that these characters may be better described sonically as character-groups instead of single characters. This is due to the recording techniques used by the band which employ a number of different percussion sounds, as well as synthesized/computer sounds.

38. The sample in question comes from Paul Lansky's *Mild und Leise* (1976–B3). The piece was composed in 1973 on an IBM 360/91 mainframe computer utilizing FM synthesis. The pitches shown in the staff (essentially four different voicings of an E♭ major 9th chord) merely represent a reduction of sorts, due to the prominent overtones. For more details on the piece, and Lansky's personal account of working with Radiohead, visit the composer's website at http://www.music.princeton.edu/paul/radiohead.ml.html.

39. The voice is part of the Sampler/Twenty character group for a number of reasons, but most importantly for the meter it exhibits. From a metrical perspective, it is consonant with the sampler parts, falling into both a ¼ meter and a five-measure cycle for a total of 20 beats.

40. I use the written-out, capitalized forms "Six" and "Twenty" to refer to the assumed characters in the plot, while reserving the Arabic numerals "6" and "20" for empirical rhythmic attributes.

41. Regarding hierarchies in grouping structure, Lerdahl and Jackendoff (1983, 13) posit a rather suggestive hermeneutic interpretation: ". . . discrete elements or regions related in such a way that one element or region subsumes or contains other elements or regions. A subsumed or contained element or region can be said to be subordinate to the element or region that subsumes or contains it; the latter can be said to dominate, or superdominate the former."

42. The key of this song is largely underdetermined due to a lack of harmonic progression. The E♭ major ninth chord, heard in the sample in all four inversions, functions like what Joseph Straus has called a "referential sonority," which is analogous to a tonic triad in nontonal music. In fact, these exact four pitch-classes form the referential sonority Straus demonstrates (1982, 266) throughout the third movement of Stravinsky's *Dumbarton Oaks Concerto*.

43. The labels "heads" and "tails" are largely borrowed from language sometimes used to describe bipartite fugue subjects, where an analyst divides the subject into two motives.

44. After Six reaches the penultimate grouping of 6 seen in Table 3.6, these death spasms can be heard in the rambling 30 beats (structured as 5*6) that follow. An alternative reading of these 30 beats before the sampled chords re-enter might hear it as one last futile counter-attack before the ultimate defeat. I am reminded here of the stubborn knight in *Monty Python and the Holy Grail*, who attempts to fight back despite having each of his limbs chopped off one by one.

45. See Letts (2010, 44).

4   Timbre

PERHAPS NOWHERE IS a theory of ecological perception more at home than in the study of timbre. No longer mediated by competencies needed for understanding harmony, rhythm, and form, timbre accesses those most ancient parts of our brain simply concerned with identifying and interpreting sounds and their sources. Timbre is therefore unique among these four parameters inasmuch as "the connotations of sounds frequently operate without reference to primary domains," allowing us to "ask questions relating to the effect listeners perceive in the uses of particular timbres, gestures, and their combinations."[1]

Timbre is then not so much a musical parameter as a perceptual process of relating sounds to their sources. In one of the earliest contributions to the ecological theory of perception, Denis Smalley calls this process "source-bonding," which he defines as "the *natural* tendency to relate sounds to supposed sources and causes, and to relate sounds to each other because they appear to have shared or associated origins."[2] Immediately recognizable, minimally altered sources in Radiohead's music range from rock-standard instrumentation (e.g., guitar, bass, drums, lead vocal), to those more associated with western classical music (e.g., glockenspiel, harp), to the idiosyncratic. This latter category includes the closely miked dog barking in "House of Cards" (2007–8, 2:50) and the porcelain radiator-cum-percussion instrument that opens "Packt Like Sardines in a Crushd Tin Box" (2001–1). Source-bonding with those timbres that fit our expectations regarding rock music is a relatively immediate affair, offering little surprise, while attempting to bond with sources that are entirely foreign to rock music (for example, a radiator) produces no meanings or connotations derived from other pieces. Radiohead's most salient timbres, which maximize arousal and prompt a listener's search for meaning, are usually not those whose sources are immediately recognizable but instead those whose sources are either (1) deformed through signal processing or (2) those for whom the only "source" is synthetic. Finding meaning in a particular timbre is possible because "the change in frequency content of a sound over time reflects the type of energy expended in its creation and thus, by extension, the types of meaning we attribute to it."[3]

Approaches to meaning via form, rhythm, and harmony are well-worn territory for music theory. Likewise, the text has always been a carrier of meaning. For whatever reason, music theory, like historical musicology and most other forms of music analysis (ethnomusicology excluded), has generally shied away from timbre in discussions of meaning. But *how* do we go about the pursuit of meaning through a timbral lens? Since the sound-sources we hear in any environment imply various meanings, we can arrive at these meanings through the process of source-bonding. In source-bonding with Radiohead, it is important to remember that our cognition of timbre is shaped by expectations. When listening to a genre for which the electric guitar is the primary signifier (rock), what kinds of meanings arise when this fundamental timbre is removed, forcing us to bond with other sources instead? Smalley's process of *spectromorphology* provides a method for source-bonding with less familiar timbres. Spectromorphology, which concerns a listener's interactions with sounds and their sources over time, was in 1997 one of the earliest music-theoretical approaches inspired by James Gibson's ecological theories of visual perception, and plays a significant role in Clarke's 2005 book *Ways of Listening: An Ecological Model of Musical Perception*. For Smalley, this direct link to the human perceptual system not only has intrinsic value as such, but is also valuable in its capacity for "helping a listener to pinpoint those musical qualities which are carriers of meaning."[4]

Recent neuroscience also sheds light on these ecological approaches. The connections our brains make between timbre and source may be the product of newly discovered receptors called mirror neurons, which "[allow] an individual to understand the meaning and intention of a communicative signal by evoking a *representation* of that signal in the perceiver's own brain."[5] Timbre as a study thus allows us to examine the causal relationships between the sound we hear, how we perceive that sound, and what referential meanings can be drawn from that perception. Simon Zagorski-Thomas goes so far as to suggest that "these developments in psychology demand a new approach to musicology: an approach based on what we know about how humans interpret sound and music and how it is physically created through the gestures of performance."[6]

Source-bonding and spectromorphology aimed at the analysis of timbre enables such a psychologically grounded approach. In order to do so we must broaden our idea of "source" from the material all the way through the cultural, social, and stylistic. Because the brain does not operate in a purely indexical manner—because our perceptual systems not only process what is specified by a source's material but also that source's circumstances—Eric Clarke suggests the following relationship between sources and specification:

> . . . the sounds of music specify a huge diversity of sources: the instruments and recording media from which they emanate, the musical styles to which they belong, the social function in which they participate, the emotional states and bodily actions of their performers, the spaces and paces—virtual and real—which they inhabit, the discourses with which they are intertwined.[7]

But a distinction should be made between this multifaceted definition of source and the perceptual process that Smalley identifies as source-bonding. Smalley, like Clarke, wants source to connote a wide range of referents beyond the physical. Despite this aim, both authors spend considerable amounts of time applying their methodology to the physical. An ecologically oriented theory of timbre should then distinguish between two modes of perception: one for the identification of pure, material sources, and another aimed at meaning and reference (though the latter is obviously dependent on the former). Clarke's theory of *affordance* can be used to connote all meanings which stem from, but do not emanate as sound waves from, materials connected to the process of music-making. We might fruitfully visualize affordances as those meanings reaching out in all directions from the listener's imagination *after* the sound waves from the material source have been processed. For most listeners, the *meaning* of a timbral utterance surely stretches beyond mere identification. For that more immediate affair of understanding and identifying the material source of a sound, the physical source from which sound waves emanate, Clarke's other primary theory, *specification*, in which a heard timbre instantly specifies its source through material properties (e.g., hollow, metal) is a good initial step, followed quickly by Smalley's concept of source-bonding, which describes the mutualism between perceiver and perceived.

Smalley proposes the term source-bonding for the analysis of timbre for its potential to make meaningful relationships that move "from inside the work to the sounding world outside."[8] For Smalley, the bond is a process, one which is very much subjective. Clarke seems to have been influenced by the profound link Smalley draws between source-bonding and meaning:

> The word "bonding" seems particularly appropriate since it evokes a binding, inescapable engagement or kinship between listener and musical context. The bondings involve all types of sounding matter and sound-making, whether in nature or in culture, whether they arise as a result of human agency or not. Source bondings may be actual or imagined—in other words they can be constructs created by the listener; different listeners may share bondings when they listen to the same music, but they may equally have different, individual, personalised bondings; the bondings may never have been envisaged by the composer and can occur in what might be considered the most abstract of works; wide-ranging bondings are inevitable in musics which are not primarily weighted towards fixed pitches and intervals. *Bonding play* is an inherent perceptual activity.[9]

Source-bonding in Radiohead

Smalley and (to a lesser extent) Clarke are not concerned with rock music, but rather electro-acoustic music and western classical music, respectively. Recent scholarship has adapted these foundational approaches to an idiom closer to Radiohead's own. In an article on timbre in the music of the British rapper known as The Streets, Mark Slater proposes a "poetic-ecological model" that latches onto Clarke's more subjective "bonding play" to explain how multiple listeners may interpret synthesized timbres as bonded to different material sources, though the physical source in all cases is merely a computer—all sounds are sampled and/or synthesized. Zagorski-Thomas gets the closest in adapting this to pop–rock genres that rely on both acoustic and electronic instruments. Like Slater, he focuses on the role of the listener in source-bonding. In analyses of songs recorded by acts as diverse as The Civil Wars, Shania Twain, and Trent Reznor, timbre is continually linked not only to perceptual principles, but also to contemporary studio production technology. In a particularly lucid analysis of Twain's "The Woman in Me" (1995–5), he shows that source-bonding with the kick drum sound is a remarkably contingent affair. Because of modern pop–rock's extensive use of close-miking techniques, to perceive the sound as a kick drum is not to perceive it as we would in a room, or even in a concert hall, but to perceive the intricate details we would only hear if our head were actually *inside* the kick drum with the front head removed—a listening experience for which few of us have any prior experience (thankfully). This effectively blurs the line between source-bonding with an acoustic instrument and an electronic one, but also demonstrates the quantum leaps our perceptual systems are instantly capable of making.

Source-bonding with traditional instrument sounds in Radiohead's music can be an equally instant affair, despite the significant amount of processing those sounds undergo in studio production. The combination of close-miking and abundant hall reverb used to shape Yorke's voice in the verse of "Exit Music (for a Film)" (1997–4) is a physical contradiction. This imaginary, created space in which we are close enough to hear the detailed sounds coming from his lips, teeth, and nose— yet also far enough away to hear those sounds transformed as they bounce off the back wall in a cathedral, for example—does little to keep us from instantly bonding with the material source: Yorke's voice. But given enough digital processing, source-bonding approaches an event horizon where its material origin is sufficiently obscured.

Source-bonding becomes a more difficult affair in tracks such as these, resulting in one of two marked timbral families: *source-deformation* and *synthesis*. As an example of the former, in "15 Step" (2007–1, 2:23–3:10) who among us instantly recognizes the instrument playing those chords? The properties we might immediately latch onto include looping (the sharp cuts in amplitude followed by immediate swells back to the original volume), reversing (the "whoosh" sound that comes from playing a sound backwards from nil, through decay, up to full volume), and envelope filtering (the kaleidoscope effect of moving from more to less treble and back). But these most audible invariants are all production techniques, rather than properties of physical construction. This is a particularly difficult case of source-bonding because not only is the material source almost completely obscured by the processing techniques, but the material source itself—an autoharp—is not even within a reasonable set of timbral expectations for those inculcated in the rock genre.

Bearing in mind that source-bonding is highly subjective, we might speculate on what kind of listener might actually identify this material source. Listeners steeped in folk music traditions would have a better shot at identifying the autoharp, but unlike modern rock listeners, would have almost no frame of reference for the kinds of source-deforming signal processing applied to it. The opposite goes for a modern rock listener, who knows the effects but not the instrument. In other words, there may be no "ideal listener" for this timbre. But timbral perception is not necessarily a right or wrong affair. A much richer conception of source-bonding resists the ultimate teleological urge to know, and rather focuses on the process itself. Ten listeners paying attention to this single timbre for long enough will likely develop ten unique explanations for the source, a beautiful process that is all too often foreclosed upon prematurely by simply looking up "the answer" on Internet chat forums.

Bonding with sources in Radiohead's music relies upon our ability to recognize the *specifications* and *affordances* of a certain timbre. We might first begin by untangling those two terms. Both are noun forms of a verb: to specify, to afford. Grammatically, the usage is subtly different, especially in terms of transitivity. In Clarke's usage,[10] all forms of the verb [to afford] are necessarily transitive, usually taking a gerund as their direct object (the couch affords sitting; the ball affords throwing). Elsewhere, Clarke suggests that affordance provides the closest link to musical meaning, and in this sense of the term he means that a certain musical stimulus affords a noun—namely, a certain meaning. Clarke's sense of affordance is clearly aimed at referential rather than behavioral meaning.

[To specify], on the other hand, is not transitive, and for Clarke more rightly connotes the domain of properties *directly specified* by objects themselves, rather than perceptual processes.[11] Objects produce sounds due to properties of their material construction. Even when dealing with guitar effects pedals, the resulting sounds are specified by the signal path and wiring of the stompbox.[12] Of course, this is a matter which a listener learns over time from being surrounded by objects making sounds.

Specification then seems more properly the domain of the direct relationship between object and sound—something closer to what Smalley means by source-bonding—while the meanings gleaned from said specification may be deemed affordances. For example, the sound ahead and to my left as I attempt to cross a busy intersection in Chinatown on my bike instantly specifies "whistle" by nature of the invariant properties of the aperture and agitator, while my prior experiences in such situations affords the meaning "crossing guard," that latter being confirmed when I naturally orient my head toward the direction of the sound and see a uniformed officer in approximately the same location. Because referential meaning leads to certain behaviors, sources specified by recorded sound should move beyond the physical into the cultural. In a sustained analysis of Jimi Hendrix's iconic rendition of "The Star-Spangled Banner" from Woodstock (1969), Clarke shows just how far the web of specifications stretches from beyond the recorded sound itself. Several timbres specify "instability" of the sound itself, including distortion, feedback, and the rotating mechanism of the Leslie speaker cabinet.[13] These specifications may then in turn afford meanings such as <counterculture> through their association with certain rock scenes in the late 1960s.

Identifying the timbral sources in Radiohead's music leads us to these kinds of material- and culturally driven meanings. Meanings driven by other parameters in Radiohead's music, including harmony, rhythm, and especially form, are often contingent upon timbre as well. The robotic pace and minimal pitch fluctuation of the primary voice throughout "Fitter Happier" (1997–7) are invariants that specify a computer, rather than human source. Identifying this computer source then leads to meanings connecting computers to dystopian themes expressed here and elsewhere on *OK Computer* (1997), the source now sounding something like "Hal" from *2001: A Space Odyssey*. The through-composed form provides the structure for a seemingly benevolent set of instructions near the beginning of the track to malfunction and derail toward apocalyptic prophecies including nuclear winter and horrific factory farming practices. Similarly, in "2+2=5" (2003–1, 1:54) the seam between the B and C sections results from the cooperation of timbre, harmony, and rhythm. The heavily distorted electric guitar playing power chords in ⁴⁄₄ time—conventional timbres, harmonies, and rhythms which have not yet been heard in the track—instantly affords <rock> for the first time on the album, and perhaps even <grunge> for the first time since *OK Computer*.

The stark contrast in timbres between sections in "2+2=5" is a striking example of spectromorphology, in which "[a] listener moves in time with the recognition of some objects also moving in time. The musical experience is to establish relations among these objects according to the musical culture, a set of values and functions that creates auditory models."[14] We can also think about such transformations as oriented not in time, but rather space. By making sense of changes over time based on analogous physical situations in which said changes would occur, sound can be linked to motion. Sometimes this is a relatively straightforward affair directly linked to specification. When we hear a violin playing pizzicato, for example, our motor neurons respond sympathetically by imagining the motions required of the right hand to produce those sounds. Most sound production is a direct result of physical motion (even the movement of air through the respiratory system), and we as listeners respond to this through embodied cognition, mirror neurons, and, quite often, through actual sympathetic movement ourselves.[15]

But because timbral perception is learned, we have come to associate the same "real-world" movements in sound with those now produced by electronic means. Even when we are aware that certain timbral shifts have no physical genesis, we still interpret them as having a motional characteristic. In analyzing FatBoy Slim's "Build it Up, Tear it Down" (1999–1), Clarke latches onto a particular moment wherein an electronic bass instrument is processed through a variable low-pass filter, which allows high frequencies to emerge only slowly over time. He links this to a physical sound source that is first hidden behind some object, but which gradually comes into view:

> . . . in everyday circumstances, the acoustic array from a sound source that is concealed in relation to a listener (behind a large object like a wall or a building, or below a horizon) will possess attenuated high frequencies due to simple masking principles . . . As the distance to the source decreases, or the degree of

occlusion declines, the high frequencies increase in relative intensity, shifting the timbral balance towards increasing brightness.[16]

A similar use of the low-pass filter can be heard in the drum sounds of Radiohead's "Airbag" (1997–1). The change over time experienced in Phil Selway's snare sound starts in the instrumental bridge at 2:24. With the voice no longer present, our attention is drawn more to the instrumental sources. At 2:30 the high frequencies of the snare and hi-hat are immediately and unexpectedly attenuated. It is not a change in volume, only in tone. These high frequencies then slowly fade back into the mix until reaching an apex at 2:38, only to roll off again, this time gradually. After reaching another valley around 2:47, the high frequencies then incrementally reappear in a constant approach to the return of the chorus at 2:58, at which point they are permanently reinstated. Listeners cognizant in the shape of waveforms will see something like the cliffs of Dover: a precipitous drop to a series of more predictable and gradual waves. And listeners with exposure to a radio's tone knob will immediately sense the gestural motion inherent in this timbral shift: a brusque motion counter-clockwise followed by undulating motions between five o'clock (high frequencies reinstated) and seven o'clock (high frequencies attenuated). The timbres generated by this low-pass filter are contingent upon our sense of time, but also have direct correlates in space and motion.

Spectromorphology need not be limited to transformations in a single sound, but also linked timbral groups. "2+2=5" (2003–1) provides a rather radical example of a spectromorphology with a sharp seam occupied on either side by disparate timbral groups. More often than not these timbral shifts are more gradual. The opening of "Everything in its Right Place" (2000–1), for example, begins with a timbral family composed of distinct electronic sources. Yorke's sampled, electronically processed vocal fragments blend seamlessly into the electronic fabric created by the keyboard and programmed four-on-the-floor kick drum. At 0:34 a different timbre emerges: Yorke's minimally processed singing voice with a delivery that specifies acoustic live performance. The change in timbre over time is thus not so much a change in source (both ultimately came from Yorke's vocal cords), but in electronic processing. Oppositions between the spectromorphologies of acoustic and electronic source-families can be heard throughout *Kid A* (2000) and *Amnesiac* (2001). In this opening track, we can already sense a division emerging between organic and technological timbres. This line is, however, always blurred by the labor involved in the production of these timbres. Most electronic instruments, including the Sequential Circuits Prophet-5 keyboard in "Everything in its Right Place," require a human to play them, and acoustic sources are often filtered through subtle electronic processing if not actually triggered entirely by samplers.

Spectromorphology can thus provide a more empirically grounded way to assess the division between the technological and the organic that so many critics read into Radiohead's turn-of-the-millennium albums. In tracks such as "Idioteque" (2000–8) these can certainly be interpreted as a battle, especially since the individual timbres are also bound to particular rhythmic identities. But more often than not, a closer examination of the timbres and their sources reveals contradictions unresolvable through a pure binary opposition between humans and technology.[17] Meanings produced by these timbral sources are contingent not only upon the actor producing them and the equipment mediating that production, but also an individual listener's knowledge of those technologies and practices.

Analysis of timbre, like other parameters in Radiohead's music, is contingent upon the expectations we as listeners have inherited from rock music. So dependent is timbre upon the receiver's reception that, in the field of speech perception, timbre is defined as "the result of a perceptual process rather than as a fixed quantity, and highlights the importance of both listeners and signals in determining quality."[18] In order to identify Radiohead's most salient timbres, passages which confront us with strange yet quasi-familiar sounds that prompt us to think about the source of that sound and the meanings surrounding its deformation, we must separate those salient timbres from timbres which are inherited directly from rock conventions.

Conventional Timbres in Rock Music

Four primary layers form the timbral basis of rock music. The sound sources that compose these four layers provide us with a coherent set of expectations regarding timbre in rock music. Rock's "explicit beat layer" is almost always contributed by the drum set, which differs from all other layers in that it is devoid of definite pitch.[19] Acoustic (and sometimes electronic and programmed) drum sets act in tandem with the "functional bass layer" to establish the song's sense of groove. Bass guitar, almost always electric in modern rock, is far and away the most common representative of this layer. Floating on top of, and interacting with these two layers is the song's most memorable timbre, the "melodic layer." Not only occupied by lead vocal, this layer may be occupied by several primary and secondary melodic instrumental layers, even simultaneously and/or alongside the voice.

Of these four layers, the "harmonic filler layer" acts as rock's most indelible timbral signifier. This includes all timbres that work to fill the registral space between the primary melodic layer and the functional bass layer. Allan Moore claims it is "the constitution of this layer, and the way it is actualized, that has the greatest impact on the attribution of a particular style by any naïve listener."[20] Radiohead's harmonic filler layer after *The Bends* is usually articulated by the electric guitar and/or various keyboards. Listeners inculcated in rock's timbral conventions have also come to expect acoustic guitar, piano, wind/string pads, and backing vocals.

But even the individual instruments which compose these four layers are not composed of an invariant spectrum. This exposes a problem in the definition of timbre. One of the earliest definitions asserts that timbre is the difference between two sounds differing in neither frequency, amplitude, nor duration[21] (a definition largely taken up by the American Standards Association). Under this definition, the electric guitar so fundamental to rock's harmonic filler layer has a potentially infinite number of discrete timbres. The other extreme can be found in the original French usage of the term *timbre*, which actually relates more to instrumentation. According to this definition of timbre, the "electric guitar," like the "clarinet," has only one *timbre*.

This contradistinction in terminology is problematic because "timbre has been used in too many contexts to mean too many different things."[22] Nearly all ecological models of analyzing recorded popular music have addressed this problem head-on through detailed descriptions of rock's conventional layers and timbres. Rock's two most conventional instruments—the voice and the (distorted) electric guitar—are capable of a remarkably wide breadth of timbral variation. Radiohead's music makes extensive use of a huge variety of instrumental timbres, textures, and production techniques whose beauty derives from their nuanced shades of individuality. The powerful distortion and double-tracking used to open "Airbag" (1997–1); the microphone selection and placement used to evoke intimacy in "You and Whose Army?" (2001–4)—a precise matter of inches and vintage materials; the puzzle-like interlocking of equalized frequencies between the drum set and bass guitar that engenders the groove in "Little by Little" (2011–3); each of these unique timbres stems from subtle and nuanced modifications to time-worn methods.

But for marked timbres that do transcend the limits of what constitutes conventional timbre in rock music, our interpretive strategy involves four steps: (1) the process of identifying unconventional material sources (source-bonding); (2) the development of, and engagement with, those sources over time (spectromorphology); (3) the interactions between timbre and other parameters such as rhythm, harmony, and form in the constructed environment of the track; and (4) the kinds of extra-physical meaning these sources afford for an individual listener. Two discrete types of timbres in Radiohead's music are particularly salient for their balance of convention and surprise: source-deformation and synthesis. When we encounter timbres such as these, the process of delineating cultural, historical, and societal affordances is just as important as identifying and bonding with materials specified by recorded sound.

Source-deformation (Instrumental and Vocal)

From time to time Radiohead imports non-rock instruments into otherwise standard rock instrumentation. Minimal processing ensures that these instruments are instantly recognized. This includes the sweeping harp glissandi beginning in the second verse of "Motion Picture Soundtrack" (2000–10, 1:39); the glockenspiel heard in "No Surprises" (1997–10, e.g., 0:13), "Sit Down" (2003–2, e.g., 0:14), and "All I Need" (2007–5, e.g., 1:42); and an array of keyboard instruments including the harmonium in "Motion Picture" (2000–10) and the Fender Rhodes in "Morning Bell" (2000–9). More often though, they do something like the opposite. Through electronic processing, a standard instrumental source—especially the voice or lead guitar—is deformed (perhaps re-formed?) in such a way as to obscure its material origins. But in terms of source-deformation, how far is too far? How much electronic processing, and of what sort, is enough to obscure the material source of the electric guitar such that a listener will have trouble perceiving it as such? The answer to this question depends on a listener's familiarity with the style and the sorts of timbral modifications that are most common. No listener even remotely conversant with modern rock music will fail to recognize the electric guitar through a veil of distortion, but a listener unfamiliar with the genre whose only experience with a guitar involves the clear and highly percussive timbre of the acoustic guitar might. Addressing source-deformation from the perspective of a listener stylistically competent in modern rock's signal processing methods—the kind of exposure a listener gleans from nothing more than listening to rock radio—allows us to reconstruct the expectations held by a majority of Radiohead's listeners.[23]

Rock music admits a great many variations on the sounds created by guitars, drums, and even voices. Distortion, an effect that started as an engineering defect in amplification technology, is a ubiquitous color added regularly to electric guitars and basses, and occasionally to other material sources (in which case the lack of convention results in the stimulus becoming a bit more perceptually marked). Distortion is measured by degrees, meaning that a sound can be more or less distorted, rather than an either/or situation. This can be neatly represented by the clipping of a sine wave.[24] Distortion produced by amplifiers utilizing vacuum tubes occurs when the input signal, a sine wave, exceeds the voltage capacities of the tube. At this point, the tube begins to "flatten" the wave, a process known as clipping. As more voltage is added, the wave becomes flatter at the top and bottom, resulting in a progressively more distorted sound that gradually approaches a fully distorted square wave. Guitarists have an impressively large vocabulary for naming discrete amounts of distortion (after all, there are an infinite number of points between perfectly clean and fully distorted); the three most common stages are known as "overdrive," "crunch," and "distortion." Understanding an effect as simple as distortion can serve as a perceptual model for understanding source-deformation more generally. Under enough distortion, the original input signal (generated by a material source) becomes noise, indistinguishable from noise generated by any other material source. Though the exact details of how an acoustic signal is distorted by each individual effect varies greatly depending on the effect in question (e.g., phasing involves the misalignment of two identical signals, while equalization manipulates the relative amplitudes of discrete frequencies), all source-deformations can be measured as a process wherein the effected output signal perceived by listeners differs from the original input signal more or less obscured by said effect.[25]

An analogy to our sense of taste is helpful here. Anyone familiar with the unique tastes of Earl Grey and genmaicha teas will be able to identify which source they are blindly tasting largely due to the invariant properties of bergamot and toasted rice, respectively. A dash of milk or honey adds a pleasing effect (much like tasteful reverb and echo), but in no significant way affects the perceiver's ability to identify the source as either Earl Grey or genmaicha. However, given *enough* honey, the effect not only becomes displeasing, but in fact begins by degrees to obscure the source until a point is reached at which the ratio of honey to tea is such that the original source, now saturated in honey, is imperceptible. Radiohead's recorded music deforms two material sources essential to rock music: the electric guitar and the voice. Neither clean input signals nor fully saturated input signals, each case occupies a different position along a linear continuum between the two extremes. For listeners with different levels of competency in the signal processing techniques used by the band, the original sources will then be more or less deformed, representing points on a continuum between immediate recognition and incomprehensible noise.

One of the more subtle source-deformations used by the band is the result of guitarist Ed O'Brien's "Sustainer Strat." Interestingly, whereas most source-deformations arise as a result of digital manipulation, this one is largely the product of a physical deformation. In 2002 O'Brien modified his Fender Stratocaster guitar, taking out the neck and bridge pickups and replacing them with a *Sustainer* system made by the Japanese guitar company Fernandes. This Sustainer system consists of two parts. The neck pickup in O'Brien's Strat was replaced with a pickup-shaped unit that creates an electromagnetic pulse that causes the strings to sympathetically vibrate indefinitely, without the usual mode of activation required by the guitarist's picking hand—and more crucially, without the transients we hear as a result of that pick attack. Numerous studies have shown that transients are essential to our perception of timbre, so much so that when they are removed electronically, subjects are considerably less reliable in identifying sources.[26] This string vibration is then picked up by a second unit near the bridge, where the traditional pickup used to be. As such, the guitar's original *method* of producing sound—string vibrations transmitted through pickups—is preserved, but the agency under which the strings were made to vibrate in the first place is now electronic, rather than human.

"The Gloaming" (2003–8) is among the first studio recordings O'Brien made with his new Sustainer Strat. Coinciding with the entrance of the voice at 0:56, the entrance of a pulsating E4 fundamental certainly specifies the source <electronic instrument>, but it does not immediately specify guitar because of the missing transients. One important invariant property of the electric guitar's traditional playing technique includes the activation of the vibrating string by either striking said string with a pick or by plucking it with fingers. Doubtless, many variations on this activation are admitted, but even in less common methods of playing such as strumming with the back of a hand or scraping with a fingernail, the string must still be activated by some sort of strike. This property of the guitar's transients, notably absent from the continuous stimulus beginning at 0:56, deforms the source in such a manner that few listeners will bond immediately with a guitar, if at all.

At least two factors other than the Sustainer Strat are responsible for this interpretation. First, the ecosystem created by the track reminds us of *Kid A* (2000) and *Amnesiac* (2001), containing no standard rock instruments. Indeed, "The Gloaming," originally named "33.3 repeating," was demoed in the same sessions. Every track besides Yorke's voice is the product of synthesis. Having heard only programmed sounds up until this point—namely three layers of programmed percussive sounds occupying three different ranges—a listener may assume that this round, attack-less sound is also produced by some synthetic means. Second, the mechanically precise rhythm with which the E4 is repeated is something we usually associate with samples rather than human performance. Certainly repetition is inherent in our modes of music-making, but with microtiming discrepancies and occasional embellishment. Humans rarely repeat something *exactly*.

Technology is responsible for this deformation as well, perhaps less timbral and more rhythmic. O'Brien in fact only plays one measure of this E4, using his AKAI Headrush pedal to create a repeating loop of that fragment. Looping pedals work on the same basic technology as the delay pedal. The output signal is a carbon copy of the input signal offset by a user-determined amount of time. Typically, looping effects such as the Headrush used in "The Gloaming" differ from delay pedals such as the Roland Space Echo used on "2+2=5" (2003–1, 1:22–1:53) in that they allow for a longer period of time between input and output.[27] This longer sample time allows for O'Brien to align his loop with every *measure*

of the percussion despite the fact that his loop shares no common rhythmic denominator with any of the percussion's attack points *within* each measure. Like
the two percussion layers in "Bloom" (2011–1, 0:14), the effect is like runners
running around the track at different speeds yet always beginning and ending
together. Since the Sustainer Strat allows for the rounder activation of the guitar,
its rhythmic onset is obscured as well, more like a quick fade-in than a definable
attack point produced by a pick.[28] Therefore, in "The Gloaming," timbral source-
deformations are integrally linked to rhythm qua attack and repetition. Table 4.1
lists timbral characteristics produced by both the Headrush and the Sustainer
Strat and, just as importantly, the timbres normally produced by a guitar which
are made absent by these sources.

A related timbral–rhythmic effect in Radiohead's music is produced by replacing
the picking/strumming/plucking attack we normally expect from the guitar with
the E-Bow. Manufactured by the Roland corporation, the E-Bow is held in the guitarist's picking hand instead of a pick. When the E-Bow is placed directly above any
one of the guitar's pickups, it creates an electro-magnetic pulse that vibrates only the
string directly under it. O'Brien's E-Bow can be heard in counterpoint with Jonny
Greenwood's ondes Martenot throughout "Where I End and You Begin" (2003–6,
e.g., 2:21), and in "Nude" (2007–3, 1:04–1:13) the E-Bow is heard in the left channel
in counterpoint against Greenwood's melody in the right.

Still other guitar deformations in Radiohead's music are largely the function of
foot-operated digital effects, widely known as "stompboxes." Distortion is usually
activated with a stompbox, as are a number of other digital effects which either do
not significantly deform the material source of the guitar (for example, reverb, delay,
compression) or do so in a manner consistent with rock expectations (for example,
small amounts of flange, phase, and chorus). Remembering again that this is (inter)
subjective based on a listener's prior experience with the relevant technology, some
stompboxes push this deformation to the point that the material source may be

TABLE 4.1

Chart of timbral specifications and affordances in "The Gloaming" (2003–8)		
Timbres that specify \<Fernandes Sustainer>	Timbres that specify \<Akai Headrush>	Absent expected timbres that afford \<deformation> meaning
soft attack/bowed sound	exact repetition of specified period	pick noise/transient no longer audible
crescendo	precise rhythmic placement	human micro-rhythm absent

sufficiently obscured. This is due to the mutualistic relationship between perceiver and environment in which "different perceivers will be attuned to different invariants and at different times."[29]

One pedal to which few rock listeners are customarily attuned, the Mutronics Mutator, can be heard in Jonny Greenwood's final guitar solo from "Paranoid Android" (1997–2, 5:47). Beginning directly after the two-minute chorale, the Mutator solo draws our attention to this novel timbre, rather than the brief recapitulation of B-section material that interrupts an otherwise through-composed form. Greenwood's Mutator solo is panned hard to the left, while a highly distorted, yet otherwise unaffected guitar track complements it on the far right. This stereo image with solo in the left channel and distorted rhythm track in the right channel is also a remnant of the B section, making the timbral alteration via Mutator pedal all that has changed in this final section and therefore worthy of sustained perceptual interest.

The Mutator pedal's source-deforming capabilities stem from its extreme envelope-filtering capabilities. Whereas a standard envelope filter pedal (perhaps most commonly associated with Bootsy Collins-era funk guitar) uses hi-pass and low-pass filters to subtly transform the tone range of a guitar over short periods of time, resulting in consistent "wah-wah" like sounds (consistent both in the frequency and amplitude of the wave), the Mutator's signal path provides the opportunity to almost wholly discard the original tone of the guitar and supplant it with synthetic upper frequency content.

The Mutator effect is best described as source-deformation, rather than synthesis, because it does nothing to disguise the fundamental frequency of each note, nor its attack characteristics. Leaving these two parameters intact allows the listener to perceive two invariants that specify guitar. First, the amplitude curve, with immediate activation and steady decay, specifies a vibrating body struck with some implement. Second, the fundamental frequencies are not equal-tempered. Neither of these two invariants is unique to the guitar. For example, the instant activation followed by steady decay in a jazz ride cymbal is an invariant property of a suspended object being struck by a wooden beater, and the pitch bend on an analog synthesizer is the invariant property of a signal path that allows for a portamento wheel controlled by the performer's left hand. While these two invariants may not directly specify the electric guitar, they do at least "hint" at its source.

Source-deformation in Radiohead's guitar timbres can be traced back to invariant properties of either modified instruments (e.g., Sustainer Strat), modified methods of activation (e.g., E-Bow), or effects pedals, which deform the source once the signal has left the instrument entirely. Several source-deforming guitar effects pedals and their uses are given in Table 4.2.[30] Bear in mind once again that any line between, on

TABLE 4.2

Selected source-deforming guitar effects in Radiohead 1997–2011

Effect pedal	Song	Description
AKAI Headrush	"The Gloaming" (2003–8, 0:55)	creates E4 loop
	"15 Step" (2007–1, 3:44)	ambient loop at end
	"Weird Fishes" (2007–4, 3:54)	pulsating high-frequency timbre
Mutronics Mutator	"Paranoid Android" (1997–2, 5:47)	squeaky envelope filter tone
	"Subterranean Homesick Alien" (1997–3, 0:10)	liquidy, crystalline frequencies
Electro-Harmonix Small Stone Phaser	"Airbag" (1997–1, 1:31)	diffuses tremolo picking in right channel
	"Subterranean Homesick Alien" (1997–3, 2:35)	throaty tone in overdriven guitar panned hard left
Electro-Harmonix HOG (Harmonic Octave Generator)	"Morning Mr. Magpie" (2011–2, 1:35)	ambient shrieking in center-left channel
	"Lotus Flower" (2011–5, 0:11)	quiet swells in left channel
Digitech Whammy IV (used for portamento effects)	"15 Step" (2007–1, 1:44)	$A\flat 4$–$B\flat 4$ portamento sounds a bit like a voice
	"Feral" (2011–4, throughout)	portamento setting slides between pitches, used in conjunction with MXR Phase 90
AMS DMS1580 Delay	"Karma Police" (1997–6, 3:38)	quarter-note based feedback loops grows in amplitude each repetition
Boss SD1 Super Overdrive (with reverb, played with coin)	"Morning Bell" (2001–7, throughout)	Jonny Greenwood scrapes coin parallel with the string to make keyboard-esque sounds
Unknown Reverb and Delay	"Go to Sleep" (2003–5, 1:23)	delay time set quite fast, guitar attacked either behind the nut or below the bridge for repeating metallic gesture

the one hand, source-deformation and, on the other hand, tasteful effects applied to an instantly recognizable electric guitar, must necessarily be subjective based on a listener's prior experiences interacting with such sounds. For example, the use of the Electro-Harmonix HOG (Harmonic Octave Generator) to produce the repeated B♭4 heard on the downbeat of every measure in the opening of "Separator" (2011–8, 0:01) will only minimally deform an otherwise intelligible guitar-source for most listeners (hence its absence from Table 4.2), while the more extreme HOG settings in "Morning Mr. Magpie" (2011–2, 1:35) will render the source near unintelligible for an overwhelming majority of listeners. Nevertheless, those provided here should provide for some level of intersubjectivity among most of Radiohead's listenership.

Thom Yorke's voice is the other source regularly deformed by effects throughout Radiohead's catalog. One such example is heard throughout "Everything in its Right Place" (2000–1). Two significant deformations heard throughout are responsible for this track's signature sound. Yorke's vocal source is altered not only in terms of upper frequency content but also attack. Some might regard only the first of these as properly timbral, the second more properly rhythmic. However, a more in-depth understanding of the sampling processes used to deform Yorke's voice in this track reveals that a source's attack—a properly spectromorphological property since it affects timbre over time—is just as integral to a source's identity as its upper frequency content.

The vocal-deformations heard on the studio version of "Everything in its Right Place" were created entirely by producer Nigel Godrich using the industry-standard audio editing software Pro Tools. As such, the "sources" responsible for this deformation are not transparent, and are more dependent on software programming than on the relatively straightforward voltage capacitors and signal routing that control effects pedals.[31] Examining how the band reproduces these vocal effects live (quite accurately, it must be said) can reveal an embodied, performative approach to the technological component of these vocal-deformations.

Korg's Kaoss Pad was developed in 1999 primarily as an interactive substitute for computer-based sampling methods, one which could easily be used live in improvisatory settings. Its touch-screen manipulates the playback of a sample, either captured live or loaded onto the unit ahead of time. This interface allows for a more performative approach to sampling. Because most live performances focus on "accurately" reproducing the recorded album, this practice is often left out of the concert setting, and a pre-recorded backing track is used instead. A notable exception to this practice could be seen on Björk's 2007 *Medulla* tour. With a ten-piece brass band as the only acoustic instruments on stage, her unusual set design highlighted the use of the Kaoss Pad, as well as a similar product, the ReacTable,[32] by placing a video camera above the surface of the unit, foregrounding the "performance" of the unit by tour musician Damian Taylor. Put differently, the Kaoss Pad provides epiphenomenal interpretations of timbre.

Jonny Greenwood uses the Kaoss Pad extensively. Many Radiohead fans had an intimate glimpse of this instrument in a live performance of "Everything in its Right Place," filmed by MTV2 in Paris on the 2001 tour.[33] From 0:26–0:42, Greenwood, kneeling on the ground with the Kaoss Pad in his lap, can be seen using the interface's sampling capabilities to capture Yorke's opening F4–C4–F4 motive "eve-ry-thing" as it is sung in real-time. Immediately afterward he begins to play back the motive, but by dragging his right index finger along the y-axis to toggle the playback position. Analogous to the manner in which you might speed up, slow down, or reverse a reel-to-reel tape, Greenwood deforms the timbre of Yorke's original utterance by making audible its reverse playback, resulting in the characteristic "whooshing" timbre experienced when we hear a record backwards. This demonstrates the role of spectromorphology in the analysis of timbre. Despite the fact that Greenwood is limited to the pitch spectrum present in Yorke's original utterance, the timbre itself is powerfully transformed by altering only the attack. Once again, transients prove vital to source-recognition: "playing a piano tone backwards gives a non-piano-like quality, although the original and the reversed sound have the same spectra."[34]

This process of sampling and playing back with altered attacks continues throughout the performance. As if the song's ¾ groove were not interesting enough, Greenwood's metrical re-placement of Yorke's motives adds rhythmic interest to the piece as well, allowing us to hear many of the motive's possible mod-10 beat-class transformations. Manipulating the order of attack points also carries a lexical component that bears directly on musical meaning. At 2:58 Greenwood loops a rhythmically altered version of the sample. Starting on Yorke's "m" consonant ("my head"), he then immediately scrubs backward to "-s in" ("colors in"). The perceptual result is that of Greenwood puppeting Yorke to say "mis-sin'" on Eb4–C4. What might Yorke be "missin'" in this moment? An individual's answer to this question, posed by Greenwood via Yorke via the Kaoss Pad, will vary based on that listener's understanding of the song's original lyrical meaning. Greenwood's lyrical/melodic alchemy may simply add a note of lack and absence to the overall theme of confusion ("I see two colors in my head") present here and throughout the song ("what was that you tried to say?").

Vocal-deformations can stem from modified attack and backwards playback, but also from direct manipulation of upper frequency content itself. Easily done in Pro Tools, in the Paris video Greenwood manipulates the pitch of Yorke's voice using an earlier version of the Digitech Whammy (1st generation) used later for portamento guitar effects in "15 Step" (2007–1, 1:44) and "Feral" (2011–4). Indeed, the pedal was a staple in his guitar effects setup throughout the *OK Computer* tour. At 1:21, Greenwood samples the F4 from Yorke's last syllable of "le-mon" and, using the Whammy, pitch shifts the source up a full octave to F5. Rather than hear this as a second vocal track up an octave (impossibly high for Yorke's chest register),[35] it deforms the F4s Yorke continues to sing live until 1:37 by adding supernatural amplitude to the first overtone: F5. Perceiving this F5 as an overtone while the camera zooms in on Yorke's slightly grinning face singing the F4 at 1:31 lends a dose of the uncanny. Our visual systems perceive a source which should make a certain sound, while our auditory systems perceive one which could not possibly be made by the visual source. Meanings abound in this visual–auditory source-deformation, perhaps stemming from the observation that Yorke's voice is definitely *not* "in its right place."

Two tracks from *Amnesiac* (2001) reveal a vocal-deformation technique largely dependent on studio production. "Packt" (2001–1) and "Pulk/Pull" (2001–3) both rely on a peculiar adaptation of the industry-standard pitch corrector Antares Auto-Tune.[36] The fact that both tracks not only disfigure Yorke's voice, but also showcase a deformed (perhaps malfunctioning?) version of the pitch correction technology itself, is reflected in the mutilated spellings in both tracks' titles.[37] As Yorke himself notes about the vocal-deformations made possible by the pitch corrector,

> There's also this trick you can do, which we did on both "Packt" and "Pulk/ Pull Revolving Doors," where you give the machine [the pitch corrector] a key and then you just talk into it. It desperately tries to search for the music in your speech, and produces notes at random. If you've assigned it a key, you've got music.[38]

The "music" created by the pitch corrector Yorke speaks of here is largely tongue-in-cheek. However, the pitches created by this unique use of the pitch corrector do not seem incidental to the rest of the track. Prior to Yorke's entrance at 0:16 in "Pulk/ Pull," the synthesized introduction consists of a single C5–G4 melodic motive, which is combined with a second C5–D5 neighbor beginning at 0:45. A rare respite from the incessant percussive thumping at 1:13 highlights the confluence of these two motives as they blend into one [027] trichord—CDG. Perceiving this pitch nexus centered on C (the G as a lower arpeggiation, the D as an upper neighbor) then prompts a reexamination of the ambient noise heard since the track's opening, in which we can now hardly help but hear a strong C4 as the dominant frequency.[39]

Yorke's opening statement begins with two low, un-pitched spoken syllables ("there are") followed by two spoken syllables ("barn doors") to which the pitch-corrected frequencies C4–D4 are applied. Perceiving this organic link between the sparse pitch content of the synthesized timbres and the pitch content generated by the pitch-corrected timbres prompts the question, When Yorke spoke of setting the pitch corrector "to a key," did he literally mean a diatonic, equal-tempered key such as C major?[40] The number of diatonic collections which contain the pitch-classes C, D, and G (five) makes this question difficult to answer, and so the more likely scenario is that a listener will bond primarily with these three reference pitch-classes themselves. In fact, the most salient of Yorke's corrected pitches appear to text-paint the different types of doors heard throughout the track, especially C4–D4 on "barn doors," and the D4 on all syllables of "sliding doors."

Each statement in "Pulk/Pull" continues this process of dividing stanzas into unpitched original speech timbres and artificially pitched timbres. Additional effects occasionally further reinforce the text-painting of door types already suggested through pitch selection. Most notably, a voluminous amount of hall reverb is added when Yorke speaks "trap doors" near the track's end. The added reverb specifies a once-closed space that has now opened out into a much more cavernous one. This implies the rather obvious interpretation that Yorke himself has fallen through these trap doors. His following statement "that you can't come back from" text-paints this interpretation through a rapid drop in pitch, which directly specifies a source rapidly moving away from the perceiver in a phenomenon known as the Doppler effect. Indeed, Yorke does not come back from this fall through the trap doors—this is his final statement in the track.

The pitches shared between the pitch corrector and the rest of the track are important because they support meanings that shift the corrected timbre from seemingly random to perhaps intentional. When we think of effects regularly used to alter guitar timbres, for example the stompboxes discussed earlier, we do not typically interpret them as a disruptive force, but rather as an effect tastefully added by the performer or producer. Yorke's interview highlights the "random," almost malevolent force of the machine, a theme which resonates precisely with the anti-technological sentiments heard on *Amnesiac* (2001) and *Kid A* (2000). Yorke found that this deformation of his voice made it possible to articulate the darker lyrical themes heard on these two albums. He notes "[t]he lyrics are absolutely brutal and horrible and I wouldn't be able to sing them straight," but the license granted by pitch corrector and other vocal-deformation technologies were "great, it felt like you're not answering to this thing."[41] The particular use of the pitch corrector in "Packt" was not to "correct" any sort of mistakes, but rather to give it a dehumanized, nasal quality, which further divorces Yorke personally from that sound as its source and, more importantly from the standpoint of the listener, cloaks that material source in a shroud of a misappropriated technology.

But perceiving the organic links between this machine and other machines heard in the track shifts this meaning away from chaos toward order, closer to a carefully orchestrated technological tapestry than an indeterminate Fluxus work. As bassist Colin Greenwood has noted, the track was produced using a Roland MC505 workstation, a sampler made available in 1998 just in time for the *Kid A* recording sessions. The MC505 provides two timbres crucial to "Pulk/Pull." First, it contains a generator for highly compressed, dance-like percussion timbres heard in the opening seconds. Second, it enables users to process and recall previously recorded sounds, such as those the band sampled in St. Catharine's Court during the preproduction for *OK Computer* (1997). These two crucial sounds that form the backdrop of the track suggest at once two separate environments: a *virtual* environment created by the onboard percussion sounds factory-loaded onto the MC505 by the Roland corporation; and a *natural* environment recorded through interaction with an ecosystem in Cambridge in the late 1990s.

Tracks such as "Pulk/Pull" and "Packt," which employ timbres both derived from the natural environment (crowd noises, human voice) and from virtual/technological environments (samplers, pitch corrector) occur throughout Radiohead's catalog, but are especially prominent on the two electro-acoustic albums *Kid A* (2000) and *Amnesiac* (2001). These songs support a plethora of meanings based on an individual listener's knowledge of source materials and prior experiences with those materials, especially the human voice and the technologies by which it is deformed.

Synthesis (Third-order and Remote Surrogacy)

Many of Radiohead's novel timbres result not from deforming recognizable sources, but from synthesizing those sources using a variety of electro-acoustic methods. Synthesis comes in two varieties. Recognizing these distinct kinds of synthesis is not necessarily important as a taxonomic activity, but from the standpoint of the listener, the different types of synthesis are largely responsible for different types of source-bonding activities and therefore meaning.

Denis Smalley introduced the term "surrogacy" to address the ecological process of bonding with sources for which there is no traditional material source. Despite the lack of this material source, the process of source-bonding remains much the same:

When we recognise that a sound has been created by human gesture we can identify in detail the type of physical energy and touch that instigated and propagated the sound . . . even when the sound (either the source, or aspects of the cause) is not "real" or does not seem entirely plausible.[42]

Though Smalley offers three types of surrogate sources—second-order, third-order, and remote—only the latter two should be considered perceptually salient. This is because second-order surrogacy is largely the result of trying to mimic acoustic sounds as closely as possible, so closely that a listener will likely not give them a second thought. This was largely the aim of early synthesizers in the 1980s, including the industry-changing Yamaha DX7. Even before the synthesizer proper, 1970s rock artists including Led Zeppelin and others were using the Mellotron to trigger orchestral sounds. Activating short loops of tape onto which live sounds have been previously recorded, the Mellotron even allows for transposition through its built-in keyboard.

Radiohead uses second-order surrogacy in only a handful of songs. The Mellotron itself is responsible for the surrogate-choir in "Exit Music" (1997–4, 1:26). We might also include bass and drum sounds synthesized to sound acoustic in this category. At the same time, bass and drum sounds that in no way attempt to mimic their acoustic counterpoints have been so commonplace in electronic dance music since the 1980s that they offer few surprises. The same goes for synthesized "lead" patches, such as that created by the Novation Bass Station in "Myxomatosis" (2003–12, 0:01), which now specify a rather generic "synth" source through their association with keyboard-driven EDM. These second-level surrogacies and conventional synthesis techniques should not concern us from the viewpoint of ecological perception, since they inhabit a perceptual world that lacks speculation:

> Surrogacy proper, as the temporary inference of a sound's cause, starts at the third order and continues into remote surrogacy. The use of the term "surrogacy" for the first two categories maintains the speculative action of the perceiver in decoding the specific sound source, although when dealing with familiar sources, such as violins, cellos or other familiar instruments, the attribution of a source may seem so natural as not to feel speculative.[43]

This is easy to recast in terms of salience: when material sources, whether acoustic or surrogate, are too easy to identify, they leave little need for contemplation of meaning on the part of the listener. On the other hand, as simulacra for sources that are not immediately recognizable, third-order and remote surrogates are perceptually marked. Third-level surrogacy arises when "[t]he nature of the spectromorphology makes us unsure about the reality of either the source or the cause, or both."[44] The "causes" of sounds in Radiohead's music are always human gestures. Listeners respond to gestures which are perceived to activate the source in question, even when that source is a synthetic surrogate for some supposed material. Drum machines provide an instructive example. The attack and decay envelopes heard in the synthetic kick and snare sounds of "Idioteque" (2000–8, 0:01) are invariant properties we experience in the world when a taut surface is struck by a hard object. Mirror neurons lead us to respond to such sounds through embodied cognition *as if someone were actually striking a physical source.* Gesture and source are intimately intertwined in third-order surrogacy.

Third-level surrogates include all synthesized sources in Radiohead's music that suggest some level of human action in their creation. Rather than actual genesis of the sound, this is a matter of what the sound implies. This includes all drum-like, voice-like, and other traditional instrument-like sounds not better described as second-level mimicry, but does not include sources for which the only human gesture is pressing a button on a computer, sampler, or the like (setting aside for now the simple observation that any human-cued electronic sound requires at least one bodily motion to cue it, be it a digit or voice command). If a listener can imagine a human gesture activating a synthetic source, it is said to be synthesis of the third order.

Most examples of third-order surrogacy in Radiohead's music result from the synthesis of bass-like or drum-like sounds. "Pulk/Pull . . ." (2001–3, 0:12) is an example of a drum-like percussion timbre produced by a drum machine—a stand-alone unit in which all necessary wiring and signal processing is housed inside a durable case. The timbres heard on "Pulk/Pull" are therefore properties of the signal path inherent to the Roland MC505 (a hybrid sampler/drum machine), while those heard on "Everything in its Right Place" (2000–1, 0:11) and the first half of "2+2=5" (2003–1, 0:14) are properties of the classic Roland TR909, the 1990s-era replacement to what had been the industry-standard drum machine for all genres of EDM for more than a decade, the iconic TR808.

Since 2000, an increasing amount of Radiohead's third-order percussion surrogacy has come not from these self-contained units, but from more complex instruments including Jonny Greenwood's ever-growing modular synth array or the synthesis capabilities of the MAX/MSP software. An early example of the former is the percussion timbre heard throughout "Idioteque" (2000–8). One of the few Radiohead tracks that began as a Jonny Greenwood demo (most are created by Yorke), the track owes almost its entire timbral identity to FM-synthesized percussion and a sample from Paul Lansky's *Mild Und Leise* (1976–B3), both of which are almost always present in the track. Acoustic vocals by Yorke and O'Brien, and a brief sample from Kreiger's electro-acoustic work *Short Piece* (1976–B2, 1:08; heard at 0:10 in "Idioteque"), are the only other timbres encountered in the track.

The percussion timbre of "Idioteque" does not constitute second-order synthesis because it does not specify an acoustic drum kit. It is also not a remote surrogate because it *does* specify the manner in which a drum set is played, and thus presents a mimesis of drum-set performance practice. Illuminating the types of cognition third-order surrogates afford is just as important as understanding the technology behind them since "the basic sounds have spectromorphologies that either are, or are mimetic of, particular types of object being acted upon in a particular manner."[45]

Percussion synthesis technology is by no means limited to those patterns which are playable by a single human percussionist. It is therefore notable from a perspective of third-order surrogacy, which specifies some sort of human action despite the timbral divorce from any real material source, that the "Idioteque" pattern specifies a three-limb pattern quite common to human drum-set performance. The snare-like sound plays accented backbeats, which are framed by syncopated kick-drum surrogates. Whereas the closed hi-hat-like source could, for example, play running sixteenth notes over this, doing so would not be mimetic of human-performed percussion because the two hands needed to produce this pattern would then not allow for one hand to play the backbeat-accented snare. But what we hear in this highly mimetic pattern is the hi-hat playing on off-beats only, which would leave a performer's other hand free to play the snare on alternating downbeats—a two-hand pattern particularly common in disco and disco-inspired dance music that lends embodied meaning to the play on "discothèque" in the song's title.

Third-order percussion surrogacy created by Jonny Greenwood's modular synth can also be heard in the frenetic climax to "Sit Down, Stand Up" (2003–2, 3:03). Around this time Greenwood was also experimenting with synthesizing similar beats on the computer using MAX/MSP, a software program popular among electro-acoustic composers. "15 Step" (2007–1, 0:01) presents an interesting case of a MAX/MSP beat that specifies drum set performance, but which would not be performable by a single human. Just as in "Idioteque," the timbral envelopes and rhythmic placement of two percussion timbres, one kick-like and one snare-like, bear comparison to their acoustic counterparts and the manner in which those instruments would be performed by a human. But unlike "Idioteque," the would-be hi-hat pattern in "15 Step" is replaced by an ambient, staticky timbre that is neither acoustically similar to a hi-hat nor rhythmically regular enough to specify any manner in which it is regularly played. Even if we were to assume for a moment that this high-frequency percussive timbre in the right channel represents a hi-hat, what would we make of the syncopated second-order handclap surrogate heard closer to the center? Hi-hat panned right and handclaps in the center present a simulacrum of watching a drummer perform on stage, but are the handclaps coming from a second performer, or have we surpassed the realm of human performance altogether? "15 Step" thus makes exquisite use of the technology made available by the MAX/MSP program in that it juxtaposes third-order synthetic timbres with those that mimic neither the timbral nor performative properties of the drum set. One example that perhaps pushes both timbre and mimetic potential too far for any third-order interpretation can be heard in the percussion layers of "The Gloaming" (2003–8)—a track rife with many distinct types of electronic mediation. Timbrally speaking, the dull attack, gargantuan reverb, and remarkably definite pitch that surround the low-frequency sound that enters at 0:11 specify not kick drum, not bass guitar, but some sort of kick–bass hydra that combines the pitch capabilities of the percussion instrument (single, invariable) with the softer attack and reverb of the string instrument. The highly syncopated mid-range frequency comes close to specifying snare drum, but its white noise generator (similar to those used for percussion on early 8-bit Nintendo games) lacks a snare's sharp attack. By contrast, the hi-hat surrogate that enters at 0:30 is so reminiscent of those heard on drum machines such as the 808 and 909 that it presents no barrier to timbral surrogacy.

Supposing these three sources are performed with three limbs, we are presented with yet another embodiment problem. With a repeating period that contains no lowest common denominator—no pulse speed that encompasses the attacks of the three instruments—we are dealing with a polytempo of sufficient complexity that you would rarely, if ever, hear it at the drum set. All three layers recycle within the same measure-length period. The hi-hat establishes a precise sixteenth-based division, the kick drum gesture at the end of the bar is *between* an eighth-based division (the last note 0.5 of a beat) and a triplet division (the last note 0.66 of a beat) relative to that hi-hat, and the would-be-snare's accents, though programmed and thus mechanically reproduced exactly each measure, align comfortably within the meters established by neither. The resulting timbres and rhythms are commensurate with very few of the invariant properties of either drum-set timbre or drum-set performance practice.

"Lotus Flower" (2011–5), on the other hand, showcases a fundamental bass layer that listeners might assume was performed by Colin Greenwood on the electric bass. But this part was performed not with the left hand sliding up and down a wooden fretboard on steel strings struck by the right hand, but by fingers on the keyboard of a MiniMoog Model D synthesizer. Its third-order surrogacy stems from its frequency envelope but not its manner of articulation. As a monophonic synthesizer, the MiniMoog is only capable of producing one pitch at a time. This is, in reality, not an invariant property of the bass guitar. If a bassist plays all pitches on the same string, that line will necessarily be monophonic, but, leaving aside the obvious polyphonic *capabilities* of the electric bass (it can play chords), when playing a supposedly monophonic groove that spans multiple strings there is never a perfect on/off between the release of the first string and the attack of the second. So much vibrational energy is activated by the instrument's large steel strings that its cessation requires the active gesture of releasing the finger from a fret, which is necessary when traversing frets on the same string but not when playing frets on different strings.

Our attention is first called to this gestural discrepancy several bars into the groove. The groove itself hovers around D1 which, on a bass guitar, would be played either on the fifth fret of the third string or the open second string. Following a complete lower neighbor to C1 and back starting at 0:26, the line jumps up to B1 before arpeggiating a diminished triad through F1 back down to D1. Fretted in any reasonable manner, this gesture traverses at least two strings, but the B1 is much closer to reach on the first string. The neighbor articulation from C1 to D1 is too perfect to involve a vibrating open D string, so the move to B1 specifies one of two gestures that should involve some degree of performer imperfection: (1) a shared fretboard position traversing two strings [ring finger on fifth-fret D1 to middle finger on fourth-fret B1] resulting in the D1 ringing through the articulation of B1; or (2) a quick enough change of position [ring finger on fifth-fret D1 to any finger on ninth-fret B1] necessitating some negligible degree of glissandi to avoid silence between the articulations. We hear no such imperfections in the bass-like timbre heard throughout "Lotus Flower," resulting in a third-order synthesis that presents a surrogate for the frequency content of the electric bass guitar, but not its manner of articulation.

A third-order bass surrogate even further removed from the invariants of the electric bass guitar can be heard throughout "All I Need" (2007–5). Its frequency envelope is much more complex than a bass guitar, and even more complex than the synth-bass heard in "Lotus Flower" (2011–5). This is largely due to the physical differences between the monophonic, single-generator MiniMoog and the five-voice polyphonic, two-oscillator Sequential Circuits Prophet-5 on which "All I Need" was recorded. Analog synthesizers generate a sound wave (e.g., sine, square, sawtooth, or triangle) which can then be filtered using various knobs. The Prophet-5 was one of the first analog synthesizers to offer ring-modulation, a process in which the spectral envelopes from two different simultaneous waves are combined such that their summation and difference tones are made audible. The resulting timbres often contain rich, metallic, inharmonic spectra.

Playing the bass line from "All I Need" on an analog synth with a single square-wave oscillator gets close to reproducing the timbre of the *fundamental*, but the metallic overtones heard in the recording, rich in inharmonic partials of combined fundamentals, specify ring modulation, an invariant property of the Prophet-5 not possible on the electric bass guitar. Even the pitch content of the line, which centers around a prominent C0, transcends the limit of a four-string bass guitar in standard tuning. Though the C0 could specify a five-string bass, the sharp attack heard here is virtually impossible to achieve on a string of that diameter. Despite these differences in fundamental pitch and overtone spectrum, "All I Need" represents a third-order surrogate that nonetheless provides a listener the kinesthetic and tactile associations with a familiar rock instrument.

Another kind of synthesis regularly encountered in Radiohead's music, remote surrogacy, differs primarily from third-order surrogacy in that the timbres perceived specify little to no human action. Remote surrogacy involves the synthesis of disembodied timbre. Instead of stemming from circuit boards encased in metal housing, as most drum-like and bass-like third order surrogate timbres, remote timbres in Radiohead's music are sometimes synthesized directly in MAX/MSP. However, the predominant source of Radiohead's remote surrogacy comes from a physical instrument that even includes a keyboard: the ondes Martenot. So prevalent is Jonny Greenwood's playing of this instrument on all records since *Kid A* (2000) that it has quickly become one of the band's signature sounds.

Kid A was the first album on which the ondes Martenot appeared. In concert with the vocal-deformation and lack of guitars heard in the album's first two tracks, this strange synthetic source heard throughout the third track, "The National Anthem" (2000–3), plays a pivotal role in their new post-millennial identity. The timbre is prominent in the mix from 0:23–1:35, an extended solo introductory passage in which Greenwood seems to improvise around the memorable A_4–$F^\sharp_4$–$B\flat_4$–G_4 motive that arrives after the song's first verse (1:57).[46] Source-bonding with this timbre must have been an alienating experience for the vast majority of Radiohead fans, heretofore conditioned to expect not remote or even third-order synthesis, but really only source-deformation before 2000. Although this timbre bears a number of invariant signatures of the ondes Martenot, the timbre had appeared on no previous Radiohead album (nor any popular music album I know of). Keeping in mind that ecological perception is mutual, relying on previous exposure to timbres, the perceptual result is a remote surrogate—a synthetic source for which no known human performance gesture exists.

Centering ourselves in this pivotal moment helps to appreciate the impact of Radiohead's *Saturday Night Live* performance on October 14, 2000, just twelve days after *Kid A*'s release date. For many Radiohead fans who bought the album the day it came out, they would have had twelve days to ponder this remote-surrogate timbre before matching it with this visual stimulus in Jonny Greenwood's SNL rig. Only then could the invariant features of the ondes Martenot's construction become linked to the recorded timbre. For a right-handed guitarist like Jonny Greenwood, performing the ondes Martenot involves an inversion in the division of manual labor between frequency and amplitude. Pitch is now controlled by the right hand through one of two methods: either by traditional keyboard (method *au clavier*) or by sliding a ring worn on his finger (method *au ruban*). An amplitude-controlling interface (*touche d'intensité*) situated in a recessed drawer is operated by the left hand. The ondes Martenot is capable of producing not only different combinations of amplitude and frequency, but also distinct wave shapes. It does this in much the same manner as an analog synthesizer. The seven wave generators onboard a standard ondes Martenot are provided in Table 4.3.[47] Each of the seven wave generators and each of the four speakers is controlled by a separate on/off switch, which means multiple timbres can be blended simultaneously. Combining and blending these seven generators with the four possible loudspeakers produces a remarkable number of timbres of which the instrument is capable, even under the same frequency and amplitude. Taking into account the two different methods of attack and the *touche d'intensité*, the instrument allows for nearly infinite variation in attack shape in the hands of a skilled performer.

Jonny Greenwood became interested in the ondes Martenot after hearing it in Olivier Messiaen's *Turangalîla-Symphonie* (1948). However, the instrument's capacity for extensive timbral manipulation reflects a philosophy of timbre more readily associated with a composer to whom Greenwood has reported an even more direct influence, the Polish avant-garde-turned-neo-classicist Krzysztof Penderecki. Penderecki went about selecting timbres in a remarkably systematic way. Unlike

TABLE 4.3

Timbral combinations of the ondes Martenot

Wave Generator (in order of sinusoidal purity)	Speaker (in order of signal purity)	Frequency Specification (in order of equal temperament preservation)
Ondes (cf. sine)	principal	*au clavier* (keyboard)
Octaviant (cf. sine)	*résonance* (principal with added spring reverb)	*au ruban* (sliding ring)
Creux (cf. triangle)	*métallique* (traditional speaker cone replaced with metallic gong)	
Petit Gambe (cf. square)	*palme* (principal with added sympathetic strings)	
Gambe (cf. square)		
Nasillard (cf. square)		
Souffle (cf. pink noise)		

Messiaen, he did not use the ondes Martenot, but his timbral method aptly describes the invariant properties of the instrument's seven distinct generators:

> ... every instrument becomes the basis for several different sound generators, which, in addition, may represent different classes ... in contradistinction to traditional orchestration, in which every instrument is ascribed a certain timbral quality, here one and the same instrument can be used in a number of different ways and operate with several different classes of sound generators.[48]

This inherent timbral flexibility—an invariant property of the instrument's seven combinable sound generators—imbues the ondes with a chameleon-like ability to provide different timbres in each of the tracks listed in Table 4.4.

It is this inherent malleability which preserves the remote surrogacy of the instrument, virtually unidentifiable in frequency envelope alone. Unlike bass-like, percussion-like, or even club-like lead timbres performed at the keyboard, those timbres produced by the ondes Martenot bring to mind no human gesture other than for those who have seen the instrument performed. For those who have seen it performed, source-bonding with the instrument in recorded music is not a function of its frequency envelope, but rather the invariant construction of its performance interface—most notably the unique amplitude controller and dual methods of attack.

Remote surrogacy stemming from synthesis in MAX/MSP, on the other hand, has no identifiable gestural components even if you were to see the instrument "performed" (which would consist merely of pressing a button on the computer or MIDI controller). This class of timbres in Radiohead's music is the furthest removed from musical gesture, and therefore the furthest along a continuum that stretches from conventional performance of traditional instruments to timbres for which there is no imaginable material source. For *The King of Limbs* (2011), producer Nigel Godrich abandoned his Pro Tools interface entirely and MAX/MSP was used as a Digital Audio Workstation to record the entire album.

With MAX/MSP now seamlessly integrated, acting not only as the source but also the medium on which to capture that source, remote surrogacy abounds on *The King of Limbs*. The beginnings of this trend, however, trace all the way back to "The Gloaming" (2003–8).[49] Prior to the entrance of the third-order percussion surrogate in "The Gloaming" (itself a product of granular synthesis in MAX/MSP), the opening seconds are composed entirely of a remote-synthetic timbre for which there is no conceivable source. Elsewhere on *Hail to the Thief* (2003), MAX/MSP appears more foregrounded, divorced from otherwise rock-dominated ecosystems. "Backdrifts"

TABLE 4.4

Selected ondes Martenot passages in Radiohead

Song	Description
"The National Anthem" (2000–3, throughout)	mostly Ondes au ruban; multiple tracks throughout stereo field, panned hard left for solo from 1:57–2:17
"How to Disappear Completely" (2000–4, throughout)	all string parts doubled Nasillard au ruban
"Optimistic" (2000–6, 1:31–2:56)	Creux au clavier panned hard left; doubling guitar
"Optimistic" (2000–6, 3:56–4:46)	Creux au clavier doubling voice;
"Optimistic" (2000–6, 4:48–4:54)	petit Gambe au ruban glissando
"I Might Be Wrong" (2001–5, 0:01–0:35)	two tracks (Gambe au clavier, Octaviant au ruban)
"I Might Be Wrong" (2001–5, 3:10–3:44)	Gambe au clavier
"Pyramid Song" (2001–2, 2:24–3:29 and 4:10–end)	petit Gambe au ruban panned left
"You and Whose Army?" (2001–4, 2:17–2:47)	high, blends with lead and high harmony vocals
"2+2=5" (2003–1, 2:38–end)	Gambe au ruban panned hard right
"Where I End and You Begin" (2003–6, throughout except tacet 2:10–2:21)	multiple tracks, mostly au ruban, uncharacteristically low in right channel
"Scatterbrain" (2003–13, 1:46–2:14)	Ondes au clavier panned left
"Jigsaw Falling Into Place" (2007–8, 2:07–2:53)	Ondes au ruban panned right doubling backing voice

(2003–4, 1:54), for example, applies the software to a guitar sample in order to text-paint the second verse. Coinciding with the lyrics "all evidence has been buried / all tapes have been erased," the far left channel features a remote surrogate timbre which has been altered to erase any discernible trace of its material source. We can discern that it is a short sample of something (an invariant property of its quickly repeating period) and that it is has been reversed (specified through the "whooshing" effect of hearing the decay in crescendo), but MAX/MSP has rendered the original material nearly irrelevant, effectively erasing the possibility of source-bonding with the original material.

Plotting Radiohead's synthetic timbres on a continuum from second-level to remote surrogacy demonstrates yet another instantiation of salience. Timbres too quickly identifiable will be understimulating to the listener, while those that lack any sort of gestural component (whether they are surrogate sources or not) will be potentially alienating from the standpoint of embodied cognition. We might reimagine this continuum in terms of a composer's achievement or failure in understanding how to exploit the electronic medium for ecological purposes:

> . . . an electro-acoustic music which is confined to the second order does not really explore the potential of the medium, while a music which does not take some account of the cultural imbedding of gesture [remote surrogacy] will appear to most listeners a very cold, difficult, even sterile music.[50]

Radiohead's recorded music, especially *Kid A* (2000) and *Amnesiac* (2001), should be regarded as an electro-acoustic music. Their timbres are so perceptually salient because they specify sources of indeterminate materiality but nevertheless afford mimetic and gestural meanings grounded in a listener's expectations inherited from rock music.

More so than any other parameter in this book, a chapter's worth of theory and analysis has seemingly only breached the threshold of interesting timbres in Radiohead's music. No longer mediated by the rubrics of equal-tempered pitch classes, measurable metric divisions, and relative ratios between formal units, each individual timbre is unique, and is perceived uniquely. Each timbre spins a web of multivalent meanings without recourse to a preconceived metric. Timbre as an analytical pursuit is thus a relentless pursuit of the descriptive, its elucidation qualitative rather than quantitative. It is toward such a sustained pursuit of only one song's timbres, sources, affordances, and spectromorphologies, that I now turn.

Analytical Coda: "Like Spinning Plates"

The radical expression of timbre heard throughout *Kid A* (2000) and *Amnesiac* (2001) represents a distinct shift in Radiohead's idiolect. After this stark juxtaposition of timbres between 1990s guitar-rock and post-millennial electro-acoustic indulgence, the band begins to integrate the two rather seamlessly. It is within this understanding of Radiohead's timbral evolution that we can best appreciate the final two tracks on *Amnesiac*, as one final unrestrained experimental bombast before dialing in a synthesized electro-acoustic–rock hybrid that defines them from *Hail to the Thief* (2003) onward. "Life in a Glasshouse" (2001–11) is unique among

Radiohead songs in that its primary timbral identity arises not so much from specification or affordance, but from signification, namely of the New Orleans street band genre. Quite the opposite situation is present in "Like Spinning Plates" (2001–10), a track which crafts a timbral ecosystem so utterly individual that it must be understood through a process of immersion within that ecosystem itself. Our first step toward understanding timbre in this track is to understand the song's rather bewildering genesis.

In the *Kid A* (2000) sessions, the band was working out an early version of "I Will" (2003–10). Ed O'Brien's recording diary reveals that it must have sounded quite different than the final *Hail to the Thief* (2003) version. This late 1999/early 2000 demo features the same three-chord harmonic progression and melody as the 2003 version, but the accompaniment is radically different, featuring string/organ pads instead of clean electric guitar and, most notably, a sixteenth-based arpeggiated figure programmed by O'Brien on the Novation Bass Station. Yorke was deeply unhappy with this electronic arrangement, calling it "dodgy Kraftwerk."[51]

At some point the band played around with reversing this ill-fated demo tape and apparently liked it so much—particularly the percussive effects of the reversed sixteenth-loop—that it served as the accompaniment for a new track: "Like Spinning Plates" (2001–10, hereafter "LSP"). Yorke's lyrics for this "new" piece are also composed of recycled old material. The chorus's second line, "cloud cookoo land," for example, shows up in a 1998 post to the band's website ("amateur poetry for yu / cloud fucking cookoo land"), and was even printed in the penultimate page of *Kid A*'s "secret" booklet in 2000 (hidden behind the CD basket in the jewel case).[52]

During the time that Yorke was tracking the vocals for LSP, Colin Greenwood heard a BBC4 radio program about a British composer who had been experimenting with backwards singing. Greenwood does not recall the composer's name,[53] but it was almost certainly Jocelyn Pook, who in 2001 released the album *Untold Things* that featured created languages and backwards singing. Inspired by this—and surely by the fact that they had just reversed what would become the backing track—it came to pass that Yorke would memorize the reversed sound of his newly assembled lyrics for "LSP," sing them phonetically backwards, and then producer Nigel Godrich would reverse *that* track, resulting in a unique vocal-deformation: a doubly reversed simulacrum of forward-spoken English.

This history reveals that "LSP" owes its existence to technologically recorded memories later accessed by humans in the act of creation: a dodgy demo caught on tape is reversed and recycled; lyrics captured indelibly on the Internet resurface in a new song; a vocal take captured in the studio, reversed by a computer, and burned onto a CD is rehearsed phonetically. All of these are examples of something known as *voluntary memory*, the process of intentional recall, polar opposite to Proust's notion of involuntary recall commonly associated with taste and smell. Recent neurobiological research shows that this process of voluntary recall inevitably results in destruction and degradation of the memory itself.[54] Accessing our memories is not like recalling an indelible file on a computer, but more like roughing in a sketch of a lived situation. Each time we redraw our memories, we create newer, more distorted versions of the events. Worse still, the more we remember something, the less true to the actual event that memory becomes. Paradoxically, the memories most preserved, truest to the lived events are those locked away within the memory of the amnesiac, borne to an organism perfectly adept at recording the moment yet entirely unable to access it from memory.

Hearing *Amnesiac* (2001) as an album-long process of Radiohead remembering ideas from the era leading up to *Kid A* (2000), only to distort those ideas in the creative process of voluntary memory, allows for a historically situated understanding of the album as a whole. Applied to "LSP," this perceptual strategy helps us understand how lyrical and timbral memories resurface in this track. Three sources arouse the highest levels of timbral surprise: the vocal-deformation of Yorke's anti-war lyrics; the third-order synthesis that was O'Brien's original synth loop from the "I Will" demo; and the corrugaphone present throughout the track.

Yorke's vocal-deformation technique heard in "LSP" is one that many listeners will recognize instantly from the infamously creepy "Dwarf Scene" from the third episode of David Lynch's series *Twin Peaks*. Both involve the actor/singer spending considerable time memorizing their own recorded speech in reverse. Even if Yorke were able to memorize the pitch of his own backward speech perfectly and recall it perfectly into a microphone, the vocal-deformation effect would still occur for the same reason that a reversed piano timbre sounds different than its original. Spectromorphologically, the attack and release of a timbre cannot be reversed without the perception of timbre being altered, despite the fact that the frequency spectrum of both is the same. But Yorke of course has neither perfect memory nor perfect recall. The vocal-deformation we perceive in the track makes audible the imperfection of memory itself—to recall a memory is to deform it.

But how does this vocal-deformation also deform the meaning of the lyrics? Three avenues into this inquiry seem most fruitful. First, two lines of Yorke's concise eight-line composition appear in his post to radiohead.com in 2000, which also includes a sneak preview of what would become the second verse of "Punchup at a Wedding" (2003–11): "this just feels like spinning plates a temple of hypocrits opportunist. i am no magician. our bodies floating down the muddy river."[55] Second,

In a 2003 solo-piano performance of "LSP" filmed for *Musique Plus* in Montreal,[56] Yorke dedicates the song

> ... to our glorious leaders ... who saw fit to take us to a war that nobody wanted ... kill thousands, if not tens of thousands, of innocent people, and they shall go to the grave with that on their conscience, and I hope that's okay with them.

Third, is it merely a coincidence that the lyrics in "LSP," which not only stem from the same time period as the lyrics to "I Will" but are also sung over the reversed accompaniment to "I Will," deal with the same theme of American engagement in the Iraq war? Are these really two different songs? Explaining his lyrical inspiration for "I Will," Yorke notes,

> I had an extremely unhealthy obsession, that ran through the *Kid A* thing, about the first Gulf War. When they started it up they did that lovely thing of putting the camera on the end of the missile, and you got to see the wonders of modern military technology blow up this bunker. And then sometime afterwards in the back pages it was announced that that bunker was not full of weapons at all, but women and children.[57]

Juxtaposing the *Amnesiac* version's vocal-deformation (which affords <dream> through its association with Cooper's dream sequence in *Twin Peaks*) with the solo-piano version heard in the Montreal concert offers a window into the song's possible meaning. In Montreal Yorke not only sings the lyrics without effects, but also provides a spoken introduction that frames those lyrics within a US occupation of Iraq. The *Amnesiac* version's vocal-deformation provides Yorke a barrier between his corporeal voice and the uncomfortably dark themes in the lyrics—a coping mechanism he had previously adopted during the recording of *Kid A*. Yorke sang the original in the studio much as he did in the Montreal concert, but in the act of recalling it obsessively in order to memorize it backwards ("I spent the rest of the night trying to learn the melody")[58] the unpleasant memory was itself destroyed.

The primary percussive timbre heard in "LSP" specifies a source played backwards through its attack envelope, but the frequency spectrum—invariant despite the tape reverse—specifies no conventional rock source. Recreating O'Brien's "lost" synth loop from the "I Will" demo helps to shed light on the surrogate nature of this timbre. We know that it was created on a Novation Bass Station, but does that make it a keyboard or a third-order bass-surrogate (as in the Novation line in "Lotus Flower" (2011–5))? This question can be answered by paying particular attention to the gestures inherent in the line itself.

FIGURE 4.1 Re-construction of "I Will" synth loop, reversed in "Like Spinning Plates."

Given that we instantly perceive the "LSP" loop as reversed through its attack envelope, it seems reasonable that our search for meaning would thus be directed toward our perception of the original source. Revealing the original Novation loop is elementary with the software included on modern computers. Loading "LSP" in a program like Audacity and pressing [reverse] takes just a matter of seconds, after which we hear some semblance of the lost "I Will" demo. Ignoring the lead vocal and corrugaphone that were added to the studio version of "LSP" leaves us with something resembling my transcription of O'Brien's lost "I Will" loop in Figure 4.1.[59]

The importance of this notation concerns gesture. As much as source-bonding with timbral surrogates concerns frequency envelope, the process is just as much, if not more so, concerned with how intimations of human performance gesture are embedded within those timbres, and, from that, what sorts of imagined sources they may mimic. Figure 4.1 reveals that the source of the Novation loop cannot be a third-order bass surrogate because the performance gestures are in no way idiomatic to a picked or plucked electric bass guitar. What they instead suggest is *arpeggiation*, a gesture which in this range could afford <bowed cello> (c.f. the compound melody in Bach's cello suites), but more accurately and more immediately specifies <keyboard>.

The harmonies arpeggiated by this keyboard-surrogate are notable, although perhaps unsurprising given the genesis of the track. The harmonic rhythm and chord progression [C♯m–AMaj7–G♯] are exactly that of "I Will." In fact, the outer voices of the arpeggiation are exact reproductions of Yorke's electric guitar part in the recording of "I Will" (2003–10, 0:03–0:16).[60] Comparing this arpeggiation with Yorke's solo performance of "Spinning Plates" from the aforementioned Montreal concert reveals even more notable meanings prompted by this arpeggiation gesture.

"LSP" is usually performed live by Yorke at the piano, with or without the Greenwood brothers providing sparse electric bass and keyboard backing. But with no piano in the album version, what part does Yorke play live? Figure 4.2 is my transcription of the chorus from Yorke's solo Montreal performance. The relationships to both the O'Brien loop and the 2003 version of "I Will" are striking. First, note that the same arpeggiated gestures from O'Brien's "I Will" Novation loop are preserved in Yorke's piano part—further evidence that the gesture inherent in the former is indeed a keyboard-surrogate. Second, note that the chord progression (G♯–AMaj7–C♯m) is exactly the reverse of the "I Will" progression heard in both

FIGURE 4.2 "Like Spinning Plates," live solo-piano version, Montreal 2003 (2:08).

O'Brien's lost synth loop, and in Yorke's recorded electric guitar part.[61] Keeping in mind that both are two-part through-composed songs, not only does each section feature the retrograde of each other's chord progression, but in fact the forms themselves are reversed: the A–B form of "I Will" becomes the B–A form of "LSP."

The corrugaphone is the only timbre in the album version of "LSP" not heard in live performances or in recorded versions of "I Will." Jonny Greenwood's dense organ pads are heard in all three, and O'Brien's loop is replaced by Yorke's piano in the live version. Furthermore, the corrugaphone is the only timbre *not* subjected to tape reverse (ironic since it is the only one whose gently sloped attack transients would remain relatively unaffected by tape reverse). This suggests that its presence on the album was for a purpose—that merely reversing "I Will" resulted in a somehow incomplete accompaniment which the corrugaphone augments.

In highlighting the corrugaphone's role within the ecosystem of the recorded track, we might first start with pitch designations. The pitches D$\sharp$4–G$\sharp$4–B$\sharp$5 are the invariant properties of an instrument bound exclusively to the overtone series whose fundamental lies at G$\sharp$3.[62] Corrugaphones are used with some frequency in physics classrooms because they present a tactile and sensory link with the harmonic series. Pitch is an invariant property of the speed at which the instrument is swung, and so the ascending pitches heard throughout the recording mean the tube was swung faster. However, the fundamental and second overtone of the instrument are almost impossible to activate. These unspeakable pitches, the G$\sharp$3 fundamental and the G$\sharp$4 second partial, are notable because the pitch-class G$\sharp$ is the only common tone between all three chords in the chorus of "LSP." With a G$\sharp$ fundamental, that corrugaphone's third, fourth, and fifth partials (D♯, G♯, and B♯ respectively) perfectly arpeggiate the dominant half-cadence that accompanies the song's title in each line of the chorus.

Contrary to what meanings this corrugaphone source might afford for many—<toy, a.k.a. "whirly tube">, <found/spontaneous>—paying closer attention to the invariant properties of *this particular corrugaphone*, whose overtone spectrum is only possible by cutting a piece of pipe to the exact length necessary for a song in C♯ minor with leading tone, affords altogether different meanings including <exactitude>, <intention>, and <design>.[63]

Notes

1. See Moore (2012, 30).
2. See Smalley (1997, 110).
3. See Zagorski-Thomas (forthcoming).
4. Smalley (1997, 111).
5. See Molnar-Szakacs et. al (2006); quoted in Heidemann (2014, 20).
6. See Zagorski-Thomas (forthcoming).
7. See Clarke (2005, 189).
8. Smalley (1997, 110).
9. Ibid., 110.
10. Clarke's normative usage of [to afford] and [to specify] correspond with the *Oxford English Dictionary*'s entries II.3.b and 3.5, respectively.
11. Clarke (2005, 17), italics his.
12. This starts to break down once we consider computer software programs, such as those programmed to emulate rooms or add effects which would not be physically possible, such as Yorke's voice in "Exit Music (for a Film)" (1997–4).
13. Clarke is here not only concerned with timbre. Indeed, many of the specifications he notes in a large chart (2005, 60) are more properly the domain of melodic/harmonic instability, rather than timbre.
14. Tuzan (2009, 56).
15. Cox 2011 shows that motor neurons are active in listeners' brains whether or not they are physically moving.
16. See Clarke (2005, 81).
17. Such as that offered by Tatom Letts (2010).
18. See Kreiman et. al (2004).
19. Though it obviously exhibits differences in absolute frequency between its constituent drums (e.g., the snare is higher than the kick).
20. Moore (2012, 21) uses the term harmonic filler without citation, but it can be found within quotation marks in Clarke (2005, 82) in a discussion of Mozart's String Quartet K. 515, where it refers not to the cello (functional bass) or the first violin (primary melodic layer), but to the consort made of two violas and second violin. Names for the other three layers (functional bass, melodic, explicit beat) are used throughout Moore (2012).

21. See Helmholtz (1954).

22. See Slawson (1981, 132)

23. This is of course a flexible and imperfect guideline, by no means a definitive criterion. It also assumes that listeners have had enough "training" to know the basic instrumentation of the rock band and the range of sounds they usually make. In other words, they have not only heard the sound of a bass guitar, but know what a bass guitar looks like, sounds like by itself, and understand some basic techniques by which its sound may be colored by effects. Readers interested more in modern signal processing trends are encouraged to consult Hodgson 2010.

24. For an impressive study on the structural link between degrees of distortion and song forms enabled through distortion, see Scotto (2016).

25. More formally, any modification to t in the transfer function equation $y(t) = F(x(t))$—a representation of a noise-free system, known in stompbox lingo as "true bypass"—such that the signal at the input, $F(x(t))$, no longer equals the signal at the output, $y(t)$, results in source-deformation. See Scotto (2016).

26. See, for example, Berger 1964.

27. This is due to the fact that while a looping pedal actually *records* the input and then plays it back, delay pedals split the signal such that the original comes through immediately, and a copy of that original is run through multiple capacitors to "delay" the signal from sounding for a user-determined number of milliseconds (usually only up to 2,000). The AKAI Headrush is actually three separate pedals housed within a single unit. It contains a looper (tape recorder), tape delay, and digital delay.

28. Guitarists can also remove the transients by picking the string with the guitar's volume knob all the way down, then quickly roll the volume knob up while the string is still vibrating.

29. See Clarke (2005, 191)

30. Most of these are documented with photographic evidence from studio sessions by the "King of Gear" website: http://thekingofgear.com.

31. Discussing specifications in terms of software programming seems to be pressing Clarke's original conception a bit too far, since now the source has no physical attributes and thus no invariant properties. However, the coding inherent in such programming does have particular mathematical properties which produce particular sounds, and so could therefore be treated in much the same way if we are willing to consider the possibility of sound sources which are not visible. As primarily visual creatures, my suspicion is that our sense of perception is not as attuned to invisible sources such as computer programming.

32. Developed by the Music Technology Group at the Universitat Pompeu Fabra in Barcelona, this highly interactive table-top interface differs most notably from the Kaoss pad through its use of an upward-pointing video camera, as well as its substantially larger size.

33. At the time of this printing, the video could be accessed on YouTube at https://www.youtube.com/watch?v=hvMql9XgIgo.

34. See Risset and Wessel (1991). Radiohead's second single from *A Moon Shaped Pool*, "Daydreamers" (2016–2), takes this principle a step further. The same reverse playback techniques heard in "Everything in its Right Place" are used throughout the verses, with comparably minimal levels of source-deformation. In the outro, however, Yorke's voice is not only played backward, but with significantly altered speed and pitch, resulting in a much more extreme source-deformation.

35. In a 2003 performance at Glastonbury, Greenwood goes further by playing back fragments of the "tried to say" lyric with the fundamental itself altered to impossibly high frequencies, creating something more akin to the "Chipmunk" effect, which, in its lack of subtlety, is far less effective.

36. "Auto-Tune" is a trademarked name for the pitch-correction software created by the Antares company. After the millennium it becomes more accurate to speak of a generalized pitch-correction software due to the proliferation of this technology under various names.

37. "Packt" (2001–1) is undoubtedly more subtle in its use of this technique, largely because it is used to deform Yorke's *singing* voice, rather than to make his speaking voice *sing* in "Pulk/Pull" (2001–3). Arguably, this pushes "Packt" perhaps closer back to the conventional side of things, perhaps only different in degree from Cher's "Believe" (1998). Both tracks seem to highlight the pitch corrector's glissando capabilities, though to different aesthetic ends.

38. See Reynolds 2001.

39. Subjecting this ambient noise to a spectrogram indeed reveals C_4, and its second overtone G_5, as the loudest frequencies.

40. The factory presets on most pitch correctors convert any input frequency to a member of a certain diatonic set. They are programmable to convert input frequencies to as few as one pitch (i.e., every input signal becomes C_4), or to any one of twelve equal tempered pitch classes (i.e., any input signal will be "snapped" to the nearest member of the chromatic scale). Further tweaking of the programming allows for gross or fine tuning of those frequencies such that a user can either pivot all frequencies around a reference pitch other than $A_4=440$, or even adjust the frequency of individual scale-steps.

41. See Reynolds (2001).

42. See Smalley (2007, 39). One can sense a debt to Robert Gjerdingen's (1998, 5ff.) work in schema theory here, since such a perceptual leap relies at least as much on a top-down model as it does a bottom-up.

43. See Slater (2011, 372).

44. See Smalley (1997, 112).

45. See Zagorski-Thomas (forthcoming).

46. Comparing the recorded introduction on *Kid A* (2000) to Greenwood's ondes Martenot performance on *Saturday Night Live* in October 2000 reveals enough discrepancies to suggest that the introduction was improvised in one or both cases.

47. It should be noted that several models of ondes Martenot are now available, including a newer variant known as the Ondes Musicales. While all of these work on the same basic principles, some are missing one or more of the wave generators shown in Table 4.3 (especially *Souffle*), which represents Jonny Greenwood's 1983 reissue model. Greenwood only owns one true ondes Martenot, and it rarely leaves his home studio. For touring purposes, he commissioned the electronics company Analogue Systems to build a controller (the "French Connection") whose circuitry and interface mimics the original well enough for live performance.

48. See Mirka (2001, 435).

49. Though not composed in MAX/MSP, one of the earliest remote surrogate sounds in Radiohead's catalog can be heard in the outro of "Let Down" (1997–5, 4:40). According to Hale (1999, 149), these sounds were produced on an early PC model called the Sinclair ZX Spectrum.

50. See Smalley (1997, 112). As an exception to this rule, the "cold, sterile" music that avoids surrogacy altogether was put to great use in the forward-looking 1956 science fiction

film *Forbidden Planet*. The first completely electronic score, its "alien" sounds (composed entirely with ring modulators and homemade oscillators) depict the otherworldly landscape in the film.

51. Notable excerpts from the band's online diary for each song have been carefully archived by a German fan website called Citizen Insane: http://www.citizeninsane.eu.

52. Because Radiohead demoed a good number of songs in this period that would later appear on *Amnesiac* (2001) and *Hail to the Thief* (2003), you can comb through this hidden booklet and see many such "Easter eggs" that seem to foretell the band's future.

53. Excerpts of this interview can be found at http://www.greenplastic.com/radiohead-lyrics/amnesiac/like-spinning-plates/.

54. See, for example Mendelsohn et. al (2009).

55. See http://www.citizeninsane.eu/likespinningplates.html.

56. See video here: https://www.youtube.com/watch?v=IGWSy1YnhNI.

57. Interview with *XFM Magazine*, June 2003; see transcript at http://www.citizeninsane.eu/t2003–06–03XFM.htm. A curious reversal of this meaning is achieved by an unlicensed YouTube video that presents images of military food drops accompanying a live recording of the song. The video, which at the time of this printing has been viewed over 200,000 times, can be accessed here https://www.youtube.com/watch?v=WGxNnnXTvKs.

58. See Reynolds (2001).

59. Both the destruction of attack and the indefinite pitch of the Novation loop itself make the inner voices of this transcription a difficult affair. However, the outer-voice counterpoint and chord quality are easy enough to hear despite the lack of clarity in the timbre.

60. For example, all Yorke does to move from the C♯m with E in the upper voice to the next chord is move the lowest note down to A, since all three other pitches in the first chord are common tones with the second. That upper-voice E then moves down by step to D♯ over the G♯ chord, but only after an inner voice plays the C♯–B♯ suspension just under.

61. In the same concert, Yorke in fact gives a solo rendition of "I Will" in which he reproduces the album's electric guitar part exactly. Given these similarities, it is shocking that he gets away with these as two different songs in such stripped-down arrangements.

62. Though it may be tempting to spell these pitches enharmonically in flats, using sharps here facilitates comparison between all sounds in "LSP" and "I Will."

63. In the former camp we might include YouTube user David Layzell's comment which mentions "those whirly tube *toys*" as the source of the sound (italics mine; see https://www.youtube.com/all_comments?v=DQBDsNiCCNM&page=2). For an example of the latter meaning, I strongly encourage the reader to listen to a cover of the song by the contemporary group Odd Appetite, who accompanies their cello and wine-glass driven arrangement with a corrugaphone cut to precisely the same length to yield the exact same overtone spectrum; see http://www.oddappetite.org/audio/LSP.mp3. As far as I know, these two acknowledgments of the corrugaphone (one active, one passive) are the only citations of its existence in "LSP"—it has not been documented by the band, Mark Brend's (2005) book, or any major fan sites. I am even open to the possibility that there is no physical corrugaphone present in "LSP," but rather a corrugaphone-surrogate that mimics its spectral and amplitudinal profile remarkably well.

5   Harmony and Voice Leading

PLOTTING RADIOHEAD'S MOST salient formal, rhythmic, and timbral aspects on a continuum between expected and surprising relies on a one-dimensional line segment. But in the domain of pitch—harmony, when thought of simultaneously and voice leading when heard or imagined melodically—the case may not be that one-dimensional. A second dimension (call it depth) may be in order for processing our harmonic and melodic expectations. Because we all have different listening backgrounds, a dimension of depth added to the expectation–realization reaction can account for one of two things. First, this depth can account for a "pocket" of expectations we inherit regarding pitch behaviors in various harmonic languages. Listeners immersed in jazz harmony will have no problem understanding the bizarre and complex harmonic substitutions in "We Suck Young Blood" (2003–7), which nonetheless substitute for clear E♭ minor functional tonality. Likewise, stylistically competent connoisseurs of rock harmony might find the Neapolitan sixth chord at the beginning of "A Wolf at the Door" (2003–14) to be a rather strange dominant preparation, while connoisseurs of Schubert and Schumann will find it somewhat unremarkable. These pockets of expectation on an otherwise one-dimensional continuum (predictable<<>>surprising) can open up like a butterfly net to catch all such learned realizations.

TABLE 5.1

Three conventional harmonic systems

Functional tonal (FT)	Functional modal (FM)	Contrapuntal (CP)
Major and minor tonality. Keys established by descending fifth bass motion supporting supertonic and/or leading-tone scale degrees resolving to tonic; may contain stylistically appropriate chromaticism and substitutions.	Dorian, Lydian, Mixolydian, or Aeolian centers established by descending fifth bass motion supporting the supertonic or subtonic scale degree moving to tonic; may contain stylistically appropriate chromaticism and substitutions.	Centricity created through contrapuntal means rather than functional tonic–dominant motions; includes plagal, neighbor, arpeggiating, and passing chords acting in place of functional descending fifth motions.

Table 5.1 shows the tonal, modal, and contrapuntal systems used extensively in Radiohead's music. These underlying three systems are the source of many of the band's harmonic-melodic expectations. A listener well-versed in western tonality would have little trouble hearing these types of pitch centers, allowing for appropriate rock-specific substitutions.

When Radiohead's harmonies escape the orbit of these three sets of expectations, they usually do so in one of four ways. Radiohead songs often present multiple pitch centers at different times in the song (sectional centricity), or project an unsupported pitch emphasis for one span that actually functions subordinately within a different pitch center (absent tonic). In the case of "underdetermined" and "double-tonic" Radiohead songs, certain pitch features may cause one listener to hear one pitch center and another listener to hear an entirely different center. These four salient harmonic designs, shown in Table 5.2, represent a pocket of learned expectations which may be gleaned upon sustained exposure to Radiohead's music. But why might this be more true for harmony and voice leading than for form, rhythm, or timbre? Harmony and voice leading concern the interactions between all pitches heard in a song, and "no matter what the central musical topic might be . . . pitch relations are the matter that is colorized by timbre, shaped by formal design, and measured by rhythm."[1] These systems of harmony and voice leading, which we cultivate upon spending significant time listening to Radiohead's music, help us to understand all other parameters. Whether conventional or idiosyncratic, these systems should be considered essential *sources* that promote various affordances in an ecological sense. Although one might consider these systems more abstract than a

TABLE 5.2

Four salient harmonic designs in Radiohead

Absent tonic	Double-tonic complex	Sectional centricity	Underdetermined
Voice leading points to a tonal center whose tonic chord is not literally present; "absent" tonic is part of FT system.	Pitch center continually divided between two FT centers.	Pitch centers between two sections irreconcilable at larger levels of structure; can be part of any primary system.	Tonal or modal centricity not convincingly established or irrelevant; CP system still possible, or no discernable primary system present.

backbeat or an electric guitar, "a cadence in A minor, a dominant prolongation, or a gavotte rhythm can be regarded as the (structural) sources of a sound that a listener hears."[2]

Voice-leading analysis of Radiohead songs exhibiting one of our three conventional systems helps reveal differences between the general and the particular. The aim is not to demonstrate that all of Radiohead's music plays by these "rules" (that would seem largely antithetical to my thesis indeed). Instead, it is only through a demonstrated grounding in the general that we can begin to appreciate the particular. The three overarching systems provide the underlying "architecture" within which the harmony and voice leading operates. Though each house has unique and individual interior design, every house has a foundation. Most of Radiohead's songs have one of three different foundations—tonal, modal, or contrapuntal—which support their individual designs. The three primary systems not only provide a foil against which the four more salient designs work, but in fact also provide a lens through which the pieces operating within them may surprise us. For example, it is only through the lens of functional, goal-directed G major tonality that we can appreciate the surprise C♯ half-diminished chord substituting for tonic in "Motion Picture Soundtrack" (2000–10, 2:43). Likewise, Yorke's clever text-painting of the word ghost ("like it's seen a ghost") on B♯3 in "The Tourist" (1997–12, 0:53) can only be appreciated by recognizing the underlying I–V–I structure as it moves toward a modally functional cadence in B Mixolydian only to replace the expected cadential B3 in the melody with its Doppelgänger B♯. The voice-leading structures that unfold alongside these harmonic systems—whether one of the three primary systems or one of the four salient ones—are the source of each song's unique beauty.[3] I regard this melodic domain—especially the lead vocal—just as integral to analyzing the pitch content of Radiohead's music as the chordal harmony, sometimes more so.

Functional Tonal (FT) Systems

Whereas the other two systems for harmony and voice leading require some methodological support and argumentation, the FT system needs little because it is firmly rooted in common-practice tonal function.[4] The FT system represents music in which tonal centers are established by descending fifth root motions and leading tones resolving to tonic. This does not necessarily mean that there is only one such pitch center in a piece, only that, for any given pitch center, that center is established by a dominant-functioning chord relative to some tonic, present or implied, the root of which lies a perfect fifth below (or perfect fourth above) the dominant functioning chord. In all cases (and this will be important for contrasting tonal vs. modal systems), there must be a leading tone present, even in minor. This can manifest in three different ways, and must be accompanied by counterpoint at some level of structure appropriate to each harmonic move: (1) the dominant function can be a half-cadence in which the dominant does not resolve down a fifth to tonic; (2) the dominant function can resolve down a fifth to establish an authentic cadence on the tonic; (3) the dominant function may appear somewhere in the middle of a phrase or as part of a looped progression, and, while engendering either an elided cadence or no sort of cadence, still signifies a dominant–tonic axis.

Each of these criteria for functional tonality is couched in terms of the dominant chord and not the tonic. In FT systems, the tonic chord is only established through its relationship to a dominant functioning chord whose root lies a perfect fifth above. This is why in the third case above, for example, we cannot identify an FT system by a *tonic* functioning chord appearing in the middle of a progression. Indeed, without a dominant functioning chord present, there can, by definition, be no FT center.

The voice-leading structure of "Let Down" (1997–5) demonstrates just how much Radiohead's music can, from time to time, behave like common-practice music. Functional A major tonality is established firmly at the first entrance of the voice. Even though there is no cadence during the verse, the presence of the E major and A major chords forms a dominant–tonic axis. These chord roots alone are not enough to produce functional tonality, but when coupled with the attending $\hat{1}$–$\hat{7}$ and $\hat{5}$–$\hat{1}$ melodic gestures in the second and eighth measures of Figure 5.1, respectively, strongly assert an FT system directly on the musical foreground. The structural basis of most rock voice leading is a function of essential outer-voice counterpoint between the bass and lead vocal, with other instrumental parts usually providing inner voices or cover tones.

FIGURE 5.1 FT system in "Let Down" (1997–5, 0:22) verse 1.

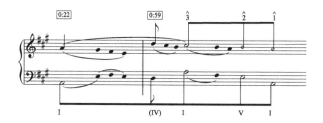

FIGURE 5.2 Voice-leading graph of "Let Down" (1997–5) verse/chorus pair.

The first chorus makes an immediate move to the subdominant chord, but, far from representing a move to "D Lydian," as a modal interpretation would imply, we can hear this move as a hypermetrically (and formally) emphatic composed-out plagal neighbor within the broader monotonality of A major.[5] The end of the first chorus at 1:21 also provides the song's first cadence, this one a perfect authentic cadence when the dominant chord that ends the chorus resolves to tonic with clear $\hat{2}$–$\hat{1}$ counterpoint against the V–I bass motion.[6] Since the only cadence occurs at the end of the chorus, the voice-leading graph in Figure 5.2 demonstrates one continuous phrase composed of an overarching motion from tonic, through plagal neighbor to dominant, ending in tonic.[7]

This simplified system of voice-leading notation can quickly impart the basic principles of a passage's contrapuntal structure. While this notation will be immediately readable by music theorists, it should also be readable to anybody who reads musical notation, as it essentially shows that *this note leads to this note*.[8] Additional symbology on the graphs demonstrates levels of depth wherein some notes remain in our ears despite other notes intervening on the musical surface. Stems indicate notes not only with harmonic support, but those that possess more structural function than those related through passing motion or arpeggiation. Flags clarify neighbor tones (only when they require additional clarification), but also the predominant harmony of a phrase if beamed below with a thick beam. Slurs connect notes which are related through arpeggiation (with or without

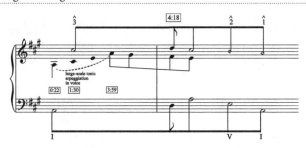

FIGURE 5.3 Background graph of "Let Down" (1997–5).

unstemmed passing or neighbor tones placed between) or by stepwise motion if part of a linear progression or neighbor-tone configuration. Dashed slurs indicate a note which is retained or coupled in more than one octave. Beams represent notes that are connected through stepwise motion, with thicker beams representing deeper-level significance. Finally, open noteheads, roman numerals, and scale-degree numbers indicate only notes which form the fundamental structure of a phrase.[9]

As in many pop–rock songs, the verse–chorus pair forms the basic voice-leading unit of "Let Down."[10] While the second and third verse–chorus pairs do little to alter the basic harmonic/melodic structure shown in Figure 5.2, a plausible background structure such as that shown in Figure 5.3 can be heard by comparing the first, second, and third verses. In the first verse–chorus pair, there is little sense of an arpeggiated ascent to the primary tone C♯. Yorke reaches up to this C♯4 several times throughout the second verse, emphasizing it further with its dissonant upper neighbor D4. In the third verse, Yorke reaches all the way up to E4 ("one DAY") as an upper third of the C♯4 before entering falsetto range to intone, on A4, a variation of the guitar's descant motive from the chorus ("you KNOW who you AR-e"). While not quite a textbook arpeggiated ascent (there is good reason to hear E4 as the upper third of C♯4, rather than the primary tone itself), this large-scale structural arpeggiation of the tonic triad does provide a deeper structural reinforcement of the A tonic, and rewards a hearing that recognizes the hierarchical relationship between, on the one hand, the structural verse–chorus core of the song, and on the other, the unfolding of the tonic triad that guides the song's dramatic narrative.

FT systems such as this can be heard at least twice on every record between 1997 and 2007.[11] Table 5.3 represents selected FT systems in Radiohead concisely only by key, fundamental structure, and cadence. The notable features that decorate these standard structures (chromatic or otherwise) can help us to appreciate their particular voice-leading designs.

TABLE 5.3

Selected FT systems in Radiohead (1997–2011)

Song and section	Key	Ursatz and cadence (if applicable)	Notable features
"Exit Music" (1997–4, verses e.g., 0:01–0:54)	Bm	$\hat{5}/i-\hat{4}/IV6-\hat{3}/V64-\hat{2}/V-\hat{1}/i$ (PAC)	Cadential tonic inflected major (guitar E–D♯–D)
"Exit Music" (1997–4, bridge 2:49–3:20)	Bm	$I-\flat II-\hat{5}/V7$	Serves as dominant preparation for verse 3's higher octave
"No Surprises" (1997–10, Verse–refrain pairs e.g., 0:26–1:50)	F	$\hat{3}/I-\hat{2}/V-\hat{1}/I$ (PAC)	Plagal neighbor B♭ chord inflected as minor throughout
"Motion Picture Soundtrack" (2000–10, verse–chorus pairs e.g., 0:39–1:37)	G	$\hat{3}/I-\hat{2}/V$ (HC)	No functional progression to ending $\hat{1}/I$; C♯ half-diminished seventh delays tonic arrival
"Like Spinning Plates" (2001–10, chorus couplets e.g., 2:28–2:42)	C♯m	$\hat{3}/VI-\hat{2}/V$ (HC)	C♯ minor triad arpeggiates VI (no tonic function)
"Glass House" (2001–11, choruses e.g., 1:46–2:17)	Am	$\hat{3}/I-\hat{2}/V-\hat{3}-I$ (IAC)	VI (F major) deceptive resolution delays tonic arrival
"Wolf at the Door" (2003–14, verses e.g., 0:16–1:02)	Dm	$I-\flat II6-V6/4-5/3$ (HC)	Fundamental structure in guitar only—voice is non-pitched
"2+2=5" (2003–1, A section couplets e.g., 0:25–0:53)	Fm	$\hat{5}/i-\hat{4}/ii-\hat{3}/V64-\hat{2}/V$ (HC)	D♭4 and B3 double chromatic neighbor to primary tone. Cadential 6/4 function is inverted (F in bass) with many added tones
"We Suck Young Blood" (2003–7, all non-bridge strophes e.g., 0:01–0:52)	E♭m	$\hat{3}/i-2/V$ (HC)	Recurring; contains many chromatic inflections including B♭ minor arpeggiating tonic
"I Will" (2003–10, A section 0:01–1:20)	C♯m	$\hat{3}/I-\hat{2}/V$ (HC)	Recurring; opposite of "Spinning Plates" in that VI arpeggiates tonic (no predominant function)
"Codex" (2011–6, all non-bridge strophes e.g., 1:06–1:39)	F	$\hat{3}/I-\hat{2}/V-\hat{1}/vi$	Deceptive resolution disassociates tonic triad from tonic scale degree in cadence

Functional Modal (FM) Systems

Functional modal systems, as the name imparts, are still based on the functional descending perfect fifth motion from dominant to tonic. However, whereas tonal systems only come in two flavors, major and minor, functional modal systems are free to color the remaining five scale steps (besides tonic and dominant) to yield any mode. These can be synthetic, as in the bizarre parallel major voice leading in "Pyramid Song" (2001–2), but are more often one of the diatonic modes, including Dorian in "15 Step" (2007–1), Lydian in "All I Need" (2007–5), or Mixolydian in "Separator" (2011–8).[12] Of the remaining two, Phrygian would be extraordinarily rare inasmuch as it would require a V chord with a consistently flattened fifth, and Locrian, under the current definition of "functional," would be logically impossible since there is no perfect fifth above the tonic.[13]

A clear illustration of this functional modal system can be heard in the C Aeolian song "Where I End and You Begin" (2003–6). Figure 5.4 demonstrates the FM system heard in the counterpoint between the bass and lead vocal. Tonic C minor and dominant G minor triads control almost the entire verse, despite the fact that there is no leading tone (B♮) present. The A♭ and F in the bass merely act as double neighbor tones around the G, and unlike the C and G, which are adorned by E♭ and B♭, respectively, these double neighbors are not supplied with the requisite thirds to promote them as bona fide chordal sonorities.

FIGURE 5.4 FM system in "Where I End and You Begin" (2003–6, 0:48) verse 1.

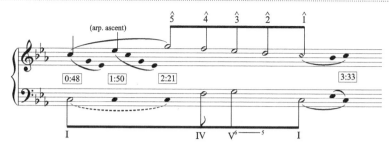

FIGURE 5.5 Background sketch of "Where I End and You Begin" (2003–6).

In terms of large-scale voice leading and form, like "Let Down" (1997–5), "Where I End and you Begin" unfolds successively higher members of the tonic triad in each of its verses: C4 in verse one (0:49), E♭4 in verse two (1:50), and finally G4 in the final verse (2:22). Unlike "Let Down," this song contains no contrasting chorus. Instead it features a strophic design where verses one and two each present a couplet of phrases. Unlike traditional strophic forms in blues-based and Tin Pan Alley-derived rock music, the song's requisite contrast comes not from an internal bridge, but through a terminal climax.

However, the Figure 5.5 background sketch reveals that the terminal climax at 3:33 does not play a role in the piece's overarching background structure. Following the culmination of the arpeggiated ascent (the attainment of primary tone $\hat{5}$ at the beginning of verse three at 2:21), the expected descent occurs completely within that verse. Given that verse three is half the length of all previous verses, this is somewhat unexpected, providing a hasty conclusion.

Functional modal systems must rely on the same fundamental structure as FT systems, and are not (1) rotated versions of FT systems, (2) intermediate prolongations within FT systems, or (3) the result of a pitch center derived through largely contrapuntal means.[14] Table 5.4 presents a cursory outline of selected FM systems at work throughout Radiohead's catalog.

Contrapuntal Systems (CP)

Even in the absence of any discernible tonic-dominant harmonic axis, Radiohead's music can still establish one or more pitch centers through contrapuntal means. Contrapuntal systems predate functional tonality by several hundreds of years, but also enjoy a newfound resurgence in so-called "neotonal" works of the early twentieth century. Figure 5.6 shows voice-leading sketches for all contrapuntal bass gestures analyzed in this section. Three such gestures are absolutely fundamental to establishing pitch centers in Radiohead's music, and rock music in general.[15]

TABLE 5.4

Selected FM systems in Radiohead (1997–2011)

Song and section	Mode	Description and cadence (if applicable)	Notable features
"Lucky" (1997–11, verses e.g., 0:23–1:10)	E Aeolian	$\hat{3}$/i–$\hat{2}$/ v–$\hat{1}$/i (PAC)	Apparent relative major G chord is always treated as larger tonic arpeggiation (Em–G–Bm)
"Lucky" (1997–11, choruses e.g., 1:10–1:38)	E Dorian	German+6 to $\hat{5}$/V (HC)	A major neighbor prolongs verse tonic
"The Tourist" (1997–12, verses e.g., 0:32–1:35)	B Mixolydian	$\hat{3}$/I–$\hat{2}$/ V–#$\hat{1}$/VI♯	Bizarre chromatic substitution in both voice (B♯ for B) and harmony (VI♯ for I)
"15 Step" (2007–1, verse–chorus pair e.g., 0:54–1:25)	A Dorian	$\hat{3}$/I–$\hat{2}$/ v–$\hat{1}$/i (PAC)	$\hat{3}$ prolonged throughout verse; functional predominant and dominant arrive at beginning of chorus
"Jigsaw Falling Into Place" (2007–9, bridge 3:11–3:47)	B Aeolian	I–V (HC) // I–V–I (PAC)	Parallel Aeolian period with interrupted 5-line; elided PAC
"Give Up the Ghost" (2011–7, throughout)	D Mixolydian	I–v	No discernible larger structure, D and Am triads are not part of absent tonic; borrowed III (F)
"Separator" (2011–8, verse–chorus pair e.g., 0:25–1:23)	B♭ Mixolydian	$\hat{3}$/I–$\hat{2}$/ V–$\hat{1}$/i6	Like "15 Step," verse prolongs $\hat{3}$, $\hat{2}$ arrives in chorus; D♭ in chorus supports $\hat{1}$ through large-scale chromatic voice-exchange (D/B♭–B♭/D♭)

Because the underlying structure in CP systems is an essential *bass motion* rather than root motion, these gestures are described in terms of voice leading only, and include no description of harmonic function other than "I," which is simply an expedient way of labeling "pitch center." In CP systems, "despite the presence of chords, the patterns that result are thoroughly melodic."[16] This explains the lack of roman numerals other than tonic, since each of the characteristic motions only serves to prolong a given scale-step. These characteristic bass motions may be paired with myriad inner-voice and lead vocal melodic patterns. Often these additional voices move in parallel octaves, fifths, and thirds—even parallel tritones, ninths, and other dissonant intervals in heavier rock styles.

To be clear, contrapuntal prolongations such as these are integral to all harmonic systems, FT and FM included. "Motion Picture Soundtrack" (2000–10), for example, contains one example each of passing, neighbor, and arpeggiated tonic prolongations within the first verse alone. What differentiates CP *systems* is that, while FT and FM systems feature pitch centers established by functional harmonic progressions and directed linear motion to the tonic, CP systems feature no such functional root motions. In CP systems, pitch centricity is established *only* through surface-level contrapuntal gestures such as the motions shown in Figure 5.6.

"Lotus Flower" (2011–5) demonstrates how these systems function within the environment of a song completely devoid of functional root progressions. The central groove of the song, transcribed in the bass staff of Figure 5.7, demonstrates contrapuntal gestures at two levels of structure. In the first four bars the upper third F and the lower neighbor C form a repeated riff that, in conjunction with the voice's passing motion (A3–G3–F3) and the upper boundary pitch C4, embellishes a Dm7 sonority with no harmonic movement. The only change of bass in measures five and six of the repeated riff further emphasizes the Dm7 prolongation by adding a pair of upper neighbors (G above F and E above D), which is interpreted in the Figure 5.8 sketch as an unfolded neighbor over the eight bars.[17]

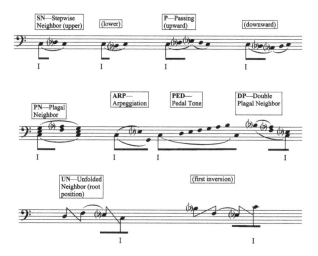

FIGURE 5.6 Basic CP bass motions.

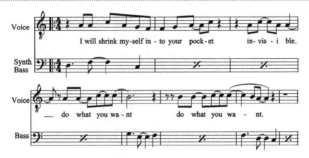

FIGURE 5.7 "Lotus Flower" (2011–5, 0:58) verse 1.

FIGURE 5.8 Unfolded neighbors in "Lotus Flower" (2011–5, 0:58) verse 1.

The B♮ in the voice that accompanies this change of bass, in addition to engendering a prominent C4–B3–A3 stepwise voice, could also be heard as a G-based plagal neighbor, the E in the bass prolonging G through arpeggiation. Already in this opening verse we can see how the D pitch center is reinforced on two different levels through contrapuntal motion. Crucially, that pitch center is not created through any sort of modal harmonic function. CP-system songs such as this and others establish pitch centricity in a manner wholly different than FT- or FM-system songs, which contain directed linear and harmonic motion generated by traditional dominant–tonic axes.

Without a functional tonic–dominant relationship anywhere to be heard in "Lotus Flower," the entire song, neither modal nor tonal, must be analyzed as a CP system. If a functional tonal progression did occur in a contrasting section, a background graph would reveal a fundamental structure in which the verse's contrapuntal system acts as a mere prolongation within a functional FT system. However, conspicuously absent from this analysis is any attempt at a background graph that might reconcile the three main sections of the song into a larger fundamental structure. While this was desirable in FT systems like "Let Down," due to the chorus containing both the intermediate and dominant scale-steps, songs whose pitch centers are governed entirely by CP systems contain no real scale-steps. They contain a pitch center established by contrapuntal motions, which may functional analogously to a tonic. But, without a dominant-functioning harmony present, the term "tonic" is potentially misleading in its association with common-practice harmonic structures.

The fact that "Lotus Flower" is not functionally tonal or modal does not mean that it is musically insufficient in any way. On the contrary, the various voice-leading gestures taken up by the verse, pre-chorus, and chorus do much to reveal strong connections between neighbor and plagal contrapuntal functions and the formal functions they enable. Table 5.5 presents several concise descriptions of other CP systems in Radiohead's music. The table presents a set of abbreviations to describe

TABLE 5.5

Selected CP systems in Radiohead (1997–2011)

Song and section	Pitch	Contrapuntal motions
"Subterranean Homesick Alien" (1997–3, verse couplets e.g., 0:28–0:49)	G	a) F/G–E/G–E♭/C–D/G [**PN**] supports B3, B3–A3–G3 in voice
"Electioneering" (1997–8, verse–chorus pairs e.g., 0:33–1:28)	D	a) verse D4/D–E4/C–A3/A [**N+ARP**] b) chorus Asus4 is [**ARP**], not modal
"The National Anthem" (2000–3, throughout)	D	a) main riff F♯–F–E–D [**P**] b) lead vocal uses same pitch classes
"Optimistic" (2000–6, verse–chorus pairs e.g., 0:42–1:31)	D	a) verse D4/F–C4/E–E4/G–D4/F [**DN**]; b) chorus bass F/A–E/B♭–F♯/D [**UN**] supports A4–G4–F♯4
"Packt" (2001–1, verse couplets e.g., 0:51–1:08)	D	a) D inner-voice [**PED**] b) A3–G3–F(♯)3–D **ARP** c) bass inverts voice's A–G–F to F–G–A
"I Might Be Wrong" (2001–5, verse–chorus pairs e.g., 0:38–1:52)	D	a) verse D4/D–C4/D–B♭3/D–A3/D [**PED**] b) F4/D–E4/D–G4/D–F/D [**PED**] c) chorus B♭3/G–A3/F–C4/A–B♭3/G [**DN**]
"Sit Down, Stand Up" (2003–2, 0:19–2:55)	F	Fm–F/A♭–G/B♭–F/A♭ [**ARP+PN**] piano riff supports myriad vocal gestures including a) D♭4–C4 and b) E♭4–C4–B♭3–A♭3
"Backdrifts" (2003–4, verse–chorus pair e.g., 0:31–1:53)	B	a) Verse D♯4/B–C♯4/B–B4/B [**PED**] b) D♯4/B–E4/A–E4/E–D♯4/B [**DP**] c) chorus F(♯)4/B–F♯4/D–E4/A–E4/C–D♯4/B [**ARP+UN**].

(continued)

TABLE 5.5

Continued

Song and section	Pitch	Contrapuntal motions
"All I Need" (2007–5, throughout)	C	[**ARP**]; entire pitch collection saturates CM13 chord
"House of Cards" (2007–8, verse–chorus pair e.g., 0:51–1:59)	F	a) verse C4/F–B♭3/B♭–A3/F [**PN**] b) verse E♭4/F–D4/B♭–C4/F [**PN**] c) chorus E♭4/E♭–D4/B♭–C4/F [**DP**]
"Bloom" (2011–1, strophes e.g., 0:59–2:10)	D	a) verse D4/D–D4/G [**PN**] b) verse A3/D–G3/G [**PN**]
"Little by Little" (2011–3, verse–chorus pairs e.g., 0:33–1:31)	D	a) verse A3/F–G♯3/E–B♭3/G–A3/F♯ [**DN**] with inner-voice D pedal b) verse D4/B♭–E4/C–F4/D [**P**] c) chorus F♯4/A–F4/B♭–E4/C–D4/D [**P**] with bass D pedal
"Feral" (2011–4, throughout)	G	a) G minor triad [**ARP**] b) B(♭)3–A3–G3 [**P**] c) B♭/G–C/A bass line from 1:30 [**UN**]

Legend for bass CP motions (refer to Figure 5.6 for illustrations): **SN**=Stepwise Neighbor **P**=Passing, **PN**=Plagal Neighbor, **ARP**=Arpeggiation, **Ped**=Pedal, **DP**=Double Plagal, **UN**=unfolded neighbors.

bass contrapuntal motions, which support complementary vocal gestures (notated with octave designations). This notation for CP systems comes closer than FT and FM systems in describing the particular surface-level features of each song, since it is these contrapuntal details themselves which comprise the structure.

It would be a mistake to assume that all songs exhibiting FT, FM, or CP systems are devoid of surprises—only the *systems* underlying these songs are conventional. Most contain momentary flights of fancy that attempt to escape those systems, if only briefly. Though functionally grounded in E♭ minor, the enharmonically puzzling escape to B (or is it C♭?) in the progression [B–C7–D] in "We Suck Young Blood" (2003–8, 1:32–1:41) will surprise any listener. Surprises such as these, brief as they may be, are not uncommon in Radiohead's treatment of conventional systems.

Their songs in which the underlying system resists classification in one of these conventional systems do not reinvent individual modes of organizing pitch for each song. Rather, four particular salient models of voice leading and harmony emerge. Neither wholly conventional nor entirely devoid of precedent in western tonality, they activate a sweet spot if we are willing to attune to deeper levels of harmonic structure.

Absent Tonic

"How to Disappear Completely" (2000–4) begins with a two-chord shuttle in the guitar—D Major with an added ninth moving to an F♯ minor triad—which does very little to establish a sense of tonic due to the third-relation between the two chords. Its harmonic system is therefore underdetermined. But rather than continue as such its sense of ambiguity abates gradually over the course of the track. The D and F♯ chords which begin the song belong to an *absent tonic* that emerges tentatively, and is finally confirmed only in the final section of the song (literally at the last minute).[18]

Each of the three conventional systems—FT, FM, and CP—establishes a single pitch center. In FT and FM systems, this is governed by a fixed harmonic system that pits the dominant and its supertonic scale degree against the tonic pitch and chord. In CP systems, the matter is more straightforward: a pitch can only be confirmed as center if it is literally present most of the time (as in a repeated riff), adorned occasionally by neighbors, passing tones, and the like. But "How to Disappear Completely" relies on a tonal center for which the tonic chord is itself absent in the first verse. In most cases such as these, the tonic chord does emerge at some point later in the piece to provide confirmation of this heretofore absent center, and in this case we can speak of an "emergent" tonic.

When the bass enters at 0:23 with its signature riff transcribed in Figure 5.9, this extra pitch information helps to refine a sense of key-finding, but only so much.

FIGURE 5.9 Bass and guitar, "How to Disappear Completely" (2000–4, 0:23) verse 1.

Because the riff exhibits a pitch collection that is pentatonic, rather than diatonic, it neither confirms nor denies either of the possible keys present in the original two-chord progression. For example, the first two pitch-classes C♯ and A are already present between the D major and F♯ minor triads strummed by the guitar. What the bass does seem to be doing is unfolding pairs of adjacent thirds in a pentatonic collection, except for one crucial pair, E and B, both as a descending fifth and ascending fourth. This inconsistency sets the stage for the emergence of an A major tonic.

Listeners who clue into chords, especially hypermetrically emphasized chords, will want to hear the D as tonic. As such, the opening two notes of the bass could be interpreted as the major seventh and fifth of the chord. F♯ minor would then sound like a mediant chord, with the C♯ and A now arpeggiating the fifth and third of that chord. Indeed, this D major interpretation seems viable even when the voice enters on A3–F♯3 ("that there") at 0:41, a familiar *sol-mi* opening gesture. Almost immediately afterward, Yorke dismisses this identification, singing "that's not me," melismatically intoning his true identity, "me—" on C♯4–B3–A3. He is, in a sense, pointing out the opening D major tonic only to express his true identity as something "other," namely a clear *mi–re–do* in A major.

The tonic A major is now less-than-absent, but is still quite fragile, lacking harmonic support. It is only at the arrival of the chorus ("I'm not here") that the root-position A major chord arrives, exactly when Yorke sings the word "here." The payoff for hearing the E/B dyad in the opening bass riff comes now, as we hear Yorke sing "not here" on the fourth A3–E3, creating a link between the moment we heard our first "clue" pointing to A major—a dominant B/E interval-class five—and the inversionally equivalent A/E interval-class five at the moment in which that key is confirmed.[19] Listeners who have held their ground in D major might hear this as a dominant-functioning chord, but one which falls rather unusually down a third to F♯ minor.[20] The irrefutable proof for an overarching A major tonal center does not arrive until the E major harmony at 4:54, which undergirds Yorke's wordless melismas as he lands squarely on the G♯4 leading tone for the song's first cadence.

"Codex" (2011–6) also begins with an absent tonic. This relationship between a hypermetrically strong relative minor (D minor) and an absent relative major (F major) is much more common in pop–rock music than the mode-preserving perfect fifth relationship (D to A) in the previous example.[21] The same relationship can be heard in "Nude" (2007–3). The opening vocalise (the structure of which is similar to that graphed at 3:10 in Figure 5.10) clearly outlines an E major pentachord, though the hypermeter reinforces the C♯ minor triad and there is no trace of E's dominant. Once the verse begins, a weak E major triad appears only as part of a sixth arpeggiation prolonging A (IV) on the way down to its third C♯. Further destabilizing any potential E major FT system, Yorke inflects all texted instances of the third scale degree in the upper register as *me* (G♮).

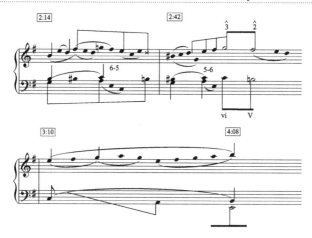

FIGURE 5.10 Absent, then revealed E major tonic in "Nude" (2007–3).

The reward for hearing this "fragile" relative major tonic lurking in the background throughout the verses of "Nude" comes in the climactic half-cadence at 3:07. For the first time, Yorke rights the third scale degree as G♯4 to begin a melismatic scalar descent down to the leading tone D♯4 ("thin-king"). Ironically, it is only in the seconds before this half-cadence in the relative major that Yorke sings the leading-tone of the relative minor (C♯m). Throughout the previous verses, the G♯m triad (iii) is only momentarily inflected as major so that the B♯ acts as an inner-voice chromatic passing tone to C♯ over IV, a stock gesture for rock. Following the half-cadence, the song ends with a recapitulation of the opening vocalise with roughly the same progression as the intro. But, the preceding half-cadence having finally cemented the underlying E tonic for the first time in the piece, the nevertheless absent E tonic now shapes its melodic pentachord unequivocally for a full minute before the piece simply ends on an imperfect tonic chord at 4:08.

In other cases involving this relationship between relative minor and major, an unequivocal tonic is not as easy to establish.[22] What we may find instead is that the two centers vie for tonic status throughout the piece. What sets this apart from the absent tonic situation is that both of these tonics, as per FT systems, must have a functional V–I harmonic progression with leading tone and supertonic scale degrees surrounding the tonic. If absent tonics are underdetermined, two simultaneous FT centers are then, in a sense, overdetermined, forming a double-tonic complex.

Double-Tonic Complex

Within the first 45 seconds of the signature guitar and bass groove of "Reckoner" (2007–7), we only hear three distinct chordal sonorities: C, D, and Em. Whereas there are those who might want to hear this as VI–VII–i in E minor, our expectations inherited from centuries of diatonic harmony suggest "major until proven other-wise." That is, even though there is no functional cadential progression in this al-ternation of three chords, if we wanted to *predict* what key center would emerge from the ensuing melody, our best guess would be the major key which contains all three chords: G major. When the voice enters on the song's title "Rec-kon-er" (G4-A4-B4) at 0:46, it satisfies the G major prediction, or at least serves as a reward for already having G major in our ears. But, for a truly FT system in G major, we need a functional dominant–tonic axis. Two long verses provide plenty of D chords within the aforementioned three-chord shuttle, but provide no tonic chord. Furthermore, all vocal utterances of the leading-tone F♯4, sung several times, step down to E4 rather than resolving to G. Thus, it may seem as if we are dealing with an absent tonic to reveal itself shortly.

However, the bridge at 2:32 brings not the arrival of a G major tonic, but instead the half-cadential progression Am–CMaj7–B7 that harmonizes G4 falling to F♯4. This repeats again, with Yorke's vocal melody now falling down stepwise from F♯4 down to D♯4 over the B7 chord at 2:51, as shown in Figure 5.11. This is of course not the expected tonic arrival in G major, but an unmistakable half-cadence in E minor. At the end of the bridge, Yorke intones what would be the perfect authentic cadence on E4 ("oooh-oooh-oooh"), but the chord support is still B7, and these notes are actually an anacrusis to the arrival of the C major chord that begins verse three at 3:20. Just as in the verses, the leading-tone is never allowed to rise to the tonic pitch with tonic chordal support.

We are then left with the curious situation in which two competing tonal centers each have a compelling dominant chord and vocal melody suggesting a tonic, but no authentic cadence. Tonal allegiance is in a sense spread between two divergent tonal centers. This tension between two harmonic centers is heard frequently in nineteenth-century art song, where it has been called a *double-tonic complex.*[23] Pieces bearing a double-tonic complex are not always as underdetermined as "Reckoner." Indeed, the two tonal centers can pull harder, as it were, apart from each other when each has functional harmonic progressions and cadences. The particular feeling of

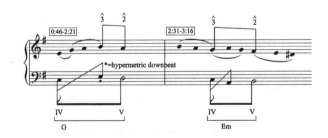

FIGURE 5.11 Double tonic complex (G major and E minor) in "Reckoner" (2007–7).

perpetual motion in "Reckoner" derives from the sense that each tonal center is merely suggested, and a moment of tonic arrival is never confirmed.

While songs bearing functional harmonic progressions and cadences in two different keys (usually relative major and minor) are common in the Romantic era, such harmonic structures are relatively foreign to modern rock music. This is because, by and large, tonicized minor keys are fairly rare. The situation is not unlike professional baseball where it is unusual to find a skilled pitcher who can also bat well. Pitchers are not intrinsically poor batters, but good batters and good pitchers are both rare. So rare is the tonicized minor key in rock music that the odds of finding one in a song which *also* features functional harmonic progressions in major are low. Indeed, no song in Radiohead's catalog 1997–2011 features an authentic cadence in both the relative major and minor. Furthermore, songs like "2+2=5" (2003–1) and "Exit Music" (2000–4) exert their tonicized minor modes so strongly that it is difficult to escape the gravitational pull of that tonal center—in both cases it remains throughout the track.

Sectional Centricity

More common than double-tonic complexes in Radiohead, and in pop–rock music generally, is *sectional centricity*, in which multiple pitch centers align squarely with sectional divisions of the song.[24] In this manner of pitting two or more pitch centers against one another, both need not be functional tonal systems. When two pitch centers represent different sections of Radiohead's songs, no more than one is an FT center, and these FT centers are almost always major. This major FT system is then pitted against a different pitch center in a different section of a song, usually established (weakly or ambiguously) by a contrapuntal system.

"Karma Police" (1997–6) is exemplary of sectional centricity. Of the three main sections of the song (verse, chorus, terminal climax), only one, the chorus, features an FT center. The faux-taunting lyrics "this is what you get" clearly express G major with the leading-tone F#3 over D major resolving to the tonic.[25] Following this quick perfect authentic cadence in G, the harmony slips perilously in parallel fifths and octaves to F# *major*. When this F# major wraps back around to the C major chord that begins the four-chord loop,[26] a retrograde relationship is heard between the roots of those two chords (F# to C) and Yorke's vocal motive that bookends the progression (C3 to F#3).

The verse places strong hypermetric emphasis on the A minor triad at the beginning of each of four two-measure phrases. Its recurring E minor chord is not an FT dominant (it lacks a leading tone), but does support scale-degree 2 at the end of each of the first two phrases, producing an FM system on A (either Dorian or

Aeolian).[27] The terminal climax, though it features a melody that strongly suggests D major (especially F♯4–E4–D4), utilizes neither an FT or FM center. Its sense of pitch center on either D or its relative B minor is only due to a CP system. The D major harmony appears on beat three of each of the first three measures of the four-measure loop, preceded twice by its plagal neighbor (G major) and once by the third-related Bm triad.

As the Figure 5.12 sketches show, these three different pitch centers in the verse, chorus, and terminal climax (A, G, and D, respectively) are thus established by three very different systems. Sectional centricity in this song can then be heard not only as three distinct pitch centers corresponding to the three main sections, but also three distinct systems of establishing said pitch center over the course of the song.

Lacking any FT or FM center, "You and Whose Army?" (2001–4) presents a more difficult case of sectional centricity. The song is composed of three main sections (verses 0:01–1:11, transition 1:12–1:52, terminal climax 1:53–3:10) proceeding in an ABC fashion.[28] "We ride tonight / Ghost horses" is clearly the song's terminally climactic highpoint and, fittingly, also the moment in the song that features the clearest pitch center, C♯. Established neither through FT or FM systems,[29]

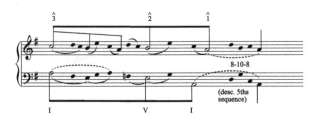

FIGURE 5.12A "Karma Police" (1997–6) FM sketch (A Dorian or Aeolian) verse.

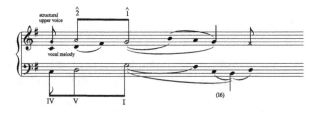

FIGURE 5.12B "Karma Police" (1997–6) FT sketch (G Major) chorus.

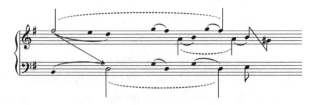

FIGURE 5.12C "Karma Police" (1997–6) CP sketch (D pitch center) terminal climax.

FIGURE 5.13 Terminal climax of "You and Whose Army?" (2001–4, 2:01).

Figure 5.13 demonstrates that this C♯ pitch center emerges largely in the chordal accompaniment though bass arpeggiation and the Dorian neighbor chord F♯ major. Yorke's voice does little more than arpeggiate the C♯ minor triad, arpeggiating the E4 above and reaching the G♯3 below through two consonant passing tones.

Any attempt at relating this C♯ pitch center to the song's verse is fraught with frustration.[30] The verse's harmonic progression resists categorization based on either FT, FM, or CP systems because it is instead based entirely on the ergonomics of the guitar fretboard. Guitarists learn early in their training that a single hand position will play both (1) major triads whose root lies on the lowest string and (2) minor triads whose root lies on the second lowest string. This guitar shape is none other than the familiar power chord (root, fifth, octave on adjacent ascending strings), with an added third on the next highest string. For example, if beginning on the second lowest string's sixth fret, this shape creates the song's opening D♯ minor triad on the fifth through second strings (D♯A♯D♯F♯), and when moved to the lowest string's fourth fret, begets the subsequent G♯ major triad on the lowest four strings (G♯D♯G♯B♯).[31]

Examining the triads played in this verse thus reveals a chromatic sequence resulting from this chord shape being transposed by interval-class five (alternating descending perfect fifths and ascending perfect fourths). To even begin to relate this fretboard geometry to common-practice notation involves considering whether to spell the chords using flats or sharps. A chromatic sequence might begin on one or the other, but if continued sufficiently long, will necessitate an enharmonic spelling at some point. Figure 5.14 provides one possible notation of the chord sequence, as well as the modified "box" pattern it traverses on the guitar fretboard.[32]

But what is a singer to do over such chromatic frenzy? Examining Yorke's lead vocal reveals some rather casual approaches to coordinating melody with harmony, suggesting what some have called the "melodic-harmonic divorce" in rock music.[33] Without a single scale to fit all of the tones in the chord progression, Yorke uses a collection that gets at *most* of the pitch classes (five sharps), and seems to have an E center in his ear. However, both E major and E minor triads occur continuously throughout, juxtaposed flagrantly on the title lyric: "You and who-se ..." (B4–G♯3–F♯3–E3) "a-r-my?" (G♮3–F♯3–E3) at 0:23. This harmonic mixture imbues

FIGURE 5.14 "You and Whose Army?" (2001–4, 0:01) harmonic reduction with fretboard diagram, verse.

the song with a vaguely bluesy and perhaps "old-timey" vibe, a harmonic reading that complements guitarist Ed O'Brien's claim that the close miking of Yorke's voice and other timbral elements in this track were influenced by early twentieth-century recordings by The Ink Spots.[34]

There is good reason to hear the E major triad in the guitar as more prominent than any of the other chords because its bass note, E2, occupies the lowest possible pitch on the standard-tuned guitar. Despite this apparent congruence between Yorke's E major chordal emphasis and the registral center suggested by this E chord, a monotonal reading of the verse is still largely untenable due to the nearly saturated chromatic sequence (containing ten pitch classes) and Yorke's insistence on A♯3 throughout despite its tritone relationship to his emphatic E center. Thus, not only is it undesirable to unify the entire song monotonally, but, lacking any FT, FM, or CP structures, the pitch center within the verse alone is less than certain.

"Life in a Glass House" (2001–11) is unique among Radiohead's catalog in that it provides a direct stylistic allusion to New Orleans Jazz. By compartmentalizing its form, timbre, and rhythm almost entirely within these stylistic conventions, the track foregrounds its bizarre harmonic design. Two choruses, appearing at 1:45 and 3:03, are squarely centered in A minor. We hear this through the inescapable functional tonal orbit between the A minor and E dominant seventh chords, as well as Yorke's stepwise traverse from the tonic A3 to the mediant C4.

Despite this clear A minor tonality in the chorus, the introduction and previous two verses, beginning at 0:28 and 1:07, do nothing to secure this tonal space prior to the chorus's arrival. Instead, the uncertain harmonic environment from 0:01–1:44 forces a listener to perceive and attempt to understand a single focal chord. This opening piano chord [A-G♯-C-E, hereafter known as AmM7], which is the first acoustic timbre we hear following 19 seconds of electronics including an A3 pedal, resounds throughout the two verses and is perhaps the single most identifiable sonic marker of the track.

According to standard harmonic vocabulary, seventh chords come in five configurations. They each consist of either a major, minor, or diminished triad, with the seventh added above the root of that triad. Seventh chords containing a major triad as their base feature either a major or a minor seventh; those with a diminished triad as their base feature either a minor or diminished seventh; but seventh chords built from minor triads only feature minor sevenths. A minor triad accompanied by a *major* seventh does not appear in standard reference texts on Western classical harmony, and is in fact so rare that there is no commonly accepted name for it (in either common-practice or rock music). So what associations might we, as listeners, make of this sonority when it is presented with such austerity in the track's opening?

We could of course hear the entire four-measure entity transcribed in Figure 5.15 as a standard A minor seventh chord, but to do so would be to assert the G♯ in the first two measures as an extremely accented non-chord tone, waiting to resolve to the "real" seventh on G♮. This strategy may sound familiar—it is what some analysts have done in order to understand the "Tristan Chord" in the prelude of Wagner's eponymous opera as an altered secondary dominant of E (or French augmented sixth, depending on whom you ask).[35] Reductive voice-leading analysis has its place, to be sure, but from a perceptual standpoint, asserting that a sound marking a piece's very identity is somehow not the "real" sound is at odds with a theory concerned with our response to novelty. Personally, I can see the value of a combined structural/perceptual approach: the G♯ in the first two measures grabs our attention sensually, even if we were to understand the G♮ as forming the structural foundation of the prolonged Am7 sonority.

Accompanied by the standard jazz backbeat (hi-hats on beats two and four), The Humphrey Lyttelton Band's wind ensemble (jazzy clarinet, trombone, sax, trumpet, etc.), and Yorke's voice singing in an uncharacteristically drawn-out and amplified vibrato (bordering on camp), one of the broadest interpretations possible to a large number of listeners will be <jazz chord>.[36] One of the many hallmarks of jazz is the use of extended tertian sonorities, especially ninths and thirteenths. Even Yorke's opening melodic statement ("once a-gain" on B3 to C4), which spans exactly the duration of the mM7 chord, begins on an accented ninth awaiting its resolution

FIGURE 5.15 "Life in a Glass House" (2001–11, 0:19) signature piano riff.

to the tenth. This parallelism between the original $G\sharp_3$–$G\natural_3$ figure in the piano and the B_3–C_4 creates a rhythmic diminution lasting half the length of the piano semitone, and those two semitones, $G\sharp$ and C, are inversionally symmetrical about the A_3–B_3 axis.

However, when the chord reappears after the first chorus at 2:14 accompanying Yorke's lyrics "but someone's listening in," these lyrics may sway a previously structural interpretive framework to a more intertextual one. There is one particular cultural association that listeners may have with mM7 sonority: the so-called "James Bond chord," which can be heard throughout most titles in the eponymous movie franchise. Yorke's lyrics, concerning espionage and an invasion of privacy, instantly reward this association. In this chorus, the narrator longs for relaxed conversation with an old friend ("of course I'd like to sit around and chat / of course I'd like to stay and chew the fat"), but then comes back to his senses, realizing that this will not be possible because of a perceived threat. Combined with the chorus's brightened/relaxed texture (full drum set now, winds improvising more freely) and more consonant melody harmonization (Yorke's C_4 now harmonized by an F major triad instead of the mM7 chord), the return to the troubled mM7 chord after "someone's listening in" brings about a profound sense of remorse, failure, and even dread.[37]

Underdetermined

Two songs in Radiohead's catalog stand out as the most harmonically perplexing. They are in fact so bizarre that grouping them together seems a matter of convenience at best. Both rely on a technique standard to popular music, that of presenting a repeated harmonic progression in a sort of circular loop. What they share in common is the fact that this repeated loop seems to begin in one key and end in another, rendering the "wrap-around" back to the beginning in each case less of a Möbius strip and more of a garden sprinkler that traverses a path only to snap back abruptly to its starting position.

The two sections in question are the verses of "Knives Out" (2001–6, e.g., 0:19) and the hymn-like chorale section in "Paranoid Android" (1997–2, 3:33) that loops for a full two minutes. Shuttling back and forth between two keys over and over again gives the harmony-attentive listener something akin to seasickness. Furthermore, neither section seems to serve any substantive role in terms of prolonging a pitch center crucial to the rest of the track.

"Paranoid Android" begins like a chromatic sequence, but, unlike the consistent circle of fifths pattern heard in "You and Whose Army?" seems to go terribly awry

FIGURE 5.16 "Paranoid Android" (1997–2, 4:03) chorale.

just as the pattern is underway. The first four bass notes establish a descending semitone pattern: C–B–Bb–A. Perceiving the first pair of triads as a root-position C minor followed by G major in first inversion leads to the expectation that a root-position Bb then F major in first inversion will follow. However, as the Figure 5.16 transcription shows, these next two chords are altered in such a way as to subvert this harmonic expectation. First, the Bb that appears in the bass of the third chord is not the root of a major triad, but rather the minor third of the previous G major triad. Second, the A that arrives in the bass of the fourth chord is no longer the third of an F major triad, but now the root of an A major triad, effectively creating a reversal in the order of expected triad positions (6/3 goes to 5/3, rather than vice versa).

The voice part follows the bass in parallel thirds, and is also subject to the reversal in position. Having sung the third then fifth of the harmony, in the second measure that pattern flips to the fifth then the third of the harmony. The compositional logic of this substitution is clear at the downbeat of measure three—the A in the bass plays the role of a root-position secondary dominant tonicizing D minor. And since Yorke's counterpoint lands now on the leading-tone (rather than the expected fifth) of this secondary harmony, his plaintiff cries "rain down" might be read as ironic since, though he arrives at this moment by way of descent, his C#4 leading-tone is now bound to ascend to D. Yorke's C#4 dutifully passes through D en route to F4. His pleas for rain now become sincere as the pathos-laden passing tone E4, harmonized in a thoroughly FT manner with the root-position dominant, firmly establishes the somber key of D minor.

This immediate juxtaposition of C minor and D minor pitch centers creates the "tonal pairing" that we hear in each of the song's major sections.[38] From D minor yet another sequence begins to take effect, this one a diatonic sequence whose bass descends stepwise in a one-flat collection. The harmony turns entirely nonfunctional and sequential. Yorke's voice seems stuck on text-painting the fall "from a great height" of F4 down to C4 until the sequence arrives at an E in the bass. Über-functional tonality presents itself in the way of a secondary dominant of V (rather than the E minor the sequence would predict) resolving up a fourth to yield a tonicized half-cadence that would be perfectly at home in Handel's *Messiah*. Given this extended glorification of D minor with its own tonicized half-cadence, the wrap-around back to the beginning (indicated by repeat signs in Figure 5.16) is undeniably jarring. Since no functional harmonic logic explains this surprise move from a half-cadence in D minor to a C minor triad, we are then left with two choices: (1) accept wholesale that rock music tends to repeat ostinati, thus the beginning must come after the ending despite any harmonic non sequiturs; or (2) appreciate the smooth stepwise voice leading between the A major and C minor triads on its own, hearing the C♯ and E falling parsimoniously to C and E♭, respectively.[39]

"Knives Out" (2001–4) starts as a more garden variety diatonic sequence—a minor mode version of the Pachelbel Canon with smooth stepwise bass. Because this sequence is so recognizable, it establishes a stronger sense of expectation. A harmonic rhythm of 1+1+3 measures divides the progression into two symmetrical halves, each containing three harmonies, with the final harmony of each lasting three times longer than the first two. The first half features the stepwise bass motion C–B♭–A♭. When the second half begins on G, we thus expect the continuation G–F–E♭. With the lead vocal beginning the first half on E♭4–C4, the counter statement in the second half starting on D4 would progress down to C4.[40] As the first half of the Figure 5.17 voice-leading graph shows, the expected result of this stepwise Pachelbel sequence would then be a large-scale voice exchange between the C/E♭ dyad first heard in the bass and voice (respectively) and the E♭/C dyad.

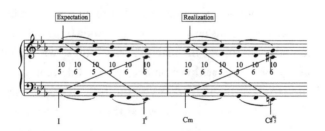

FIGURE 5.17 Expectation and realization for "Knives Out" (2001–6) voice exchange, verse.

However, like so many surprises heard in Radiohead's music, this one comes about through a subversion of this strong expectation. The last harmony heard in this progression does not provide the expected dyad C/E♭, but the twice chromatically inflected C♯/E♮. Chordally, this sonority could be interpreted either as a C♯ half-diminished seventh chord, or alternatively as E minor with an added raised sixth. In either case, the sonority is a profound departure from the established C Aeolian pitch center. But its real surprise stems from the break it causes in this expectation–realization chain. So strong is the sense of continuation toward a C/E♭–E♭/C voice exchange that the replacement of that final dyad with one shifted up by a semitone in each voice comes as a great shock.

Just as in the chorale of "Paranoid Android," this ostinato is then looped back to the beginning. And, just as the modulation in "Paranoid Android" provides a jolt when wrapping back around to the beginning, so the doubly chromatic inflection at the end of the "Knives Out" ostinato clashes with the diatonic version as it begins again. Mirroring the earlier C/E♭–E/C♯ cross relation, we now hear the reverse: C♯4 in the voice goes up to E♭4 ("look into" at 0:38), and the E♮ in the bass returns to C. Ultimately, it seems that the sharp-side ending of this ostinato prevails. The chorus replaces the first half of the phrase (C–B♭–A♭) with a circle of fifths sequence featuring chromatically inflected applied dominant chords (Am inflected as V of D, Dm inflected as V of G) which lands directly onto the second half of the verse ostinato to wrap back around, again, to the C♯/E to C/E♭ cross-relation at the beginning of each successive verse. What was once a surprise, very gradually, becomes learned and thus accepted over the course of the track.

Walter Everett's work in theories of harmony and voice leading for pop-rock music,[41] among other findings, demonstrates that pitch, more so than rhythm, form, or timbre, tends to exhibit the least amount of stylistic allegiance. In looking for a voice-leading schema involving typical rock progressions such as V7/IV, II♯ moving to IV; or, in looking for rather bizarre progressions that defy rock expectations, Everett finds examples across disparate genres that share little else in common. Relating specifically to Radiohead, Moore and Ibrahim "believe the patterns [of harmony and melody] to be less characteristic of what it is to sound like Radiohead."[42] We can thus extrapolate that, while experimental forms, timbres, and rhythm/meter combinations tend to be markers of certain experimental genres, harmony tends to be more catholic.

Radiohead's use of harmony and voice-leading schemes that range from the conventions heard in "Let Down" (1997–5) to the experiments in "Knives Out" (2001–4) should thus not be taken to reflect some outsider position within the larger rock milieu. While their experimentation in the other three parameters positions them as outside the norms of pop–rock music, we can search hard enough to hear many of the harmony and voice-leading schemes I've outlined in this chapter in blues, Motown, progressive rock, pop, Krautrock, and other genres.

I agree that pitch is central to the experience of hearing and interpreting music even for those who do not possess the language or graphic skills necessary to communicate those observations. However, for the analysis of Radiohead's music, I ultimately disagree with Everett's assertion that pitch is the single most important analytical parameter. We can understand, and even participate in, these other musical domains through gestures inherent within those domains themselves. We headbang, tap, or dance to rhythm based not only on the ways in which they shape emphatic pitch arrivals, but rather we move in patterns sympathetically with a rhythm's repeated groove pattern. Songs tell stories, and though tonal centers have a supporting role to play in those stories, so do the inherent proportions, ordering, and thematic materials of the formal sections. Finally, though timbre can be empirically defined as the relative amplitudes of discrete frequencies, this is a different conception altogether of pitch, and an ecological method of discerning sounds, their sources, and their specifications needs neither a tuning fork nor an oscilloscope.

Ultimately, then, our understanding of complex pitch relationships in Radiohead is an exercise in nuance. Hearing their predictable, often surprising, and occasionally bizarre voice-leading structures as a conversation with rock history that sometimes veers off into interesting tangents facilitates a rich approach to a pitch-based understanding of meaning in this music.

Analytical Coda: "Faust Arp"

A close reading of "Faust Arp" (2007–6) demonstrates that two salient designs in disparate domains—sectional harmonic centricity and terminally climactic form—can work in tandem to shape a compelling narrative. While songs like "Karma Police" (1997–6) seem defined by stark shifts of pitch center between sections (A in the verse, G in the chorus, D in the terminal climax), others seem content to revel in monotonality, articulating their climactic finishes through statistical means, usually by presenting the loudest dynamic (e.g., "Sit Down, Stand Up" (2003–2)), highest vocal pitch (e.g., "There, There" (2003–9)), or both (e.g., "All I Need" (2007–5)). "Faust Arp," on the other hand, seems torn between these two archetypes. The unusual formal/harmonic design of "Faust Arp" makes the most sense in tandem with a reading of the song's voice-leading structure. From a perceptual standpoint, harmony and voice leading in the song's four primary sections shown in Table 2.3 (verse, pre-chorus, chorus, and terminal climax) depend entirely on the various degrees of organicism an individual is willing to hear over three different spans of music:

> **Listener #1:** The most patient listener will hear a developing motivic structure that embellishes interval-class five—expressed as either an ascending fifth or inversely as a descending fourth—transposed to different pitch-classes in each of the song's four sections.
>
> **Listener #2:** Though two distinct tonal centers separate the song's constituent sections, this semi-patient listener attempts to unify the verse, pre-chorus, and chorus through an absent tonic prolongation that is only realized in the chorus.
>
> **Listener #3:** Because all of the song's tonal centers are fragile, threatening to unravel just as they are being established, this least patient listener hears no intersectional coherence, and struggles to incorporate various degrees of expressive chromaticism within each pitch center.

Differentiated by their willingness to hear larger voice-leading structures as connected to one another, these three listeners face a number of perceptual hurdles. These three approaches to perceiving organic unity lead to variously possible interpretations of meaning.

Verse (Bm–Bm/A–Bm/G–B/F♯)

Despite the fact that B receives undisputed hypermetric emphasis, the verse's distinct lack of tonal function leaves the status of that pitch center in relation to the pre-chorus and chorus a matter for debate. As a self-contained pitch center the verse can only be a CP system. It cannot be an FT system because, while it has a tonic–dominant axis, it does not have a dominant *chord* or a leading-tone. For the first of these reasons, it can also not be an FM system, and the alternation of D with D♯ calls into question the identity of any such mode altogether.

Listeners #1 and #2 may choose to forestall any harmonic interpretations awaiting further information from successive sections. For listener #3, who is largely concerned with harmonic understandings of individual sections, attempts to foreclose on this passage are met with some frustration. The opening sonority, an F♯3 in the voice supported by a B minor triad, seems a fine candidate for tonic. Given this perception, the descending stepwise bass transcribed in Figure 5.18 is completely in line with our expectations inherited from lament bass norms of the seventeenth century or, if you prefer, Ray Charles's rendition of "Hit the Road Jack" (1961).[43] Two surprises materialize simultaneously just as this expectation is realized on the

FIGURE 5.18 "Faust Arp" (2007–6, 0:05) verse.

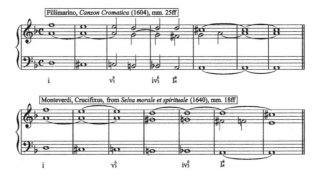

FIGURE 5.19 Two comparable seventeenth-century progressions.

arrival of the bass F♯ in the third measure. First, the assumed tonic of the passage, B minor, is now swapped out for its modal opposite, B major. Second, whereas the expected arrival harmony in a lament bass is a root-position dominant, scale-degree five is here harmonized as a consonant six-four chord. While I cannot say for certain that the resulting progression occurs *nowhere* in the pop–rock or common-practice tonal literature, suffice it to say that I have never heard it anywhere else and my informal queries among colleagues have revealed no other examples. This is the first of two cases in "Faust Arp" where a single deviation from an otherwise statistically abundant progression (e.g., the lament bass) proves to be a limiting factor which reduces the exact matches to zero. The closest we can get to a lament bass in which the originating root-position minor triad (i/1̂) gives way to a major six-four chord on scale-degree five (I/5̂) is heard in two rare examples from the early seventeenth century.[44] My rhythmic reductions in Figure 5.19 nevertheless display two striking conventions that disqualify these two examples and may further prove the originality of "Faust Arp." First, they fill in the gaps between natural minor 7̂ and 6̂ heard in "Faust Arp" with major mode inflections of those scale degrees to create

FIGURE 5.20 Arpeggiated ⁶/₄ in Beethoven, Symphony no. 3 in E♭, III, mm. 167ff. (reduction).

a smooth chromatic scalar passage.[45] Second, and most damning from a perceptual standpoint, the striking tonic six-four is probably heard, to some degree at least, as an intermediate step along the way to the phrase's goal harmony of the root-position dominant (A major).[46]

The chromatic details of the verse harmonic structure of "Faust Arp" render the progression unique. Lacking any intertextual clues, we may turn to the last half of the song's title in order to better understanding its voice-leading structure. Disregarding modal mixture for the moment, we can understand the B/F♯ at a deeper level as an example of the "arpeggiated six-four" heard throughout common-practice music, which also arises in various styles of popular music whenever the bass player opts for the chordal fifth rather than the root. Listener #3 could then hear the entire verse as an "Arp" (not unlike those heard in the similarly titled "Weird Fishes/Arpeggi" (2007–4) earlier on the album) that prolongs its initial root-position harmony through an arpeggiated six-four much like Beethoven does throughout Figure 5.20.

Pre-chorus (C/B♭–A♭–D♭)

Listeners #1 and #2 become more engaged in the structural function of the verse's mode-mixed B prolongation only upon the arrival of the pre-chorus. When the Bm chord colors itself as B major en route to C major in the pre-chorus this opens the possibility that B is not tonic, but rather *mediant* within an absent G tonic. In terms of classical harmony, we might then understand the inflection from B minor to B major as a move from iii to V/vi, which would then resolve "deceptively" to IV4/2. The B♭ in the bass of the IV chord not only creates a linear descent in the bass, but also cleverly avoids the parallel fifths and octaves associated with root motions by ascending step.

Within the realm of expectations of its native genre the move is much simpler, as III with a raised third moving to IV is a staple of rock harmony which facilitates the smooth semitonal motion ♯$\hat5$/III–$\hat6$/IV, often enharmonically reinterpreted as $\hat6$/IV–♭$\hat6$/iv afterward. This progression is in fact the signature riff heard throughout Radiohead's "Creep" (1993), shown in Figure 5.21. The fact that "Creep" is unequivocally centered in G may serve to justify even further Listener #2's monotonal endeavor.

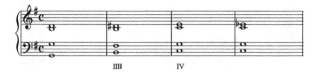

FIGURE 5.21 Rhythmic reduction of "Creep" (1993–2).

The A♭ chord which follows breaks with the rock-centric idiom heard in "Creep" despite the fact that it supports the same ♭6̂ as the C minor that should follow. This substitution of ♭II for iv suggests, however, the completely different perception of the root-position Neapolitan chord native to common-practice harmony. Such chord-by-chord leaping between harmonic idioms separated by centuries creates a jarring flow of ideas. We hear IV as rock, then ♭II as common-practice, but the D♭ chord which immediately follows subverts both, as the flattened dominant chord is native to neither style. Strangely, either of these divergent predictions—hearing C as IV (rock) and/or hearing A♭ as Neapolitan (common-practice)—leads to a satisfactory arrival on G at the onset of the chorus, but the D♭ chord that intervenes obliterates either understanding just before providing said satisfaction.

Here is the second time in the song in which a sufficiently rare harmonic progression (IV–♭II) has been rendered statistically unique by the addition of one extra harmony (♭V). Once again, there is no precedent for this progression in common-practice, pop–rock, or even jazz.[47] Needless to say, listeners of all types will be confused by this pre-chorus. As in the unique descending tetrachord progression in the verse, the song's title can provide a clue to understanding this harmonic oddity.

Despite the fact that Yorke himself seems opposed to understandings of this song based on the myth of Faust,[48] the cultural reference will be immediately present for any listener who knows the song's title. Though none of the myriad nineteenth-century compositions inspired by Goethe's two-volume play contains the exact progression in question, the pre-chorus of "Faust Arp" does resemble one particular moment from Schubert's 1823 song "Gretchen am Spinnrade." Just as the B in "Faust Arp" can be understood as a subordinate prolongation within G, the prolongation of E (mm. 18–25) in Schubert is subordinate to the nascent arrival of A. And, just like the B-to-C surprise of "Faust Arp," Schubert's E resolves unexpectedly up by a semitone to F in anticipation of its goal. Figures 5.22a and 5.22b illustrate the voice leading and harmonic similarities between these two moments, which coincidentally occur at roughly the same place in both examples.[49]

Most notable perhaps is the lyrical contrast between these otherwise congruent moments. Gretchen, having been stalked for quite some time by Faust, an aging doctor recently given the gift of youthful exuberance by Mephistopheles (who Yorke name-checks later on the album in "Videotape" (2007–11, 0:37)), is beside herself

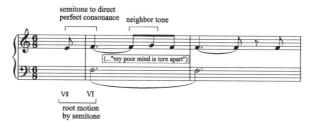

FIGURE 5.22A Franz Schubert, "Gretchen am Spinnrade," mm. 25–26.

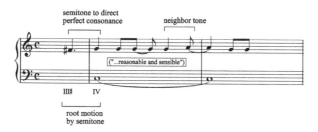

FIGURE 5.22B Radiohead, "Faust Arp" (2007–6, 0:24–0:26).

with love. As she continues to spin her wheel, her mind spins with it, and beginning at measure 26 she begins to lament how this lovesickness is clouding her ability to think straight. (Only a Romantic poet could render the sheer bliss of new love so much like death.) The narrator of "Faust Arp" on the other hand bemoans the opposite extreme, where reason and sensibility have made him "dead from the neck up." Radiohead's songs containing deeply embedded literary references within their titles might seem contradictory on one level (c.f., the Orwellian/Handelian in "2+2=5" (2003–1)), yet individual listeners might also find higher levels of congruent meaning through conceptual blending. Here, the Radiohead/Schubert/Faust nexus might, for some listeners, make more palpable and immediate the nineteenth-century sense of organic unity I espouse throughout my reading of the voice-leading structure, as well as the relentlessly chromatic harmony that resembles other Faust-inspired music by Schumann, Liszt, Berlioz, and Mahler.[50]

Chorus (G–G/F–G/E♭–G/D)

Listener #2's primary strategy for interpreting the voice-leading structure of "Faust Arp" hinges on a monotonal interpretation of the verse, pre-chorus, and chorus. Figure 5.23 presents a voice-leading graph that visualizes Listener #2's experience. Connecting the verse to the chorus relies on the same III♯–IV progression heard in "Creep" and countless other rock songs. We might be careful to note that from a purely prospective experiential standpoint the "III♯–IV" hypothesis is just that.

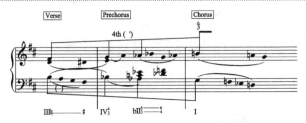

FIGURE 5.23 Monotonal voice-leading interpretation of "Faust Arp" (2007–6) verse/pre-chorus/chorus.

Semitonal ascending root motions between major triads are also heard between V and ♭VI (e.g., "Gretchen am Spinnrade"), and so the chorus's arrival on G realizes the hypothesis only retrospectively.

As the Figure 5.23 voice-leading graph shows, Listener #2's willingness to hear these three sections as a unified whole entails some palpable degree of difficulty. The A♭–D♭ progression now serves a larger purpose as part of a descending progression in the bass (B–B♭–A♭–G). As opposed to a *root*-centered analysis in which C (predominant) and A♭ (stronger predominant) cue expectation for a dominant arrival on D♮, hearing the B♭ in the bass of that C chord leads to more of a contrapuntal understanding of the line. Now the D♭ in the bass can be heard as a cast-out root demoted to a 5/3–6/4 figuration over the A♭ in the linear progression.

Hearing the three sections as unified in one key has an obvious "economical" benefit—a sort of Gestalt picture of the whole through its parts. But a further benefit may arise from hearing the connection between the opening fourth motive in the bass line, B down to F♯ (annotated with the Greek letter Alpha), and the chromaticized, inverted form that only unfolds as a fourth-progression over these three sections, F♯ up to B.

Yet another tetrachordal connection is available to Listener #3 precisely because of the puzzlement experienced previously in the verse. This arrives less through a higher-level synthesis so much as a failure to understand either. Heard thusly, the chorus presents the opposite obstacle to diatonicism as the verse. While the verse's tetrachordal descent matches its initial triad quality (B minor diatonically implies the continuation A–G–F♯), the chorus's tetrachordal descent contradicts its initial triad quality (perceiving the G major triad does not imply the F–E♭–D continuation). Essentially flipping the position of the surprise, Listener #3 now experiences it at the beginning of the descent, rather than the ending.

Terminal Climax [B♭–F/A–C/G–G]

After all the harmonic turmoil of the verse/pre-chorus/chorus unit subsides (either unified in G or not), the terminal climax spins on its heel to present yet another

TABLE 5.6

Highest lead vocal pitch in "Faust Arp" (2007–6) by measure

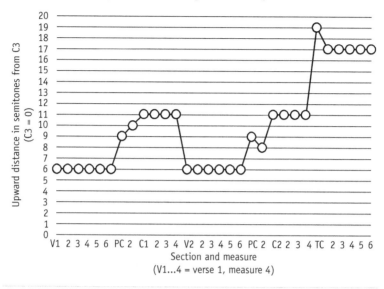

unrelated section. In this way it is quite like other terminal climaxes. But this syntactical gesture is only one way in which "Faust Arp" articulates its climax. Table 5.6 shows the inherent statistical climax in this section as the culmination of a process wherein lead vocal pitches are heard climbing higher into Yorke's register as the song moves from section to section.

Resisting any sort of FT or FM system, the climax's entire harmonic progression is best heard as a CP-system chain of plagal neighbors. Like the double-plagal progression heard throughout blues-influenced guitar rock,[51] this entire root progression—B♭–F–C–G—can be heard as a *triple plagal* progression. That is to say B♭ is plagal to F, C is plagal to G, and we can also hear F's plagal relation to C mediating those two pairs (though perhaps less explicitly). What this means for the ever-patient Listener #1 is another sort of culmination similar to the statistical climax heard in the lead vocal register. Each of the previous three sections elaborates interval-class five—expressed as either an ascending or descending fourth, either in pitch space or through root motion—in some meaningful way. As Figure 5.24 shows, the verse, chorus, and verse/pre-chorus/chorus unit feature stepwise gestures spanning interval-class five; the pre-chorus presents a perceptually marked interval-class five root motion at the surprise at D♭; and the terminal climax outlines not a single instance of interval-class five, but three in a row.

FIGURE 5.24 Interval-class five motivic development throughout sections of "Faust Arp" (2007–6).

Listener #2's connection between the terminal climax and the rest of the song may be more immediate. Paying attention to the exact voicing of the four chords in the terminal climax reveals that, while the last two contain the pitch-class G as part of their triadic structure, the first two also contain a G_3 ringing as the third open string of the guitar. Forming an oblique inner-voice counterpoint against the descending stepwise bass (G/B♭–G/A–G/G), the ringing G may be heard as confirmation of Listener #2's G tonal center heard throughout all previous sections of the song.

Throughout "Faust Arp," three different levels of focus in the perception of harmony and voice leading may be present. I have identified these strategies as belonging to three imaginary listeners. Listener #3 has trouble understanding the verse by itself, the chorus by itself, as well as the connection between them due to a rather myopic focus on intra-sectional harmonic detail. Listener #2 exhibits a higher level of organic unity through a willingness to forestall interpretation of the verse and pre-chorus until reaching the chorus, which affords the perception of these three essential sections as one tonal motion toward a G major goal. Where Listener #2's strategy falters at the onset of a wholly unrelated terminal climax, Listener #1's focus on the motivic development of interval-class five, though perhaps a bit detached from common-practice modes of harmonic perception, finds the entire composition, including the terminal climax, unified.[52] For both Listeners #2 and #3, two different references in the song's binomial title—one literary, one harmonic, both of which appear elsewhere on the album(!)[53]—may play a supporting role in the song's voice-leading structure. Of course, the interpretive strategies of these three listeners need not be sovereign. The most rewarding experience of perceiving and interpreting the voice-leading structure of "Faust Arp" may come from freely blending these approaches.

Notes

1. See Everett (2008, 168).

2. See Clarke (2005, 190).

3. The analytical symbology I use in graphs throughout the chapter belies a transparently Schenkerian methodology, though I prefer the term "voice-leading analysis" because much

of the sophistication of Schenker's system was aimed at classic-era voice-leading idiosyncrasies. Otherwise, it is a simple system of diagramming voice leading. Approaches that introduce modifications to orthodox Schenkerian voice-leading structures that make it more suitable for the analysis of pop–rock music can be found in Everett 2004, Burns 2008, and Nobile 2011.

4. Walter Everett's (2004, 32) thorough study provides significant proof for this assertion: "in a manner that approaches quantifiable significance . . . the majority of listeners who hear an array of tonal approaches in the hit records that reside in and out of today's mainstream also possess many of the same tonal-hearing mechanisms that were present one, two, and three hundred years ago."

5. Despite the fact that the bass $\hat{4}$ is not a neighbor tone to $\hat{1}$, IV is considered a neighbor to I because it supports the neighbor-gestures $\hat{3}$–$\hat{4}$ and $\hat{5}$–$\hat{6}$ *above* the bass.

6. Note in Figure 5.2 that there are two differently shaped noteheads: the diamond-shaped notes represent pitches that appear in the instrument parts rather than the voice. For example, the B and A at the end of the graph appear in the arpeggiated electric guitar chord and the strummed acoustic guitar chord, respectively.

7. Technically, the D-C♯-B slurred at the beginning of the chorus cannot compose out a harmonic interval because the D only serves as a neighbor tone to begin with. However, I find the motivic parallelism between that third and the composed out C♯-B-A that follows to be worth the slip in Schenkerian orthodoxy.

8. More properly (and admittedly, more abstractly): *these notes group together.* Agency and directionality might be evocative as metaphors, but they also belie the fact that these listening strategies are not always so immediate. In other cases, the left-to-right temporal ordering of notation complicates the metaphor "leads to," since previously sounding notes may be either more or less structurally significant.

9. As suggested by Lori Burns (2008, 219), I will not distinguish graphically between *Ursätze* at different levels of structure.

10. Both Nobile (2011) and Summach (2011) argue for this alignment of the song's primary *Stufenkreis* or phrase structure with its verse–chorus or strophic structure.

11. Everett (2015, fn 11) notes that some rock artists are more mindful of classical voice-leading tendencies, including Radiohead and the Beatles. This opinion is, to my mind, much more nuanced than say that of Trevor de Clercq (2013, 173) when he states, "The Neapolitan sixth chord, for instance, is essentially foreign to pop-rock music." Radiohead uses *functional* Neapolitan chords, both in root-position and first inversion, in "Subterranean Homesick Alien" (1997–3, 0:02), "Exit Music" (1997–4, 3:10), "A Wolf at the Door" (2003–14, 0:05), and "Decks Dark" (2016–3, 1:18).

12. "All I Need" is probably better characterized as a large-scale arpeggiation of the CMaj13 chord, with the bass G functioning more as tonic prolongation than functional dominant.

13. Indeed, Everett (2008, 157) states "[t]he pure Phrygian and Locrian modes are probably nonexistent."

14. Everett (2004, 19) echoes this narrow definition of modal harmony based exclusively on the presence of a dominant–tonic axis: "examples truly in the Aeolian mode would typically use a minor dominant."

15. Biamonte's study (2010), ironically focusing on modal patterns, provides ample support for these three contrapuntal gestures as the structural basis for 1970s guitar-based rock music.

16. See Everett (2004, 19).

17. A more orthodox Schenkerian take on the Dm7 chord would treat the C beamed in the reduction as a passing tone from an implied D above it (since Schenker treats all sevenths as passing tones). My choice to promote the C to a higher level of salience reflects the Dm7's role as a stable referential sonority throughout this section.

18. Spicer (forthcoming) coins this term for a pitch center whose tonic chord is absent from the section or song as a whole. He also makes use of the related terms "emergent" and "fragile" tonic. I will use these last two terms only when they are applicable to individual songs, using the more general "absent" as a category that includes all related entities.

19. Interval-class five includes both the perfect fifth and the perfect fourth. Interval class is a useful concept for the analysis of rock music inasmuch as it abstracts the octave of any pitch in a given interval. The interval class between any two pitches is the lesser of the two possible intervals (mod-12) when you change the octave of either pitch. For example, the pitch interval between C and D is either two (if D is above C) or ten (if C is above D), and so the interval-class is two.

20. There is at least collection-based support for a D major tonic to be heard in the bridge (3:30–4:06) where Yorke consistently sings G3 (foreshadowed in verse two at 2:23), which stands in a tritone relation to the C♯–B–A motive that reappears. This clash between competing D and A tonics comes to a head as Yorke finishes the bridge on a dissonant, quasi-cadential E4–D4 against the F♯ minor triad just before the chorus returns to confirm A major.

21. While most absent relative major tonics hold out until the arrival of a "breakout chorus" (see Doll 2011), this absent tonic is revealed relatively early at 1:12. The introduction can thus be heard as a vi–V–IV third prolongation, with the tonic chord arriving only in the verse along with the tonic pitch in the voice which is nonetheless never given simultaneous tonic support.

22. Rob Schultz (2012) demonstrates this irreconcilability of relative keys in several songs by Elliott Smith. It should be noted that Schultz does not consider FT systems to be a necessary condition for establishing a competing minor-mode tonal center.

23. See Krebs 1981 for discussion of the double-tonic complex in music analytical literature (including its original usage by Robert Bailey), its relationship to the related concept of "tonal pairing," and the presence of both in Romantic-era *Lieder*. Robert Gauldin (1990) has even applied this concept of the double-tonic complex to the music of The Beatles. Within this chapter, I will use "double-tonic complex" to describe all such situations, despite the fact that several contributors have argued for a stricter definition that requires a single motive encompassing both centers. For example, a motive that uses the pitch classes A, C, E, and G could reflect both A and C centers.

24. This term stems from a short article by Guy Capuzzo. Capuzzo (2009, 164–168) provides reductions of the three sections of "Karma Police" that differ from those presented here in significant ways. First, in his sketch of the verse, he shows an overall $\hat{3}$–$\hat{2}$–$\hat{1}$ motion with ♭VII acting as the "dominant," which promotes said sonority as more structurally significant than I have graphed it, as merely an equal participant in the circle of fifths sequence. Second, his representation of the chorus ignores the D dominant and renders the chorus a IV–I neighbor motion. Lastly, Capuzzo hears a B minor pitch center in the terminal climax despite the lack of a functional leading-tone.

25. As Capuzzo is careful to point out, the tritone relationship between F♯ major and the C major that immediately follows complicates a G major hearing, as does the unidiomatic

6/4 voicing of the guitar's D chord. Given that neither the guitar nor piano are playing in a true bass register, I do not find the latter to be problematic, as I can hear an absent and paradigmatic scale-degree 5 bass implied.

26. This may also be heard as an example of what Scott Murphy (2006) has identified as the "major tritone progression" in film music, which he associates with distance, unfamiliarity, and ambiguity.

27. Capuzzo (2009, 162) analyzes the verse's entire pitch content as a diatonic octad that can be understood as the confluence of A Dorian and A Aeolian [ABCDEFF#G]. Given that the voice never articulates either the F or F#, I hear these as inner-voice tones which do not affect the overall FM center on A.

28. The song is either terminally climactic or a through-composed terminally climactic hybrid. This depends on whether you hear the root position E-major chords at 0:29 and 1:06 as articulating the ends of two separate verses.

29. Malawey (2014, 26) notes a "hybrid modal collection" that mixes Dorian and Mixolydian modes.

30. Though a fuller examination of this song might include the way that the transition bridges these two sections, my analysis focuses only on the song's two main thematic parts: the verse and the terminal climax.

31. This discrepancy between the chord quality of two identical shapes stems from the guitar's tuning, which is built entirely of ascending perfect fourths (five semitones) *except* between the third and second strings, which is one semitone less—only four. This accounts for the third of the minor triad built on string five being one semitone lower than the third of the major triad built on string six. Alternating minor and major triads in a circle of fifths could also be heard as a sequential series of ii–V progressions.

32. A box pattern on the guitar is one in which chords or notes move "vertically" up or down by two frets while at the same time moving "horizontally" across adjacent strings, creating what looks like a series of connected squares on the fretboard. I have chosen to notate this with sharps for two reasons. First, guitarists are typically more adept at reading sharps. Second, because starting with D# and working our way flat-side on the circle of fifths means that we gradually work our way toward fewer sharps. If beginning, for example on E♭ and moving flat-side, the spellings quickly become full of flats, passing C♭ minor en route not to E major, but to the unwieldy F♭ major.

33. The term originates from Allan Moore (1995, 189), is theorized by Tempereley (2007), and is reconsidered significantly by Nobile (2015).

34. Moore and Ibrahim (2005, fn 49) reproduce the relevant passage from O'Brien's online diary, in which he describes the recording of this song as "inkspots-esque."

35. Nattiez (1985) gives a summary account of various authors' approaches to analyzing the Tristan Chord.

36. In fact, jazz is just about the only style in which the mM7 chord is commonly found.

37. Retrospectively the AmM7 chord may now be understood as a highly chromatic verse-prolongation of a global A minor tonic. Two significant barriers to such a monotonal hearing should be cautioned: (1) the A minor tonic is only confirmed at 1:45, thus a prospective hearing of 0:01–1:44 must necessarily ignore it; (2) the verse's progression [AmM7–Cm–Gm–F#m7♭5/F] not only never presents a stable tonic triad, but, containing the chromatic pitches B♭, E♭, and F#, is only one semitone shy of saturating the chromatic scale.

38. In analyzing this song, Rusch (2013) uses the related concepts of tonal pairing and double-tonic complex nearly synonymously, providing relevant citations for each. Her figure 5a demonstrates a C/G tonal pairing in the intro and A section, A/C pairing in the B section and coda, and echoes my C/D pairing for the chorale.

39. The total voice-leading work (see Cohn 2012, 6) inherent in this chromatic third relationship is four semitones—not efficient at all by typical Neo-Riemannian standards. The C♯ moves to C (parallel), A to G (relative), and E to E♭ (parallel), yielding the doubly chromatic PRP operation.

40. Another possible expectation might involve moving the voice down another complete third D4–C4–B♭4, rendering the expectation of the final chord an E♭ major seventh chord.

41. See Everett 2004 and 2008, especially.

42. See Moore and Ibrahim (2005, 141). They find more specific compositional strategies in Radiohead to stem from formal design, although with a suspect methodology of analyzing form where lettered sections (e.g., A, B) are not necessarily thematically independent.

43. This descending [0135] tetrachord is ubiquitous in popular music (cf., the chorus of The Beatles' "We Can Work it Out" (1965) also from B to F♯).

44. Close calls abound in early pop–rock music but even still the presence of the tonic six-four is a rigorous requirement whose search returns zero results. Hear, for example, Robert Knight's "Everlasting Love" (1967, 1:34–1:40), which, despite having a perceptible lament in the inner voice and returning a major tonic triad on the final chord, puts said final tonic in root position, rather than six-four position (thanks to Walter Everett for pointing me toward this example over the Society for Music Theory listserv).

45. Though not discussed or transcribed these two pieces appear in Kyle Adams's index (2006, 258 and 264).

46. This is more obvious in Fillimarino's setting, where the A lasts for three more measures past the tonic six-four. In common-practice keyboard music, we occasionally hear mode mixture at the point of the six-four. But unlike these nascent states shown in Figure 5.19, the "cadential six-four" suspension over the dominant solidifies by the mid seventeenth century to the point that said six-four should no longer be regarded as perceptually marked. Nineteenth-century lament basses sometimes lead to secondary dominants of IV in four-three position, yielding the same tetrachordal structure but with a dissonant seventh chord on the tonic rather than a stable major triad.

47. The lingua franca of common-practice harmony includes significant use of the ♭II chord (as Neapolitan sixth) which proceeds directly to the diatonic V chord as per its predominant function. Jazz sees the same pairing of the diatonic dominant with the lowered supertonic, more often than not reversing the order of the common-practice version (V–♭II) wherein the ♭II acts as a tritone substitution for the dominant. The closest relative to this pre-chorus progression may be heard in another rock pre-chorus. Silverchair's "Ana's Song" (1999–3, 0:36) uses the progression B♭–F as a transition into the E major chorus, yielding the reverse (♭V–♭II–I) of "Faust Arp." A decade later Radiohead would use a transpositionally equivalent progression—B♭ major–E♭ major–A major—in "Decks Dark" (2016–3, 1:15), but the tonal orientation is different. Strongly centered in D previous to this moment, we must hear this progression as a dominant preparation that eventually works its way back to the D tonic.

48. When asked about this connection in an interview by *Observer Music Magazine*, Yorke answered in his characteristically faux-aloof manner: "I vaguely know the story of Faust. But

that would involve me having remembered it in some detail or picked it off the shelf. Which I didn't. But yes, hmm, Goethe's Faust. I'm going to have to look that one up, actually, 'cause that sounds suitably pretentious. We live in Oxford, after all."

49. The ratio of 25 measures of "Gretchen" to the total 116 measures in the piece approximates the ratio of 24 seconds of "Faust Arp" to the 130 total seconds in the song.

50. This connection has nothing to do with whether or not Yorke knew the Schubert song in question. Rather, the connection to Faust in the song's title makes all related cultural references available and relevant to a large number of listeners.

51. Nicole Biamonte (2010, 99) provides several examples of the double-plagal progression heard in blues-influenced rock songs released between 1957 and 1987.

52. Though perhaps in a manner more Schoenbergian than Schenkerian.

53. Arpeggios are heard even more clearly in the track "Weird Fishes/Arpeggi" (2007–4) and the myth of Faust is sufficiently evoked by the album's closing track "Videotape" (2007–10) ("Mephistopheles is just beneath").

6 "Pyramid Song"

NO OTHER SONG in Radiohead's catalog has generated so much speculation as "Pyramid Song" (2001–2). What is with the meter? Was it really inspired by Mingus? Are the lyrics from the Egyptian Book of the Dead? Fans and critics alike seem quicker to offer personal interpretations of meaning for this song than any other in Radiohead's catalog. I take this outpouring of affective response to be indicative of the song's salience. One just does not find comparable levels of debate surrounding "Fake Plastic Trees" (1995–3) or "Hunting Bears" (2001–9). The former is just too predictable, while the latter, in its timbral, rhythmic, harmonic, and formal austerity, offers scant avenues into interpretation. "Pyramid Song" exhibits a Goldilocks zone between these two extremes. It invites speculation through its repeated chord progression, clear lyrical declamation, and familiar voice/piano/drums instrumentation, but its swinging Euclidean rhythm and chromatic voice leading provide ample surprise. The evocative lyrics and computer-generated music video only intensify our desire to understand this song.

How do the expectations cued by "Pyramid Song"—as well as the surprises it presents—relate to similar phenomena heard throughout Radiohead's catalog? In this final chapter, I'll attempt to synthesize the major theories and analytical methods in the book's first five chapters into a holistic analysis of what guitarist Ed O'Brien once called "the best song we've recorded."[1]

Genesis

Between 2001 and 2013, four main theories about the inspiration for "Pyramid Song" circulated among fan sites and in the published critical discourse: (1) the Tibetan and/or Egyptian books of the dead; (2) Charles Mingus's "Freedom"; (3) a complicated intertextual "clapping" connection linking "Freedom," Shirley Ellis's "Clapping Song," and Tom Waits's "Clap Hands"; and (4) Egyptian funereal rites.[2] However, in 2013, Yorke gave an unusually candid interview, essentially ending the mystery of the song's genesis once and for all:

> We were in Copenhagen, we just started recording the first session after *OK Computer*, and we were all deeply dysfunctional, especially me. And there was an exhibition, they had a whole Egyptian section where they went on about religious beliefs and stuff, and they had these figures in these little boats ready to go wherever it is they were going to go. We were having a really shitty session, but we got in the morning afterwards, sat down, played these chords and I just said, "That's nice," made a note of it and then wrote words, and it was very quick. We recorded the drumming a few months later, and it sounded like something from a Charlie Mingus record. It was just one of those weird things of, when you make a record, eventually you get to a flow and that was just part of the flow. We were going through this bad period where nothing was going right and this was a big breakthrough. But I never expected it to be such a popular single. When we play it live people go nuts for it, and we're like, "Really?"[3]

Yorke is referring to the Copenhagen sessions in March 1999 when the band recorded some of the first takes for *Kid A* and *Amnesiac*. Though released as two albums, songs from both were recorded in the same sessions, which took place not only in Copenhagen, but later in Paris and Oxford. Though Yorke recorded the piano part in Copenhagen in 1999, Jonny Greenwood's string arrangements on "Pyramid Song" were recorded later by the Orchestra at St. Johns in the same sessions as those for "How to Disappear Completely" (2000–4) and "Dollars and Cents" (2001–8).[4]

Taking Yorke at his word about the Egyptian inspiration (which was most likely the extensive Egyptian display in the Collection of Antiquities at Ny Carlsberg Glyptotek), we must also admit that the imagery of boats taking one to the afterlife is far too universal to connote anything specifically Egyptian. Most of Radiohead's western listenership will sooner associate the lyrical imagery with Dante's depiction of the river Styx in Canto VII of *The Divine Comedy*.

In order to fully appreciate this lyrical imagery in "Pyramid Song," as well as the visual imagery in its corresponding video, we must first understand the musical elements both animate. Drawing from all previous chapters' theoretical models, I will now highlight the most salient formal, rhythmic, timbral, and harmonic moments of "Pyramid Song." Beginning with the relatively straightforward formal and timbral elements, I will then discuss the song's perplexing parallel voice leading before shedding light on its most defining characteristic, the palindromic rhythm. Finally, I will draw on these most salient moments to craft a narrative that runs throughout the song's music video.

Form

"Pyramid Song" is best described as a strophic form with end-refrain. Like "I Will" (2003–10), the form unfolds not so much from repetition, but from subtle motivic variation over the course of the track. Table 6.1 reflects this process by naming variations of the introductory piano motive "pyramid," "radix," and "BACH." These motives, along with the "intro" motive itself, are transcribed in Figure 6.1. The rationale for naming these motives will be discussed later in the harmony and voice leading section.

Each of the motives has a duration of 32 eighth notes. Though the rhythm for each motive can be divided into two 16-count halves, the pitch–rhythm motive cannot, and unfolds over the full 32 counts. "Radix" and "BACH" both have a chord change on this symmetrical seam, but the pitch content of the second half is not a copy of the first. This discrepancy between, on the one hand, a shared 16-count rhythmic motive and, on the other, four different asymmetrical 32-count pitch motives, is partially responsible for the track's dizzying, hypnotic undulation.

Three of the four motives (essentially piano riffs) combine in predictable ways. First, the introduction begins with the "intro" motive alone. When the vocalise is added in the third phrase, Yorke changes to a "pyramid"/"intro" couplet. This pairing of the vocalise with the "pyramid"/"intro" couplet is consistent—it reappears between the verses. Two verses are formed by pairing the "pyramid" and "radix" motives into couplets. Yorke sings a line ending on C♯4 over each "pyramid" motive, then a lower line usually ending on B3 (or prolonging B through lower ornaments) over the "radix" motive. Four of these couplets comprises the first verse. Selway's drum fills interrupt a recap of the intro, after which the second verse precedes much like the first (the lyrics are the same). The end of verse two's fourth couplet is modified to reveal the first instance of the "BACH" motive.

TABLE 6.1

Form in "Pyramid Song" (2001–2)

Section	Time	Motive	Description
intro a	0:01	intro ×2	solo piano w/quiet strings
intro a′	0:18	pyramid/intro	vocalise added
verse 1a	0:36	pyramid/radix	"jumped in the river"
b	0:54	pyramid/radix	"moon full of stars"
c	1:13	pyramid/radix	"all my lovers"
d	1:31	pyramid/radix	"we all went to heaven"; ondes Martenot more prominent; refrain in second half="there was nothing to fear, nothing to doubt"
intro b	1:49	pyramid/intro	vocalise returns, strings more prominent (doubling vocalise w/glissando); drum fills
intro b′	2:08	pyramid/intro	drums begin pattern
verse 2a	2:24	pyramid/radix	ondes Martenot more prominent
2b	2:42	pyramid/radix	
2c	3:00	pyramid/radix	low harmony voice added
2d'	3:18	pyramid/BACH	string/ondes drop out, leaving voice/drums/piano
2e	3:36	BACH/radix	refrain from end of 2d ("nothing to fear") repeated ×2
outro	3:54	intro ×4	strings in foreground (G–F#–D motive)
sustain	4:33–4:49	n/a	ondes and strings

FIGURE 6.1 Four mod-32 motives in "Pyramid Song" (2001–2).

A fifth couplet is inserted here to allow the song's refrain ("there was nothing to fear, nothing to doubt") to repeat. We hear it twice over "BACH" and then once over "radix." Expanding this final couplet allows the F#3 resting note on "doubt" to be harmonized three different ways: (1) as the major seventh of G; (2) as the root of F# major; and (3) in counterpoint with a higher B3 over the sustained G major chord at the end of "radix."

Timbre

There are five acoustic sources in the recording. Three of these (piano, voice, drums) are immediately recognizable and prominent in the mix. The other two acoustic sources (string ensemble and upright bass) are less so. Like many acoustic bass parts, this one is "felt rather than heard." The string ensemble plays the most dynamic role relative to the song's form. This dynamic timbral/formal role is shared by the song's only synthetic timbre, the ondes Martenot.

Timbre and orchestration are closely linked in "Pyramid Song." Because the instruments and voice are minimally processed they pose almost no barriers to source identification. Considering timbre's relation to form in this song is more interesting. When do the different instruments enter, why, and what is their role relative to the central focus of the song: the voice and piano? Visualizing this timbral flow in Table 6.2 may serve as a starting point to answering these questions.

TABLE 6.2

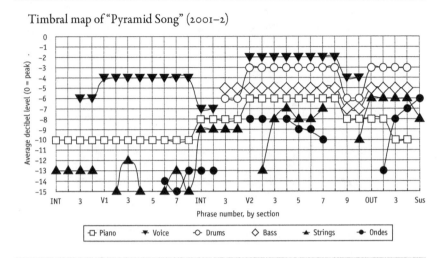

Timbral map of "Pyramid Song" (2001–2)

An explanation of the timbral method shown in Table 6.2 is in order. Using spec-trographic analysis, we can measure the loudness of any instrument at any point in the recording. For example, when the voice enters on F♯4 (370hz), I can tell that the voice is louder than the piano because the amplitude of that pitch (−6db) is louder than the amplitude of the A♯3 guide tone heard prominently in the piano (233hz @ −10db).[5] The quietest sound in the recording is the last moment of decay before each new attack in the piano-only introduction (−24db), and the quietest continuously sustained amplitudes are heard in the string and ondes Martenot's faintest moments in verse one (−15db). In digital audio, 0db represents the point of clipping. Like most modern pop–rock recordings, this track's dynamic peaks come as close to possible to that 0db ceiling without touching it.

While the voice, piano, drums, and bass all maintain an even dynamic relation-ship throughout the recording—once the drums enter everything rises an average of about 4db—the strings and ondes Martenot enter, exit, and swell in a dynamic process that shapes the song's form. Table 6.3 removes the bass, drums, and piano— all of which follow the same general curve—in order to simplify the relationship between the voice, string, and ondes.

Generally, the strings and ondes Martenot play a supporting role relative to the voice until the end of the track, when they take center stage. Rather than "pad" soft textures underneath the voice (as in many pop–rock recordings), the support-ing instruments engage in a dialogue with the voice. Verse one begins with a new texted melody in the voice. As the second phrase ends the strings swell in volume and reach a peak that sustains through the third phrase. After receding into the

TABLE 6.3

Simplified timbral map of "Pyramid Song" (2001–2)

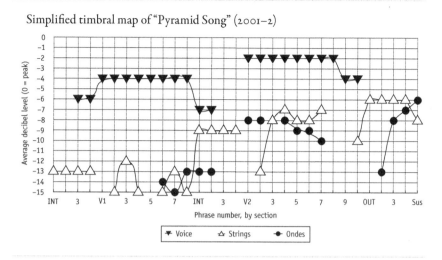

background, they crescendo again to trace a similar arc around the seventh phrase. Here the ondes Martenot joins, adding a third dynamic curve to the mix. Notice in Table 6.3 that, in the same phrase that the strings form a valley–peak–valley shape, the ondes Martenot's amplitude curve inverts that shape: peak–valley–peak.

Like the rest of the timbres in this track, the strings and ondes rise significantly in volume when the drums and bass enter just before verse two. Just as the voice enters at the beginning of that verse, the ondes Martenot takes center stage for the first time. Louder than the heretofore dominant strings for two phrases, the ondes then loses its position once they swell into the third phrase. Both the strings and ondes drop out completely, allowing Yorke to intone the refrain "nothing to fear, nothing to doubt" quietly yet prominently. With the voice part now tacet, the strings swell and peak at their highest volume level. The outro sounds largely *driven* by the string ensemble. That is, until the ondes reaches up and over, but somewhat too late—by the time it reaches prominence over the strings all other instruments have dropped out. Intoning what sounds like a sad, atonal variation on the strings' G–F♯–D motive, the ondes is left alone on the soundstage as the track ends.

Harmony and Voice Leading

Four Motives Mod-32

Four mod-32 melodic-harmonic motives that make up "Pyramid Song," traditionally notated in Figure 6.1, are graphed in Table 6.4. The 32-eighth duration shared by each motive is graphed on the *x*-axis. Using pitch-octave notation

TABLE 6.4

Guide tones of four mod-32 motives in "Pyramid Song" (2001–2)

(a) "intro" motive

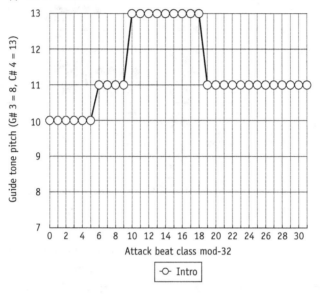

(b) "pyramid" motive

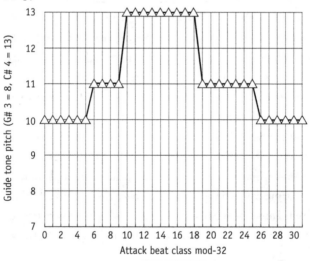

TABLE 6.4

Continued

(c) "radix" motive

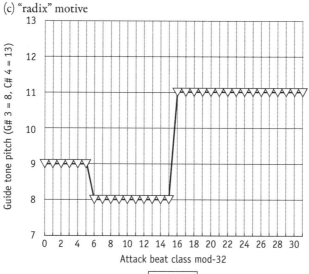

(d) "BACH" motive

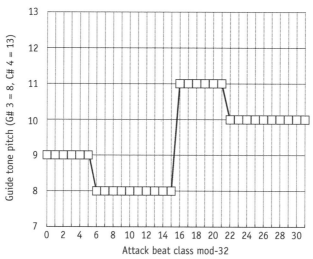

(G♯3=8 . . . C♯4=13), the *y*-axis graphs the chordal thirds of each motive, or what we might call the "guide tones." I offer three justifications for the salience of these guide tones. First, Yorke's voicings highlight them prominently and consistently. Second, the guide tones are more salient than either the roots or the bass notes of each chord; neither changes in the transition between F♯ major and minor triads. Finally, graphing the guide tones clarifies the counterpoint since the upper voice is rife with suspended or pedal tones—especially pedal F♯ over G major and even vice versa, suspended G over F♯ major.

The rise and fall of the "pyramid" motive in pitch space suggests a two-dimensional simulacrum of its eponymous polygon. Like the mod-16 rhythm that recurs throughout the song, its parallel major triads (F♯, G, A, G, F♯) form a palindrome. Something close to its mirror image can be seen in the "radix" motive (named for its resemblance to the mathematical symbol for roots). The "BACH" motive that appears only near the end of the song begins like "radix" but ends on the same A♯ that begins "pyramid." The resulting collection differs from all others in that it contains four distinct pitch-classes which form a cluster of semitones transpositionally equivalent to Bach's musical signature.[6]

Motives "pyramid" and "radix" most obviously relate by inverted contour. The up-then-down shape of the former flips to form the down-then-up of the latter. A more precise accounting for this inverted relationship must take into account pitch-class. The [10, 11, 1] guide tones in "pyramid" are transpositionally equivalent to the [8, 9, 11] guide tones in "radix."[7] Though they appear to be "inverted" in the everyday sense, they are both of the normal order [013] and therefore require only transposition to get from one to the other. Their apparent inverted shape on the pitch-octave graph is due to the altered contour of the two motives. While the first three notes of "pyramid" ascend in an <012> contour, "radix" begins on its middle pitch, dips down, then ascends to the highest, creating a <102> contour. A true pitch-class inversion relationship would only attend if the contour of "radix" were altered to <210>—say, on the pitch-classes A, G♯, F♯—which would incidentally run the bass notes of "pyramid" in retrograde.

Voice Leading

With the exception of the slippage from F♯ major to F♯ minor that occurs between the end of "pyramid" and the beginning of "radix," all triads in "Pyramid Song" are major. This parallel voice leading of major triads is also the underlying system heard in "Everything in its Right Place" (2000–1). Crucially, both songs constrain these four triads within the bounding interval of a perfect fourth. This means that the [E, F♯, G, A] triads in "Pyramid Song" and the [C, D♭, E♭, F] triads in "Everything in its Right Place" both have the *potential* for a tonic–dominant axis despite the parallel voice leading. In other words, "Pyramid Song" could engender a functional tonal system on A, with its E dominant chord, and "Everything in its Right Place" could do the same with its F major tonic and C major dominant. The degree to which the lead vocal melody in either song supports this functional tonal hearing differs, as does the degree to which the mode mixture inherent in parallel major voice leading obfuscates it.

"Everything in its Right Place" features a blatantly tonal system right at the moment its title lyric arrives. When Yorke sings F4–C4–F4 over the first appearance of an F major triad (0:34), which then leads to a C major triad, we have almost no choice but to hear this functionally in F major despite the parallel voice leading. The lead vocal melody in "Pyramid Song" never articulates an authentic cadence in A major, largely because the A major and E major triads are never heard successively. In fact, within the temporal flow of the "pyramid" and "radix" motives, these two triads are *maximally separated*—the potential E dominant is separated by three chords both before and after each potential A tonic. The functional tonal system heard most clearly in "Pyramid Song" is a half-cadential figure that spans the "pyramid" and "radix" motives. A voice-leading graph of this half-cadence is shown in Figure 6.2.

Mode mixture creates some degree of difficulty in hearing this functional tonal system. Note that "Pyramid Song" admits mode mixture on the seventh scale degree, with the subtonic G both preceding and following the leading tone G♯. Both Gs are in the bass, the first part of an ascending thirds progression, the second treated as a mode-mixed arpeggiated prolongation of the E dominant. Compare this to the mode mixture heard in "Everything in its Right Place," graphed in Figure 6.3.

FIGURE 6.2 Voice-leading analysis of "Pyramid Song" (2001–2, 0:36).

FIGURE 6.3 Voice-leading analysis of "Everything in its Right Place" (2000–1, 0:34).

FIGURE 6.4 Voice-leading analysis of "The Tourist" (1997–12, 0:54).

"Everything in its Right Place" features this same mode-mixed dominant prolongation, where E is heard as the leading tone in the C dominant chord which is then arpeggiated through E♭. Interestingly, both use an [013] passing gesture in the bass (c.f. F♯–G–A vs. C–D♭–E♭), though it prolongs the tonic in "Pyramid Song" and dominant in "Everything in its Right Place."

While both songs employ mode mixture on scale-degree seven, mixture on scale-degree three—quite detrimental to a sense of major tonic—is avoided in both songs. Though it does not affect scale-degrees 3, 6, or 7, "Pyramid Song" uses something akin to mode mixture when it mixes two different qualities of the submediant chord, both F♯ major and F♯ minor. The most striking impact of this "mixture" is that it occasionally replaces the tonic scale degree A with its chromatically inflected A♯. While exceptionally rare within the purview of rock harmony, this replacement of scale-degree 1 with ♯1 has a single precedent in Radiohead's catalog.[8] Figure 6.4 shows a voice-leading analysis of "The Tourist" (1997–12, 0:54), in which the expected tonic B major chord is replaced by the major submediant G♯ major as Yorke sings the uncanny raised first scale degree (B♯) on the word "ghost." Interestingly, both songs use the same [0135] cluster of chord roots—the E, F♯, G, A quartet of "Pyramid Song" is transposed up a whole step to F♯, G♯, A, B in "The Tourist"—though the latter differs from both "Pyramid Song" and "Everything in its Right Place" in that one of those triads is minor.

Comparing the parallel major voice leading and mode mixture heard in "Pyramid Song" to similar strategies heard earlier in the band's output contextualizes what might otherwise be perceived as a voice-leading "anomaly." It reveals a thread of continuity in Yorke's harmonic language while at the same time relating such radical expressions to a model of functional voice leading inherited from western tonality.

Rhythm

No other aspect of this song is more contentious than its rhythm and meter. Most commentators focus on the rhythm's palindromic aspects, yet some go further to speculate on potential meter signatures, the role of swing, and the drum set's role in either reinforcing or distracting from these structures.[9] I will approach most of these facets of the rhythm through the lens of maximal evenness and maximal individuation.

Mod-16 Palindrome

Though the rhythmic/melodic motives transcribed in Figure 6.1 are each 32 pulses long, the rhythm itself is only 16 pulses long. When those 16 pulses are divided by the five attack points, we are left with the maximally even distribution <33433>. The geometry of a pyramid—five sides, four of which have 3 vertices and one of which has 4—is hard to miss.[10]

What makes this rhythm so captivating is the ironic tension between its palindromic nature and the maximum individuation of its component beats. Though it is symmetrical, each beat is unique. To understand these and other peculiar mathematical properties of the "Pyramid Song" rhythm we have to understand its archetype: the Cuban Cinquillo, shown in Figure 6.5.

The maximally even Cinquillo rhythm <21212> is also a palindrome, and, when visualized on a timeline, closely resembles a pyramid. "Pyramid Song" is simply a Cinquillo played twice. More specifically, playing the mod-8 Cinquillo <02356> twice using alternating hands, as shown in Table 6.6, generates the

FIGURE 6.5 Mod-8 Cuban Cinquillo.

TABLE 6.5

Mod-8 Cuban Cinquillo

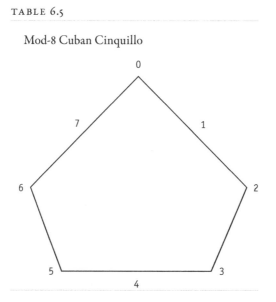

TABLE 6.6

Two mod-8 Cinquillos generate mod-16 <33433>

Mod-16	0	1	2	3	4	5	6	7	8	9	10	11	12	13	14	15
Mod-8 Cinquillo (Right Hand)	0			3			6				2			5		
Mod-8 Cinquillo (Left Hand)			2			5			0			3				6

TABLE 6.7

Maximally individuated rhythm in "Pyramid Song" (2001–2)

Duration of previous beat	Duration of previous beat	Beat	Duration of next beat	Duration of next beat
3	3	A	3	4
3	3	B	4	3
3	3	C	3	3
3	4	D	3	3
4	3	E	3	3

mod-16 <0,3,6,10,13> in each hand. This derivation from the Cinquillo shows that the "Pyramid Song" rhythm bears the same "interlocking reflection" property of most of the world's traditional rhythmic timelines.[11]

The mod-8 Cinquillo and its mod-16 offspring heard in "Pyramid Song" are both diatonic rhythms, meaning they are not only maximally even but also maximally individuated. Throughout the song, the five beats in the cycle remain as far apart as possible (maximally even) with each beat nevertheless playing a unique role in that cycle (maximally individuated).

Let <ABCDE> in Table 6.7 represent these five beats <33433>. Beats A, B, D, and E are each three pulses long, and C is four pulses long. C is obviously unique owing to its distended duration. But the other four, all three pulses long, are also unique with regards to the durations they precede and follow. An analogy to the diatonic scale is helpful here. The diatonic scale is the maximally individuated distribution of seven pitch-classes across the 12-tone scale. In the scale <CDEFGAB> there are five whole steps and two half steps. When we hear a melody in C major that uses all of these pitch-classes, we can easily discern which half-step is B–C, and which half-step is E–F—despite the fact that they are the same interval—by the number of whole-steps on either side of them.

Though few listeners perceive the mathematical processes behind diatonic scales or rhythms, it is these cyclical properties that give the rhythm its enigmatic character. In a study of diatonic rhythms heard in world music, Jay Rahn goes so far as to assert that "[d]iatonic rhythms . . . can be understood as twisting or tunneling through time, forming a special, braided structure."[12]

The Drum Part

The 16 pulses that subdivide the piano rhythm throughout "Pyramid Song" are only made audible once Selway's drum part enters at 2:07. The interaction of his quarter-note ride cymbal pattern with his syncopated kick-and-snare pattern, shown in Figure 6.6, reveals an underlying eighth-note pulse that divides the five piano attacks into <33433>. This is notable for two reasons. First, it means that hearing the piano-and-voice-driven first two minutes of the song as <33433> is only possible retrospectively. Second, while the subdivisions in Selway's drum part make possible the <33433> piano rhythm, his accent pattern actually divides those 16 pulses differently.

Though it is of course impossible to recreate the first time we heard the song's first two minutes, it should not have been possible, strictly speaking, to discern a <33433> subdivision in the piano part.[13] Yorke's voice "floats" over the rhythm with a perceptible swing in which only the *downbeat* of each mod-32 motive aligns with the beginning of each poetic line (jumped, black, moon, all . . .). Even retrospectively with Selway's subdivision in our ears, it's difficult to perceive any reliable meter from Yorke's vocal performance in the first two minutes. Being as true as possible to perceptual processes, then, we might then represent the piano rhythm in the first two minutes in relation only to this stable downbeat, in which case the relative ratios of each attack relative to the total duration are <.1875, .1875, .25, .1875, .1875>, or, more

FIGURE 6.6 Drum entrance in "Pyramid Song" (2001–2, 2:07).

phenomenologically <short, short, long, short, short>. Either of these ratios form an obvious pyramid shape if perceived vertically along a timeline.

When Selway's subdivisions at 2:07 finally provide the <33433> framework for the piano rhythm, he simultaneously divides those same 16 pulses differently than the piano: <33334>. His first three accents <kick, snare, kick> align with the first three attacks in the piano, respectively, but his snare accent just after the first barline anticipates the fourth piano attack by an eighth note, creating a grouping dissonance that persists through the rest of the mod-16 groove. When the two parts realign on the downbeat of bar three—the beginning of a new mod-16 cycle—only to pull apart again in the same place as before, a cyclical, braided pattern of alignment/dissonance between the two timelines begins to emerge.

Swing

Like "Life in a Glass House" (2001–11) and the ill-fated "Spectre" (2015)—written for, yet never attached to, the eponymous Bond film[14]—the drums and piano in "Pyramid Song" lock together in jazzy swung eighth notes. Though the exact proportions between two swung eighth notes (the first always longer than the second) are unique to individual performers, the most common approximation of this long–short subdivision is 2:1, often notated as a quarter-note triplet followed by an eighth-note triplet.

However, most jazz and other swing is simply notated using even eighth notes with the assumption that performers will add their own swinging interpretation. It is this assumption that allows for the <33433> maximally even rhythm in "Pyramid Song." If we were to take into account the rhythmic discrepancies resulting from the swing in those subdivisions, we end up with the slightly more precise rhythm mod-24 shown in Table 6.8.[15]

TABLE 6.8

Mod-24 swing durations of "Pyramid Song" (2001–2) rhythm		
Attack	Mod-16 duration; (rhythm=<0,3,6,10,13>)	Mod-24 duration; (rhythm=<0,5,9,15,20>)
A	3	5
B	3	4
C	4	6
D	3	5
E	3	4

Because attack point C always encompasses both the long and short halves of two beats, its duration is unaffected by swing. The remaining four attacks are each swung. Those that begin on a notated downbeat (mod-24 beat classes 0, 3, 6 . . .) will be longer than those beginning on the shorter swung eighth (mod-24 beat classes 2, 5, 8 . . .). This means we now have not two different durations (cf., 3 and 4 mod-16), but three different durations: 6, 5, and 4 mod-24.

If we are willing to entrain to these three different beat lengths, then the "Pyramid Song" rhythm is no longer a palindrome; <54654> is not equal to its retrograde <45645>. It is also no longer maximally even, since the maximally even distribution of 24 by 5 is [55554]. One of the only interpretive upshots to this analysis, for me, is a numerological one. Three different beat durations correspond to three different guide tones in both of the song's primary motives: "pyramid" (A♯, B, C♯) and "radix" (A, G♯, B).[16]

The Music Video

The "Pyramid Song" music video blends the Dante-inspired lyrics and imagery with a bleak view of a post-terrestrial future hastened by global warming. Both *The Divine Comedy* and global warming are omnipresent in the band's output since *OK Computer* (1997).[17] Yorke has spoken at length regarding the influence of Dante's literary work on Radiohead songs between 2000 and 2003, especially on *Hail to the Thief* (2003).[18] He explains, for example, the impetus for subtitling "2+2=5" (2003–1) "The Lukewarm":

> The lukewarm, is something from Dante. If I remember this rightly, it's the least nasty bit of hell, just as you walk through the door there're the "Lukewarm." . . . And it's quite a curious thing that Dante presents you with . . . you have these people and you think, "Well, they haven't done anything wrong, they just didn't do anything."

In a famous scene from Canto VII, Dante ferries across the river Styx ("jumped into the river what did I see?"), where the trapped souls of the sullen strain upward beneath the black water ("black-eyed angels swam with me") to reach the surface in an attempt to escape their Purgatorial state ("we all went to Heaven in a little row boat"). A particularly lucid depiction of this scene occurs in the film *What Dreams May Come* (1998) when Robin Williams's character crosses the river Styx in an attempt to rescue his wife from Purgatory. The film's release just three years before *Amnesiac* makes the Dante references all the more salient.

In addition to depicting images directly correlating to the song's lyrics, the song's music video suggests further allusions to this scene—Dante's fifth circle of Hell—not directly found in those lyrics ("let us descend now unto greater woe; already sinks each star that was ascending").[19] The greater woe of the music video is the environmental fallout of a warming planet—precisely what Yorke identifies as Dante's "lukewarm" (both *literally* in terms of global temperature, and *figuratively* regarding humankind's collective inertia for change). Global warming reappears continually in Radiohead's multimedia output. Take for example the short *Kid A* promotional video—affectionately refereed to by fans as "blips"—that promoted "Motion Picture Soundtrack" (2000–10). In this video the iconic "minotaur" that accompanies nearly all of the *Kid A* and *Amnesiac* artwork is reimagined as a polar bear stranded on a sinking floe of ice. What immediately follows cements the link between global warming and Dante. As the polar bear slowly sinks to the tune of "I will see you in the next life," a sinister, red-eyed, black-cloaked minotaur sails across the river—now blood-red—in a tiny row boat brandishing a sickle.

The video for "Pyramid Song" features only computer-generated graphics, imbuing Radiohead's anti-technology critique with a sense of irony. It opens with a fly-over shot of a ramshackle atoll floating in the sea. In a post-terrestrial earth, it is conceivable that this is one of many such havens. Our main character, the polygonal simulacrum of a future-human I'll call "Diver," now comes into the frame. Diver has no hands, but instead something resembling flippers. Later in the video, floating skeletons reveal a similar anatomical design, suggesting, yet never confirming, the possibility that this takes place in the far future when humanoids have adapted to a watery planet.[20]

The majority of the video's action essentially replicates a scene from the 1995 film *Waterworld* starring Kevin Costner. Diver discovers an old scuba tank and map and descends to find the ruins of a modern city. Just before Diver submerges, the camera moves underwater, trained upward on the undulating waves. This shot spans exactly the length of the "pyramid" motive in verse 1b. Diver's splash disrupts the undulation of the waves just as the opening F♯ major returns. The pyramid shape of the motive, up and down in a symmetrical pattern, has been animated in waves. Diver plunges and begins to descend, accompanied by the descent from F♯ minor down to E in the first iteration of "radix."

Throughout the first verse we survey the sunken aquatic cityscape. Skyscrapers, floating office chairs, webs of power lines, and dozens of cars; all tombstones of a past society that has literally drowned itself in technology. The second verse begins with our first close-up imagery. Accompanied by the now-prominent whir of the ondes Martenot at peak amplitude, we see the inside of a sunken automobile. As the synthetic ondes timbre recedes into the background, the organic, wooden string ensemble takes over at the onset of verse 2b. Floating books, of course also organic and, in a sense, wooden, now cement the relationship between timbral and visual representations of the technological/organic tension throughout Radiohead's output.

At verse 2c, Diver approaches a white picket fence and enters the ghostly house beyond. A crab crawls across a phone book before burrowing into a black dress shoe. Overcome with nostalgia, Diver pulls up a chair to an abandoned dinner table, still set with fine china. As the refrain "nothing to fear, nothing to doubt" plays on, Diver now retires to an easy chair in a wallpapered room. In the last iteration of this refrain, the camera zooms out to show Diver's purposely detached oxygen supply floating back up to the surface.[21] Resigned to fate, Diver would rather die in a comfortable easy chair than do anything to improve the outside world. Nothing could be more evocative of Dante's "lukewarm," or Radiohead's critique of modern technocracy.

The depth of analysis, interpretation, intertextual significance, and, through each of these approaches, meaning, that I've found in "Pyramid Song" is indicative of the richness of any Radiohead song after *The Bends*. This deep level of investigation is by no means outside the norms for a large portion of Radiohead's fan base. Comparable levels of introspection abound, recorded in numerous fan sites, and this is but a fraction of the total meaning-creation for this music that is never written down. All of this is to say that I don't think that the primary impact of this book will be to *inspire* the sorts of analyses I've given here. They are, by and large, already happening. What I do hope to have provided in this book is a coherent set of tools to analyze discrete parameters in Radiohead's music—form, rhythm, timbre, and harmony—and also a method by which to interpret those findings in relation to a song's lyrics or intertextual connections. Analyzing Radiohead entails the ability to perceive certain *intersubjective* elements in the music (e.g., A major, maximally even rhythm, ondes Martenot), but also a willingness to admit one's *subjective* understanding of those elements as viable components of the analysis.

Notes

1. http://www.rollingstone.com/music/news/radiohead-warm-up-with-amnesiac-20010524.
2. Nathan Hesselink's (2013) thorough and democratic survey of the published literature and fan sources alike documents these four theories. Though published in the March 2013 issue of *Music Theory Online*, Hesselink's article was submitted before Yorke's interview with *Dazed* was published in February 2013. We may regard Hesselink's article as capturing the culmination of over a decade of speculation just before the mystery was solved.

3. http://www.dazeddigital.com/music/article/15435/1/uni-of-yorke-class-1-flylo-the-gaslamp-killer-faltydl.

4. See Randall (2012, 188).

5. To be sure, these are rough estimates because the total amplitude of a given instrument is not measurable by its fundamental frequency alone, but by the sum total of that fundamental and the softer overtones. Furthermore, the piano has not one, but between three and five fundamental frequencies, since it is a polyphonic instrument. This kind of empirical timbral analysis is best when tempered with a healthy amount of intuitive checking. Once the data is complete, the analyst should go back through and ask questions like, Is the bass really louder than the strings at this point? and adjust intuitively if necessary.

6. Like many composers (e.g., Schoenberg, Shostakovich), J. S. Bach found a way to encode his signature into pitch-class motives: B♭ (German: *B*), A, C, B♮ (German: *H*).

7. The C♯4 was previously designated as "13" to show its location in pitch space, higher than all other tones heard in the third octave. Pitch-class space is not concerned with octave designations, and therefore uses only mod-12 integers, making 13 equivalent to 1.

8. The apotheosis of this increase in parallel major voice leading can be heard throughout "Burn The Witch" (2016–1). Composed entirely of five major triads whose roots form a diatonic pentachord—B, C♯, D, E, and F♯—it extends the [0135] set of major triads heard in "Everything in its Right Place" and "Pyramid Song" by one extra step: [01357]. The A major melody supported by F♯ major triads in the verse of "Burn the Witch" creates the same "mixture" on scale-degree 1 (A in the voice vs. A♯ in the chordal support) heard in "Pyramid Song."

9. Hesselink (2013) provides examples of these and other categories of speculation.

10. The promotional "blip" for the *Kid A* version of "Morning Bell" (2000–9), also composed of a recurring maximally even rhythm, features floating pyramids with a minotaur adorning the four-sided base.

11. See Touissant (2010, 4).

12. See Rahn (1996, 78).

13. Perceiving an underlying <33433> subdivision the first time one hears these first two minutes of the song is probably only possible by putting the cart before the horse, so to speak. Because one has heard <short–short–long–short–short> in the context of <33433> subdivisions previously—e.g., the iconic hook of Grandmaster Flash's hit "The Message" (1982–B3, 1:04)—one might then project that structure onto the current stimulus.

14. The rhythmic and timbral similarities between "Pyramid Song" and "Spectre" are remarkable. Writing a review in *Pitchfork*, Cook-Wilson (2016) goes so far as to note that "Selway's jazzy drum figures allow 'Spectre' to come into its own—a welcome 'Pyramid Song' sequel."

15. The transformation from mod-16 to mod-24 results from each beat in two measures of 4/4 (8) having now three underlying subdivisions, although the second is never accented.

16. I should be careful to note that there is no intrinsic link between pitch and rhythm in this tripartite connection. For example, both the five-unit and four-unit duration are used on the A♯ that begins the "pyramid" motive. If, for example, the duration increased as the pitch raised—e.g., A♯ for four units and B for five units—I might find more than mere numerological significance.

17. Phil Rose (2016) analyzes all of *OK Computer* through the lens of the "technopoly": a term coined by the cultural critic Neil Postman in his book *Technopoly: The Surrender of Culture to Technology* (1992).

18. See Kennedy 2003; cited in Rose (2016, 147).

19. See Dante, Canto VII.

20. Whales, for example, evolved from terrestrial mammals who became slowly more adapted to a marine ecosystem. The skeletons of some cetaceans still bear the vestiges of a hand-like or paw-like structure.

21. Curiously, the scuba tank is attached to an oxygen hose, which is what we see floating, detached.

Bibliography

Adam, Nathaniel. 2011. Coding *OK Computer*: Categorization and characterization of disruptive harmonic and rhythmic events in rock music. Ph.D. dissertation, University of Michigan.

Adams, Kyle. 2006. A new theory of chromaticism from the late sixteenth to the early eighteenth century. Ph.D. dissertation, City University of New York.

Agawu, Kofi. 1996. "Review of Robert S. Hatten. 1994. *Musical Meaning in Beethoven: Markedness, Correlation, and Interpretation.* Bloomington: Indiana University Press." *Current Musicology* 60/61: 147–161.

Attas, Robin. 2011. Meter as process in groove-based music. Ph.D. dissertation, University of British Columbia.

Bailie, Stuart. 1997. "Conversation with Jonny Greenwood." *New Music Express.* June 21.

Battistella, Edwin. 1996. *The Logic of Markedness.* Oxford: Oxford University Press.

Berger, K.W. 1964. "Some factors in the recognition of timbre." *Journal of the Acoustical Society of America* 36 (10): 1888–1891.

Biamonte, Nicole. 2010. "Triadic modal and pentatonic patterns in rock music." *Music Theory Spectrum* 32 (2): 95–110.

Biamonte, Nicole. 2014. "Formal functions of metric dissonance in rock music." *Music Theory Online* 20 (2).

Blake, David. "Timbre as differentiation in indie music." *Music Theory Online* 18 (2).

Brend, Mark. 2005. *Strange Sounds: Offbeat Instruments and Sonic Experiments in Pop.* Montclair, NJ: Backbeat Books.

Brower, Candace. 2000. "A cognitive theory of musical meaning." *Journal of Music Theory* 44 (2): 323–379.

Butler, Mark. 2006. *Unlocking the Groove: Rhythm, Meter, and Musical Design in Electronic Dance Music*. Bloomington: Indiana University Press.

Capuzzo, Guy. 2009. "Sectional tonality and sectional centricity in rock music." *Music Theory Spectrum* 31 (1): 157–174.

Clarke, Eric. 1999. "Subject-position and the specification of invariants in music by Frank Zappa and P. J. Harvey." *Music Analysis 18* (3): 347–374.

Clarke, Eric. 2005. *Ways of Listening: An Ecological Approach to Musical Perception*. Oxford: Oxford University Press.

Clarke, Eric. 2007. "The impact of recording on listening." *twentieth-century music* 4 (1): 47–70.

Cohn, Richard. 1992a. "Transpositional combination of beat-class sets in Steve Reich's phase-shifting music." *Perspectives of New Music* 30 (2): 146–177.

Cohn, Richard. 1992b. "Metric and hypermetric dissonance in the menuetto of Mozart's Symphony in G Minor, K. 550." *Integral* 6: 1–33.

Cohn, Richard. 2012. *Audacious Euphony: Chromatic Harmony and the Triad's Second Nature*. Oxford: Oxford University Press.

Cook-Wilson, Winston. 2016. "Tracks: Radiohead, 'Spectre.'" Pitchfork Media. http://pitchfork.com/reviews/tracks/17891-radiohead-spectre/. Accessed 3/25/2016.

Covach, John. 2005. Form in rock music: A primer. In *Engaging Music: Essays in Music Analysis*, ed. Deborah Stein, 65–76. Oxford: Oxford University Press.

Cox, Arnie. 2011. "Embodying music: Principles of the mimetic hypothesis." *Music Theory Online* 17 (2).

de Clercq, Trevor. 2012. Sections and successions in successful songs: a prototype approach to form in rock music. Ph.D. Dissertation, University of Rochester.

de Clercq, Trevor. 2013. "A future theory of pop-rock music: A response to Christopher Doll and Joseph Swain." *Dutch Journal of Music Theory* 18 (3): 173–179.

Doll, Christopher. 2011. "Rockin' out: Expressive modulation in verse–chorus form." *Music Theory Online* 17 (3).

Endrinal, Christopher. 2008. Form and style in the music of U2. Ph.D. dissertation, Florida State University.

Everett, Walter. 1999. *The Beatles as Musicians*: Revolver *through* The Anthology. Oxford: Oxford University Press.

Everett, Walter. 2004. "Making sense of rock's tonal systems." *Music Theory Online* 10 (4).

Everett, Walter. 2008. Pitch down the middle. In *Expression in Pop-Rock Music: Critical and Analytical Essays*, ed. Walter Everett. 2nd ed. New York: Routledge.

Everett, Walter. 2009. *The Foundations of Rock: From "Blue Suede Shoes" to "Suite: Judy Blue Eyes"*. Oxford: Oxford University Press.

Everett, Walter. 2015. Death Cab for Cutie's 'I Will Follow You Into the Dark' (2005) as exemplar of conventional tonal behaviour in recent rock music. In *Song Interpretation in 21st-Century Pop Music*, ed. Ralf Von Appen, André Doehring, Dietrich Helms, and Allan F. Moore, 9–28. Farnham, Surrey, UK: Ashgate.

Feld, Steven. 1984. "Communication, music, and speech about music." *Yearbook for Traditional Music* 16: 1–18.

Gauldin, Robert. 1990. "Beethoven, Tristan, and The Beatles." *College Music Symposium* 30.

Gibson, J. J. 1979. *The Ecological Approach to Visual Perception*. Boston: Houghton Mifflin.

Gjerdingen, Robert. 1988. *A Classic Turn of Phrase*. Philadelphia: University of Pennsylvania Press.

Gjerdingen, Robert. 1989. "Meter as a mode of attending: a network simulation of attentional rhythmicity in music." *Integral* 3: 67–91.

Griffiths, Dai. 2005. Public schoolboy music: Debating Radiohead. In *The Music and Art of Radiohead*, ed. Joseph Tate, 159–167. Farnham, Surrey, UK: Ashgate.

Hale, Jonathan. 1999. *Radiohead: From a Great Height*. Toronto: ECW Press.

Hatten, Robert. 1994. *Musical Meaning in Beethoven: Markedness, Correlation, and Interpretation*. Bloomington: Indiana University Press.

Heidemann, Katherine. 2014. Hearing women's voices in popular song: Analyzing sound and identity in country and soul. Ph.D. dissertation, Columbia University.

Helmholtz, Hermann. 1954 [1895]. *On the Sensation of Tone as a Psychological Basis for the Theory of Music*. Trans. Alexander J. Ellis. New York: Dover.

Hodgson, Jay. 2010. *Understanding Records: A Field Guide to Recording Practice*. New York: Bloomsbury.

Horlacher, Gretchen. 1992. "The rhythms of reiteration: Formal development in Stravinsky's ostinati." *Music Theory Spectrum* 14 (2): 171–187.

Huron, David. 2006. *Sweet Anticipation: Music and the Psychology of Expectation*. Cambridge: MIT Press.

Iyer, Vijay. 2002. "Embodied mind, situated cognition, and expressive microtiming in African-American music." *Music Perception* 19 (3): 387–414.

Kennedy, John. 2003. "Thom Yorke on *Hail to the Thief*." XFM, aired June 3, 2003. Transcript at http://citizeninsane.eu/t2003-06-03XFM.htm. Accessed 3/29/16.

Krebs, Harald. 1981. "Alternatives to monotonality in early nineteenth-century music." *Journal of Music Theory* 25 (1): 1–16.

Krebs, Harald. 1999. *Fantasy Pieces: Metrical Dissonance in the Music of Robert Schumann*. Oxford: Oxford University Press.

Kreiman, Jody, D. Wanlancker-Sidtis, and B. R. Gerratt. 2004. Perception of voice quality. In *The Handbook of Speech Perception*, ed. David B. Pisoni and R. E. Remez. Blackwell Reference Online.

Lehrer, Jonah. 2008. *Proust Was a Neuroscientist*. Boston: Mariner Books.

Lerdahl, Fred and Ray Jackendoff. 1983. *A Generative Theory of Tonal Music*. Cambridge: MIT Press.

Lewis, Amanda. 2011. "Microphone practice in Bon Iver's 'Skinny Love.'" *Journal of the Art of Record Production* 5.

Letts, Marianne Tatom. 2010. *How to Disappear Completely: Radiohead and the Resistant Concept Album*. Bloomington, IN: Indiana University Press.

London, Justin. 2004. *Hearing in Time: Psychological Aspects of Musical Meter*. Oxford: Oxford University Press.

Malawey, Victoria. 2014. "Ear training with the music of Radiohead." *Indiana Theory Review* 30, no. 2: 1–38.

Margulis, Elizabeth Hellmuth. 2013. "Perception, expectation, affect, analysis." *Zeitschrift der gesellschaft für Musiktheorie* 10 (2): 315–326.

Mendelsohn A., Furman O., Navon I., Dudai Y. 2009. "Subjective vs. documented reality: a case study of long-term real-life autobiographical memory." *Learning & Memory* 16: 142–146.

Meyer, Leonard. 1980. "Creating limits: Creation, archetypes, and style change." *Daedalus* 109 (2): 177–205.

Mirka, Danuta. 2001. "To cut the Gordian knot: The timbre system of Krzysztof Penderecki." *Journal of Music Theory* 45 (2): 435–456.

Molnar-Szakacs, Istvan, and Katie Overy. 2006. "Music and mirror neurons: From motion to 'e'motion." *Social Cognitive and Affective Neuroscience* 1 (3): 235–241.

Moore, Allan. 1995. "The so-called 'flattened seventh' in rock music." *Popular Music* 14: 185–201.

Moore, Allan. 2012. *Song Means: Analysing and Interpreting Recorded Popular Song.* Farnham, Surrey, UK: Ashgate.

Moore, Allan, and Anwar Ibrahim. 2005. Sounds like teen spirit: Identifying Radiohead's idiolect. In *The Art and Music of Radiohead*, ed. Joseph Tate, 139–158. Farnham, Surrey, UK: Ashgate.

Murphy, Scott. 2006. "The major tritone progression in recent Hollywood science fiction films." *Music Theory Online* 12 (2).

Nattiez, Jean-Jacques. 1985. "The concepts of plot and seriation process in music analysis." *Music Analysis* 4 (1/2): 107–118.

Neal, Jocelyn. 2007. "Narrative paradigms, musical signifiers, and form as function in country music." *Music Theory Spectrum* 29 (1): 41–72.

Nobile, Drew. 2011. "Form and voice-leading in early Beatles songs." *Music Theory Online* 17 (3).

Nobile, Drew. 2013. A structural approach to the analysis of rock music. Ph.D. dissertation, City University of New York.

Nobile, Drew. 2015. "Counterpoint in rock music: Unpacking the melodic-harmonic divorce." *Music Theory Spectrum* 37 (2): 189–203.

Osborn, Brad. 2010a. Beyond verse and chorus: Experimental formal designs in post-millennial rock music. Ph.D. dissertation, University of Washington.

Osborn, Brad. 2010b. "Beats that commute: Algebraic and kinesthetic models for math-rock grooves." *Gamut* 3 (1): 43–67.

Osborn, Brad. 2011. "Understanding through-composition in math-metal, post-rock, and other post-millennial experimental genres." *Music Theory Online* 17 (4).

Osborn, Brad. 2013. "Subverting the verse/chorus paradigm: Terminally climactic forms in recent rock music." *Music Theory Spectrum* 35 (1): 23–47.

Osborn, Brad. 2014. "*Kid A*lgebra: Radiohead's Euclidean and maximally even rhythms." *Perspectives of New Music* 52 (1): 88–105.

Osborn, Brad. 2016. "Radiohead's *A Moon Shaped Pool* (XL, 2016): reflecting, looking forward." Oxford University Press Blog. http://blog.oup.com/2016/05/radiohead-a-moon-shaped-pool/. Accessed 6/29/2016.

Poudrier, Ève, and Bruno Repp. 2013. "Can musicians track multiple beats simultaneously?" *Music Perception* 30 (4): 369–390.

Rahn, Jay. 1987. "Asymmetrical ostinatos in sub-Saharan music: Time, pitch, and cycles reconsidered." *In Theory Only* 9 (7): 23–27.

Randall, Mac. 2012. *Exit Music: The Radiohead Story*, updated edition. Montclair, NJ: Backbeat.

Reynolds, Simon. 2001. "Walking on thin ice." *The Wire.* 209: 32.

Risset, Jean-Claude, and D. Wessel. 1991. Exploration du timbre par analyse et synthèse. In *Le timbre, métaphore pour la composition*, ed. J. B. Barrière, 102–131. Paris: Bourgois Editeur and IRCAM.

Robinson, John. 2003. "Thom and Jonny's exclusive track-by-track guide to Radiohead's *Hail to The Thief*, alternative titles and all." *New Musical Express* May 10: 34–35.

Rockwell, Joti. 2011. "Time on the crooked road: Isochrony, meter, and disruption in old-time country and bluegrass music." *Ethnomusicology* 55 (1): 55–76.

Roeder, John. 2003. "Beat class modulation in Steve Reich's music." *Music Theory Spectrum* 25 (2): 275–304.

Rose, Phil. 2016. *Radiohead and the Global Movement for Change*. Madison, WI: Fairleigh Dickinson University Press.

Ross, Alex. 2001. "The searchers: Radiohead's unquiet revolution." *The New Yorker.* August 20/27.

Rusch, Réne. 2013. "Crossing over with Brad Mehldau's cover of Radiohead's 'Paranoid Android.'" *Music Theory Online* 19 (4).

Schultz, Rob. 2012. "Tonal pairing and the relative key paradox in the music of Elliott Smith." *Music Theory Online* 18 (4).

Scotto, Ciro. 2016. "The structural function of distortion in hard rock and heavy metal." *Music Theory Spectrum* 38 (2).

Slater, Mark. 2011. "Timbre and non-radical didacticism in The Streets' *A Grand Don't Come for Free*: a poetic-ecological model." *Music Analysis* 30 (2–3): 360–395.

Slawson, Wayne. 1981. "The color of sound: A theoretical study in musical timbre." *Music Theory Spectrum* 3: 132–141.

Smalley, Denis. 1997. "Spectromorphology: explaining sound-shapes." *Organised Sound* 2 (2): 107–126.

Smalley, Denis. 2007. "Space-form and the acousmatic image." *Organized Sound* 12 (1): 35–58.

Spicer, Mark. 2004. "(Ac)cumulative form in pop-rock music." *twentieth-century music* 1: 29–64.

Spicer, Mark. Forthcoming. "Fragile, emergent, and absent tonics in pop and rock songs." *Journal of Music Theory.*

Stanyek, Jason. 2014. "Forum on transcription." *twentieth-century music* 11 (1): 101–161.

Straus, Joseph. 1982. "Stravinsky's 'tonal axis.'" *Journal of Music Theory* 26 (2): 261–290.

Summach, Jason. 2011. "The structure, function, and genesis of the prechorus." *Music Theory Online* 17 (3).

Summach, Jason. 2012. Form in top-20 rock music, 1955–89. Ph.D. dissertation, Yale University.

Summach, Jason. 2014. Review of Allan F. Moore, *Song Means: Analysing and Interpreting Recorded Popular Song* (Farnham, Surrey, UK: Ashgate, 2012). *twentieth-century music* 11 (1): 183–188.

Tatom Letts, Marianne. 2010. *Radiohead and the Resistant Concept Album*. Bloomington, IN: Indiana University Press.

Taylor, Stephen. 2009. "Rhythm necklace and hemiola: Hidden meter in Radiohead, Björk, and the *Aka*." Paper presented at the Society for Music Theory national meeting, Montreal, October 31.

Temperley, David. 2007. "The melodic–harmonic divorce in rock." *Popular Music* 26 (2): 323–342.

Theeuwes, Jan. 2012. "Automatic control of visual selection." In *The Influence of Attention, Learning, and Motivation on Visual Search*, ed. Michael D. Dodd and John Flowers, 23–63. Lincoln: University of Nebraska Press.

Touissaint, Gotfried. 2005. The Euclidean algorithm generates traditional musical rhythms. In *Proceedings of BRIDGES: Mathematical Connections in Art, Music and Science*, 47–56, Banff, Alberta, Canada, 31 July–August.

Touissaint, Gotfried. 2010. "Generating 'good' rhythms algorithmically." *Proceedings of the 8th International Conference on Arts and Humanities*: 774–791.

Turner, Mark, and Gilles Fauconnier. 1995. "Conceptual integration and formal expression." *Metaphor and Symbolic Activity* 10 (3): 183–204.

Tuzan, Tolga. 2009. Contextual transformations in timbral spaces. Ph.D. dissertation, City University of New York.

Varela, F., Thompson, E., and Rosch, E. 1991. *The Embodied Mind: Cognitive Science and Human Experience*. Cambridge, MA: MIT Press.

Zagorski-Thomas, Simon. Forthcoming. The spectromorphology of recorded popular music: The shaping of sonic cartoons through record production. In *The relentless pursuit of tone: Timbre in popular music*, ed. Robert Fink, Mindy LaTour O'Brien, and Zachary Wallmark. Oxford: Oxford University Press.

Witek, Maria, E. Clarke, M. Wallentin, M. Kringelbach, and P. Vuust. 2014. "Syncopation, body-movement and pleasure in groove music." *PLoS ONE* 9 (4): 1–12.

Zbikowski, Lawrence. 1999. "The blossoms of Trockne Blumen." *Music Analysis* 18 (3): 307–345.

DISCOGRAPHY

Beatles, The. 1965. "We can Work it Out" (single). Capitol 5555, vinyl.

Beatles, The. 1968a. "Hey Jude" (single). Apple 2276, vinyl.

Beatles, The. 1968b. Self-titled (aka "The White Album). Apple PCS 7067/8, vinyl.

Beatles, The. 1970. *Let it Be*. Apple PXS 1, vinyl.

Blondie. 1980. *Autoamerican*. Chrysalis CHE 1290, vinyl.

Blur. 1995. *The Great Escape*. Parlophone 7243 8 35235 2 8, compact disc.

Buffet, Jimmy. 1977. *Changes in Latitudes, Changes in Attitudes*. ABC AB990, vinyl.

Charles, Ray. 1961. "Hit the Road Jack" (single). ABC-Paramount 45-10244.

Cher. 1998. *Believe*. Warner Bros 9 44576-2, compact disc.

Coltrane, John. 1974. *Interstellar Space*. ABC ASD-9277, vinyl.

Coldplay. 2002. *A Rush of Blood to the Head*. Parlophone 7243 5 40504 2 8, compact disc.

Danny and the Juniors. 1957. "At the Hop" (single). ABC-Paramount 45-9871, vinyl.

Fatboy Slim. 1999. *Build it Up Tear it Down*. Skint 667885 2, compact disc.

Fischer-Dieskau, Dietrich, and Gerald Moore. 1951. *Winterreise, Die schöne Müllerin, Der Schwanengesang*. EMI-Electrola 1C 127-01764/66, vinyl.

Gaynor, Gloria. 1978. *Love Tracks*. Polydor PD-1-6184, vinyl.

Grandmaster Flash and the Furious Five. 1982. *The Message*. Sugar Hill. SH 268, vinyl.

Haley, Bill and his Comets. 1955. *Rock Around the Clock*. Decca DL 8225, vinyl.

Hendrix, Jimi. 1999 (1969). *Live at Woodstock*. MCA MCD 11987, compact disc.

Knight, Robert. 1967. "Everlasting Love" (single). Rising Sons RS 45-705, vinyl.

Kreiger, Paul. 1976. "Short Piece," from *Electronic Music Winners*. Columbia Odyssey Y 34139, Vinyl.

Lansky, Paul. 1976 (1973). "Mild und Leise," from *Electronic Music Winners*. Columbia Odyssey Y 34139, Vinyl.

Oasis. 1995. *(What's the Story) Morning Glory?* Creation CRE CD 189, compact disc.

Pixies, The. 1987. *Come On Pilgrim*. 4AD MAD 709, vinyl.

Pixies, The. 1988. *Surfer Rosa*. 4AD CAD 803, vinyl.

Pook, Jocelyn. 2001. *Untold Things*. Real World CDR W93, compact disc.

Presley, Elvis. 1956. "Hound Dog" (single). RCA Victor 20-6604, vinyl.

Silverchair. 1999. *Neon Ballroom*. Murmur MATTCD084, compact disc.

Simon and Garfunkel. 1964. *Wednesday Morning, 3am*. Columbia CL 2249, vinyl.

Spears, Brittney. 2000. *Oops I Did it Again*. Jive 01241-41704-2, compact disc.

Thursday. 2001. *Full Collapse*. Victory VR145, compact disc.

Tool. 1993. *Undertow*. Zoo 72445-11052-2, compact disc.

Twain, Shania. 1995. *The Woman in Me*. Mercury 314-522 886-2, compact disc.

Index

"Fitter Happier" and, 34, 47
narrative potential of, 40
"Pulk/Pull Revolving Doors" and, 34–35
"Treefingers" and, 35
A Moon Shaped Pool, xiii, xvn1
Moore, Allan
  on difficulty of Radiohead's music,
    46, 49n29
  ecological perception research and, 4–5
  on the harmonic filler layer, 101–2
  on harmonic patterns in Radiohead, 159
  on identifying song forms, 21
  on idiolect, 11
  on *OK Computer*'s innovations, 10
  Song Means and, xiii
"Morning Bell" (Radiohead)
  King Solomon and, 61
  musical notation for, 60
  rhythm of, 60–61, 63
  source-deformation and, 103, 108
"Morning Mr. Magpie" (Radiohead), 108–9
"Motion Picture Soundtrack" (Radiohead)
  harmony of, 135, 139, 143
  promotional video for, 192
  source-deformation and, 103
musical perception
  expectation and surprise in studies of, viii–ix
  higher-level interpretation and, 8
  idiolect and, 11
  neuroscience and, 3–4
The Music and Art of Radiohead (edited
  volume), xii
music cognition research, 6
Mutronics Mutator pedal, 107–8
mutualism, 6–7, 95, 107, 119
Muzak, 9
"Myxomatosis" (Radiohead), 114

"The National Anthem" (Radiohead)
  backbeat and, 54
  harmony of, 62, 145
  musical notation for, 54, 60, 62
  ondes Martenot in, 61–63, 119, 122
  rhythm of, 54, 60–63
neuroscience, 1–2, 94–95, 125
Nirvana, 10
non-metrical beat layers, 58, 66
"No Surprises" (Radiohead)
  harmony of, 20–21, 139

lyrics of, 20–21
song form of, 20–21
source-deformation and, 103
Novation Bass Station, 114, 124, 126–27
"Nude" (Radiohead), 106, 148–49
"The Numbers" (Radiohead), 67

Oasis, 10–11
O'Brien, Ed
  "Idioteque" and, 115
  "I Will" and, 124–28
  "Pyramid Song" described by, 176
  Sustainer Strat guitar and, 104–6
  "You and Whose Army?" discussed by, 154
odd-cardinality meter
  "2+2=5" and, 41, 45, 55, 79
  "15 Step" and, 56–57
  definition of, 55
  Euclidean rhythms and, 59
  hypermeter and, 55
  musical notation for, 55–57
  non-metrical beat layers and, 58
  "Paranoid Android" and, 55
  Radiohead's music and, 55
OK Computer (Radiohead album)
  concert tour for, 111
  expectation and surprise on, 9
  innovations on, 1, 10–11, 47n1
  pre-production for, 113
  Radiohead fan base and, 45
  rhythm of songs on, 10
  song forms on, 20, 39
  timbre in songs on, 10
ondes Martenot
  "2+2=5" and, 122
  "How to Disappear Completely" and, 122
  "I Might Be Wrong" and, 122
  invariance and, 119, 121
  "Jigsaw Falling into Place" and, 122
  Kid A and, 119
  "The National Anthem" and, 61–63,
    119, 122
  "Nude" and, 106
  octatonic subset and, 62
  "Optimistic" and, 122
  "Pyramid Song" and, 122, 178–81, 192–93
  Radiohead's *Saturday Night Live*
    performance (2000) and, 119
  remote surrogacy and, 119, 121

CPSIA information can be obtained
at www.ICGtesting.com
Printed in the USA
BVHW031408111221
623743BV00003B/8